WALKING WITH BEARS

WALKING
WITH
BEARS

Terry D. DeBruyn

The Lyons Press
Guilford, Connecticut

An imprint of The Globe Pequot Press

*This book is dedicated to
the memory of my father, Claude DeBruyn,
who taught me how to use the woods, and
my mother, Lucille N. DeBruyn,
who made me curious about them.*

The Lyons Press is an imprint of the Globe Pequot Press.

Designed by Integrated Publishing Solutions

2 4 6 8 10 9 7 5 3 1

Library of Congress Cataloging-in-Publication Data

DeBruyn, Terry D.
Walking with bears / Terry D. DeBruyn.
p. cm.
Includes bibliographical references
ISBN 1-55821-642-1 (hc)
ISBN 1-58574-425-5 (pb)
1. Black bear—Michigan—Upper Peninsula. 2. Human-animal
relationships—Michigan—Upper Peninsula. 3. DeBruyn, Terry D.
I. Title.
QL737.C27D425 1999
599.78'5'0977749—dc21   99-40861
                                                                    CIP

Acknowledgments

Projects like this don't just happen—they take the work of a lot of people. And my debts are many. The project was conceived on a late-night return trip from bear watching in Minnesota. It grew under the mentoring of Dr. William Robinson at Northern Michigan University and then Drs. Rolf O. Peterson, Ann Maclean, Tom Drummer, and Peg Gail at Michigan Technological University. Dr. Lynn Rogers provided initial inspiration and support and Sandy Bonsall's third-grade class at Teal Lake School, Negaunne, Michigan, provided seed money. I received much support along the way from the U.S. Forest Service's Hiawatha Forest District, particularly Wildlife Biologist Kevin Doran and the Michigan Department of Natural Resources, especially Dr. Larry Visser. Many sportspersons' groups, organizations, and individuals contributed both in kind and financially. David "Buck" LaVasseur, Frida Waara, David Binder, and Glen Shepard promulgated the news of bears to a wide audience. Many thanks to the "bear-walkers": I learned from each of you. Also, to fellow students who helped keep tabs on Carmen and Nettie, thanks. I, of course, owe the most to Annette for putting up with all of this. And to the bears for putting up with me. The views and any mistakes contained within are mine and mine alone.

Discovering

The secret streams that flow beneath the cliffs of colored stone,
The forests thick and healthy with birch and pine and oak,
Surrounded by the greatest lakes this World has ever known,
The black bear's awesome presence as he roams the hills and fields,
The call of the timber wolf, the loon's lonesome trill,
The eagle soaring high above, the trout lies deep and still,
These are what I treasure, the only way I measure
The feeling that I have for this fine land.
There is so much to discover when you're a long time lover
Of Northern Michigan

—Mark Mitchell
Marquette, Michigan

Contents

Preface

It is winter in Michigan's Upper Peninsula, and snow covers the Hiawatha National Forest. In a den, at the base of an over-turned tree, or perhaps in a brush pile within a clear-cut stand of aspens, a female black bear gives birth to a daughter. Blind, hairless, and with ears unformed, the cub seeks out the warmth of her mother's mammae. The fat-rich milk will be the cub's sole source of nutrition for her first three months. In the spring, as melting snow gives the forest floor the patchy appearance of the side of a Holstein cow, the cub will emerge from her birth-place with her mother and embark on her life as a bear.

A little more than four years later, on a hot June afternoon in 1990, biologists Larry Visser of Michigan's Department of Nat-ural Resources, Kevin Doran of the U.S. Forest Service, and I—with blackflies swarming around our heads and one stuck in the corner of my eye—unceremoniously affix a radio collar to that cub. She has survived to become an adult female black bear. It is the beginning week of my field research for a master's degree in biology at Northern Michigan University. The re-search is aimed at understanding bears, their food habits, and their habitat use. I did not know it then, but the next summer I would teach this bear to tolerate my close presence and would spend the following six years accompanying her and two gen-erations of her offspring through the forest mosaic of the White-fish River basin in the heart of Michigan's Upper Peninsula.

During those six years, I was a privileged observer as a wild black bear carried out the circadian rhythms of her life in the north woods. On a near daily basis, up to fifteen hours a day, for over two thousand hours I was afforded glimpses of the continuum of events that make up the lifeline of a bear. Those glimpses, although they document much in the life and death of bears, do not conform well to the rigid brevity of scientific journals, where such information is cast off as "anecdotal" and inappropriate for scientific archiving. However, *single events* markedly affect the lives of wild animals, and direct observation of such events can grant insight into their lives and may further our understanding of them. If any animal in the forest could benefit from a clearer understanding by humankind, it is the bear. It is for that reason that I chose to write this book— to recount those singular events that affect the lives of bears. By training of late, I am a scientist, but I do not intend this book to be only scientific. Science occasionally censors too much mystery from the wonders in life and leaves an inadequate allowance of the magic. When I was very young, magic was a cloud of dust clearing to reveal the "white buffalo" on a television western. Later, it was the sudden presence of a white-tailed buck in the woods on a frosty morning in November. Now, I find magic in the birth of black bear cubs and images of bears ghosting through white cedar swamps or ambling unfettered through stands of mixed northern hardwoods. It is my hope here to shed light on some mysteries of the black bear while preserving all that is magical.

In writing this book, I have woven highlights of my observation of events in the lives of five litters of black bear cubs into a period of a little more than a year. Because black bears are mostly on their own after eighteen months or so with their mothers, a full year provides context to better understand events that shape the beginnings of a bear. The account is organized by seasons, because plant cycles dictate much of what bears do in the forest.

I hope you enjoy the walk.

Introduction

About five million years ago, during the late Pliocene epoch, the first identifiable bear species, called *Ursus minimus*, appeared in Europe; they are the ancestors from which present-day North American bears are believed to have evolved. Today there are three species of bears in North America: the black bear, the brown or grizzly bear, and the polar bear. Polar bears are thought to be the most recently evolved, diverging from the brown bear—by some accounts no more than 100,000 years ago—when the brown bear and the polar bear migrated to Alaska from Asia. In contrast, black bears have probably existed in America for more than 1.5 million years.[1]

Black bears are the smallest of the three North American bears. They have large heavy bodies and thick, short, and powerfully built limbs. Their noses are elongated and their ears rounded. Their tails are short—only three to five inches in length. Black bears lack the distinctive shoulder hump and the dished face of the brown bear. All bears exhibit sexual dimorphism—adult males are about 50 percent larger than adult females. In general, adult female black bears weigh between 125 and 275 pounds, while adult males range from 250 to 400 pounds. One obese male in Minnesota weighed in at 859 pounds. Cubs, which weigh less than a pound at birth, emerge from their natal den weighing between 5 and 10 pounds and may reach a weight of 100 pounds by the end of their first year. Mature male bears may attain a body length (tip of the nose to base of the tail) of 6 feet or more and stand 40 inches high at the shoulder when on all fours, although they are taller at their rump. By comparison, adult females are usually 4½ to 5 feet in length and stand about 3 feet high at the shoulder.

In the eastern United States, black bears are normally black with brown muzzles and often a white blaze on their chests. In western states, the cinnamon or brown color phase of the black bear is common. Occasionally, although it is rare, albinism may occur in black bears, resulting in totally white or cream-colored animals. In the Alaska Yukon and in British Columbia a color phase of the black bear called the blue or glacier bear is found, and the white phase or Kermode bear is found in British Columbia.[2] In the wild, if a bear does all the right things and has good luck year after year, its life expectancy is twenty to twenty-five years, but for most bears life is much shorter (although there is a record from New York of a wild black bear surviving for over forty-two years).[3]

Black bears can be found in at least thirty-two states in the United States, making them the most widespread of North American bears. They occupy forested areas from Alaska to Mexico but are absent from the plains states. Black bears are thought to have been confined to their forest dwelling niche because of their inability to defend their offspring and themselves on open ground against the larger and more powerful

Introduction

predators with which they evolved. Consistent with that notion, along the northern Quebec–Labrador border in Canada,
where the brown/grizzly bear has become nonexistent, a population of black bears has colonized the open coastal tundra.

Black bears establish large home ranges, requiring expanses
of forest from which to obtain the necessities of life: food and
water, cover (including denning sites), mates, and space. Ideal
bear habitat consists of a mosaic of upland and lowland deciduous and coniferous forests at varying successional stages
interspersed with small openings and wetlands.

The black bear is an omnivore, and most of its diverse diet
consists of vegetation, fruits, and nuts. Although seasonally
important, meat normally constitutes less than 10 percent of
a black bear's annual food intake. The skulls of bears are the
longest and most massive of the carnivores, but they lack the
flesh-cutting (carnassial) cheek teeth present in other predators
and the crescentic cusp (selenodont) style of molars present in
herbivores. Instead, black bear molars are the low, flat-crowned
(bunodont) style. The bunodont style of teeth enables bears
to crush nuts more easily but are less suited to grinding and
breaking down vegetation.

Black bears have five toes on each foot and an equal number of nonretractile claws. They walk in plantigrade fashion
(the whole foot—heel and toe—touching the ground) like humans, rather than the digitigrade (toe-walking) fashion of other
predators such as lynx and cougar. Because of this footfall,
black bears are less efficient than other predators at capturing
speedy prey.

Most black bears pass the winter in hibernation or winter
sleep, a depressed physiological condition. Although where
food is available through the year, particularly in warmer cli-
mates, some bears remain active in winter. For two or three
weeks after emerging from their dens in early spring, bears are
usually lethargic and eat little. Gradually, they begin to scavenge the carcasses of winter-killed deer, in addition to feeding

on herbs such as swamp thistle and insects such as snow fleas. As spring progresses, they eat the tender shoots of grasses and clovers; succulent wetland herbs such as water plantain, water parsnip, and pickerelweed; upland herbs like sweet cicely and jack-in-the-pulpit; buds and unfurling leaves of sapling trees such as American hop hornbeam, beech, aspen, and willow; and also insects, including beetle larvae found in decaying logs. In summer, bears feast on ripened fruits, including June-berries, blueberries, raspberries, sarsaparilla, chokecherries, and alder-leaved buckthorn berries. They also eat grasses, clovers, and wetland herbs such as wild calla and spotted touch-me-not. They may prey on white-tailed deer fawns and eat insects including vespid wasps and more than fifteen species of ants. In fall, bears fatten on the nuts of beech, oak, and hazel and the berries of black cherry trees and winterberry bushes; they also utilize vegetation including grasses and wetland herbs like cattail. Black bears are generally most active in their foraging efforts at dawn and dusk, but they may become nocturnal in areas where there is human activity or to avoid the heat of day in areas such as the southeastern United States.

Black bears normally reach sexual maturity at about age four or five. Both sexes are promiscuous, breeding with multiple mates. Female bears often begin breeding at three and a half and give birth for the first time at age four. Litters usually range from one to four cubs (litters as large as six have been reported), but two or three is most common. Once a female reproduces successfully, she will typically reproduce every other year thereafter, depending on her nutritional condition. Male bears make no contribution toward raising the cubs and remain solitary except when breeding or when congregated at plentiful food sources. In contrast, mature females may spend 75 percent of their time in the company of offspring.

A black bear cub, under most circumstances, spends the entire first year of its life with its mother, denning with her in the fall. The following spring, with the onset of the breeding season, usually from late May to early July, the ties between the year-and-a-half-old cub and its mother are severed. After the breeding season, members of the litter may temporarily reassociate with each other, or with their mother, but do not normally den together again. Adult females typically share a portion of their home range with their yearling daughters and will continue scent-marking that portion of their home range, in effect, aiding their daughters in establishing a home range of their own. A young daughter continues to expand away from her mother, establishing a permanent home range that normally is contiguous and overlapping that of her mother. In contrast, yearling males disperse from their natal areas in the fall following family breakup, which often coincides with the onset of berry ripening. A few subadult males may remain in their natal range, heading off on their own at age two or even three.

Physiography

The Upper Peninsula of Michigan (U.P.) consists of approximately 16,500 square miles of diverse terrain, an area greater than the combined states of Connecticut, Delaware, and Massachusetts. Located in the center of the world's largest freshwater ecosystem, as much as anything the U.P. offers a glimpse of the transition between northern hardwood forests of beech and maple and dense boreal forests of fir and spruce.

A line drawn from the city of Marquette, on the south shore of Lake Superior, to Iron Mountain, and southward to Menominee, divides the U.P. into two morphologically distinct areas: the Superior Uplands to the west and the Lake Plains to the east. Even the casual observer traveling across the peninsula will notice a profound difference in landscape features between the western and eastern extremities. The western U.P. is characterized by rugged rock outcroppings of Precambrian

origin. Some, dating back 4.5 billion years, are among the old-
est rocks on earth. Hardwood ridges and coniferous valleys
striate the region. In contrast, the eastern U.P. is underlain by
relatively younger Paleozoic substrates, a scant few hundred
million years old. This area, more uniform in its topography, is
covered by broad stretches of marshes and coniferous swamps.
It has often been remarked by travelers of the road between
Seney and Shingleton (the "Seney Stretch," to locals) that it is
among the flattest and most monotonous in the state.

The central U.P., however, is middle ground. Here, some ten
thousand years ago, the advance of the Wisconsin glaciation
pulsated before its final retreat north. Great torrents of cas-
cading waters carved the earth. As the water flows, so goes
the land, and in the Whitefish River basin of the central U.P.,
parent materials were thoroughly mixed by glacial meltwaters,
resulting in a diversity of landscape features and a mosaic of
soil types. While most of this area is managed for woodland
and recreation, farms dot the landscape, demarcating areas of
superior tilth. The diversity of upland and lowland forests interspersed with a myriad of openings and scores of wetlands
constitutes ideal bear habitat.

Climate

The proximity of the area to Lake Superior and prevailing
northwest winds affect the local climate markedly. During
winter, lake-effect snows are frequent, when "snow bands" set
up over Superior and pour onto the region. Average annual
snowfall at Chatham, Michigan, is 148 inches. On average, 147
days per year have an inch or more of snow on the ground.
Spring is delayed when warm southerly breezes are cooled by
the waters of Lake Michigan. Summers are cool, with readings
of 90°F or higher expected only four times a year. The onset
of autumn is not appreciably delayed by the warming effect

of Lake Superior. Average annual precipitation is 32 inches, of which 60 percent occurs between April 1 and September 30. With an average date of June 13 for the last freezing temperature and an average date of September 13 for the first freeze in the fall, the growing season averages a stingy 91 days.[1]

Vegetation

On the more fertile soils, upland climax communities are primarily maple-hemlock-fern, while lowlands are characterized by hemlock, white cedar, and miterwort.[2] Local successional cover types, after logging or burning, are aspen, birch, and/or mixed red and sugar maple, basswood, and ironwood.

On less fertile soil, climax communities of the uplands are primarily white pine–blueberry–hairgrass with some areas of maple–violet–sweet cicely. Extensive areas of these sandy uplands are managed for pines, including jack pine, red pine, and tamarack. Lowlands are predominantly hemlock–white cedar–miterwort and black spruce–fern.[3]

Winter

They tell me they have to dress bear stories up to make
them interesting, as if the truth isn't interesting enough.
—Allen Hasselborg, 1950

I watch with my back to a large white pine about twenty-
five yards upwind from the den site as the bear cub plays in
the overturned roots of a fallen aspen. It is early April, the
month for conditioning cubs to my presence. The bears know
I am here. The mother, herself having reluctantly accepted my
presence when she was a cub, rests alert outside the den in a
day bed. I speak softly to her cub, trying to familiarize it to my
voice as well as my scent. A few years before, I had introduced
myself to this cub's grandmother, and now as I sit in the warm
spring sun on frozen ground blanketed with pine needles, I am

1

attempting to do the same with her. Spring has become my favorite season, probably because of cubs and all that they are
and will become. It is a time of emergence and reemergence for
many living things in northern forests—a time of motherhood,
pure and simple. I know it won't be long before the delicate
pink-striped spring beauties are about in spectacular patches
and the erect, solitary, waxy-white blossoms of the large-
flowered trillium bedeck the forest floor. It will also only be a
short time before the bears shake off their torpor and are on
the move.

I envision the upcoming year, walking through the forest
mosaic with a third generation of bears. I will follow them
through stands of northern hardwoods, where on cool spring
days, they will feed from the forest floor on herbs such as sweet
cicely, a member of the parsley family and a spring favorite of
the bears. I hope to watch as the mother forages for succulent
wetland herbs in microvernal pools—tiny intermittent wetland areas—while her cub takes refuge in the big rough-barked
eastern hemlocks that ring the edges. I look forward to intimate
family scenes of nursing, grooming, and play. Over the next
seven months, I will be a privileged witness to those singular
events that forever shape the lives of bears and have, in past
bear walks, so greatly enriched my own. At the same time, I
am already apprehensive of the upcoming fall. September and
October are months for bear hunting in northern Michigan—a
chancy time for bears—and a time that I know through experience to be chaotic. But that frenzied time is months in the future, and much will take place between now and then in the life
of this bear cub.

❧

Six years ago I planned to select from a dozen radio-collared
bears one that would accept my presence as an observer while

2

it walked through the forest and went about its daily activities. This would augment sketchy radiotelemetry data on bear locations with direct observations of what a bear was doing at each location. (Understanding what bears forage on in different habitats, which habitats are used for resting or sleeping, and which are sought out as shelter, among other things, is critical to managing forests for bears.) It was a straightforward notion: habituate a bear to my presence and follow it. I would need a good deal of luck for this notion to work, however. In the beginning, I chose a few bears that were wrong for the plan. Then I chose one that was just right.

At the outset, I ruled out using a male bear as a subject because an adult male's home range normally overlaps multiple female bears' home ranges and would be too large. Male bears simply travel too far, too fast, for me to accompany one through the woods. Female bears, on the other hand, are more likely to range over a smaller area, making them relatively easy to locate and follow on a daily basis. Also, female bears represent the most important reproductive component of a bear population. And my intended research involved gathering information on bears' reproduction and survival as well as their food habits.

The first in a series of bears that I tried to habituate was a subadult female. Because of her age, I felt she offered some promise. The plan was to sneak in on her using radiotelemetry equipment; then, after getting close enough so she knew I was there, leave her treats—doughnuts. I would repeat this often enough that she would know I was not a threat. Over time, I hoped, she would accept my presence close enough to observe her natural feeding habits and eventually allow me to accompany her on walks through the forest. As it turned out, this bear wasn't having any of it. She ran from me on each of nine attempts to interact with her.

My next approach, I reasoned, made more sense. An adult female with cubs would be somewhat anchored by the cubs and not able to travel as fast (away from me).

3

Conventional lore has it that the worst place to be in the woods is between a female bear and her cubs (never mind that there has never been a documented human death caused by a mother black bear defending her cubs). Nonetheless, I was about to experience firsthand the most frequently used tactic that a female black bear employs when confronted with danger. She simply sends her cubs up a nearby refuge tree and flees the area, rejoining the cubs when the threat of danger has passed.

It makes little sense for the black bear, which evolved sympatric with the larger and more powerful grizzly bear, to confront unknown dangers on the ground. The genes of black bears that employed this maladaptive behavior would likely have been quickly removed from the population. This may explain why black bears, for the most part, retained the forest-dwelling niche of their ancestors.[1] Grizzly bears, on the other hand, having evolved a larger body size, could exploit not only forests but also open ground, where, unable to seek refuge in trees, they developed an ornery disposition as their tactic for dealing with threats on the ground.

Besides affording a secure refuge for their cubs, the "tree and flee" tactic of female black bears offers less opportunity for a predator to locate the refuge tree, as well as reducing the chance of injury to the female. It also offers limited opportunity for a budding bear researcher to habituate a bear.

But bears, being individuals, do not all react the same way to similar stimuli. Luckily, on my first attempt to habituate another female and her cubs, I got the break I needed. On a still afternoon in early May, after "sneaking in" for several hundred yards on the female's radio signal, I was able to get within seventy-five yards of her position. Crouched behind a stump on the ridge above, I watched as the female bear played a game of tag with her three cubs. She sat on her rump, her front legs outstretched on a wind-thrown maple that leaned about three feet above the ground. As each of the cubs ran past her on the tree, she would paw and nip at them. They would swing beneath the tree, claw their way along its underside until out of her reach, and then drop to the ground, run to the end of the tree, and mount it again to make another pass. After observing several passes by each cub, I stood up and walked toward the bears, talking as I approached. The bears were immediately startled, and with no hesitation, just like all the others, the mother bear sent her three cubs up a refuge tree as I approached. But then, in contrast to the other bears, she followed her cubs up the tree. Which was perfect. It enabled me to approach the refuge tree. I circled the tree as the bear family looked down at me. They were all huffing, blowing, and jaw-popping—blustery behavior meant to intimidate the unwelcome. It was having the desired effect. But keeping up a constant monologue in what I believed to be a soothing monotone, I spoke to the bears, tossed a few doughnuts toward the base of the refuge tree, and then exited the area. The next day I returned to the spot. The doughnuts were gone. I had made my first connection with free-ranging wild bears.

On near daily approaches over the next two weeks, the pattern was acted out in a similar manner but with minor differences. For example, I might circle the tree, leave treats, and then back off a few hundred yards, waiting until the female descended the tree to accept them. On later occasions, I would leave fewer treats at the base of the tree, remain within view (and throwing distance), and toss the treats about the refuge tree, encouraging the female to forage at a greater distance from the tree and in ever increasing proximity to me. After some time, the female bear moved about freely while her cubs remained in the sanctuary of their refuge tree. She would now approach to within a few yards of me, occasionally feeding with her head down while I stood nearby. I took this to be a good sign. Eventually, she relaxed, returning to the base of the refuge tree to rest rather than climbing back up it.

Throughout the month of May, I gradually increased the

time I spent in the presence of the bear family, always careful to leave when I felt they were becoming stressed. Each time, when leaving the family, I was mindful to talk to them as I walked out of their hearing range, reasoning that if something threatening happened to them after my visit, they would not associate it with me. As the sessions lengthened, the cubs insisted on descending the refuge tree to nurse. On occasion, the mother would accommodate them while I watched in the distance. When finished nursing, the cubs would make a few tentative movements about the refuge tree, then quickly scramble back up at the first sign of any movement on my part. After more sessions, the cubs began to remain on the ground with their mother after nursing, occasionally falling asleep under her guard.

As the sessions increased in length to several hours, the bears became restless, wanting, I supposed, to return to their daily foraging activities. When they moved away from the base of the tree, I would stand up to go with them. This sent the cubs scrambling right back up the tree, and we would start the whole affair over again.

In spite of their inherent fear of me, I felt I was getting close to a turning point with the bear family. We had settled into a routine centered on my providing treats to the mother bear—wherever I found her throughout her home range. Each day when I located her radio signal, I would make contact with her, trekking through upland hardwoods, across bogs, through cedar swamps, or around lakes to get there. It must have seemed strange to the bears. Regardless of where they traveled, here came the umbilical doughnut bag again! But any inconvenience I caused was surely offset by gain in calories. The mother bear never let the cubs forage for the treats in my presence. I did not want that to happen, either. Nor did I ever attempt to feed the bear out of my hand or touch her. I purposely kept her at a distance during habituation sessions. The last thing I wanted was a tamed pet bear. I wanted the bear to act as wild bears do in the forest. This bear was five years old. She was wild. She had had five years of lessons in avoiding humans. Fear is exactly the response that bears should have to people, and I did not want to take that fear away from her. I knew the cubs would be more trusting of me if I fed them and that the mother would accept me more quickly if I pushed it just a little, drawing her in close and feeding her out of my hand. I did not want to create what is known as a "nuisance" bear. Although, in my view, there was no such thing as a nuisance bear, only nuisance people; and I did not want to become one of them. I was doing my level best to maintain a professional relationship.

Sometimes this made for long days: the cubs up the refuge tree looking down at me and me looking back up at them, while the mother rested alert at the base of the tree, appearing anxious to resume normal activities. We both had other work to do. There were nine other female bears in the 100-square-mile study area wearing radio collars. They had to be located every day, and that took time. By the time I had spent about 150 hours with this bear family, they did not trust me enough to move from the base of their refuge tree. Spending time with the mother and cubs was, however, providing some very useful data on refuge trees and several of the plant foods she was consuming.

Refuge trees tended to be large-diameter (averaging greater than twenty inches at breast height), roughed-barked trees. Mostly eastern hemlocks were used in the upland forest stands, while northern white cedar and aspen were the species most often used in the lowlands. Long ago, black bears in the U.P. probably took refuge most often in huge white pines. At the turn of the century, even the smaller-diameter white pines—today's bear refuge trees—were scalped from the forest by greedy lumber barons.

The rough bark of an ideal refuge tree enables the cubs, with their tiny, needle-like claws, to climb them more quickly, and massive limbs provide quality resting spots for cubs. Trees of the size that the bears were selecting as refuge trees constituted less than 2–3 percent of all trees in the Hiawatha National Forest. It would seem prudent then, and make perfectly good sense, for forest managers to keep such trees around for future generations of bears.

By the end of May, the bears and I had settled into a routine of sorts. The routine was for me to approach the bears to within earshot and begin talking to them, as I homed in with the radiotelemetry equipment. My visits were no longer greeted with the blustery theatrics reserved for the unwelcome. They had begun waiting for me, the cubs up a refuge tree, the mother sitting alert at the base. Occasionally, the mother would send the cubs up a refuge tree and come to the sound of my voice. She would appear out of nowhere. I will always be amazed at how quietly bears are able to move through the forest. Sometimes, I would walk right by her only to hear her following me. I suspect that on occasion she was purposefully noisy just to get my attention. Quite a blow to my ego, as I thought myself a fair observer and something of a woodsman. Sometimes we connected a few hundred yards from the refuge tree, and after the treats were gone she would allow me to follow her back to the cub tree. Finally, on one such occasion, she returned directly to the refuge tree, calling the cubs down while I stood a mere fifteen yards from the tree.

By this time, I was becoming aware of a number of vocalizations that the bears made. Around the refuge tree the mother used four principal sounds when interacting with the cubs. She made a long blowing sound and a shorter, more rapid series of huffing sounds by expelling air through her nostrils and mouth. Both signaled discomfort or displeasure; they were often employed as alarm sounds and used to gather the cubs, send them up a tree, or make them climb higher in the tree. She also made what is best described as a plaintive *umph* and a louder tongue-clicking sound to beckon the cubs down, signal her presence, or rally the litter. The tongue-click seems to be produced by forcing the posterior of the tongue against the roof of the mouth, coupled with a simultaneous umph from the diaphragm. But a subtler version using just the umph was employed at close quarters and had a calming effect on family members. The fourth primary sound was given when the mother was at a distance from the refuge tree and out of sight of the cubs. She clunked her jaws by tapping her molars together to apprise the cubs of her whereabouts. This sound is distinct from the jaw-popping, lip-smacking, and chomping sounds bears make when perturbed. On occasion, clunking was combined with tongue-clicking, but for the most part it was used alone. I was always impressed at how the clunking sound resonated through the woods. Often it was possible to hear bears making the sound from a hundred yards or more, even on somewhat windy days.

One day the mother bear called the cubs down with a tongue-click in my presence. There was a brief rendezvous at the base of the tree (on the side opposite me, as the cubs would not come down on my side), which involved some sniffing and licking, and then the mother and cubs walked off—bear researcher in tow.

It was a little dicey at first, the tentative cubs scampering ahead of their mother and up a tree at the slightest sound of the smallest branch broken under my foot. Periodically, the mother would stop to look back at me with an intense stare. I talked to her in my now familiar calming voice, "It's OK, it's just me, I'm a friend." Satisfied or not, she would proceed. We moved in leapfrog fashion, the cubs scurrying from one potential refuge tree to the next, but at least we were moving. When they stopped, I would stop, keeping up a constant monologue. I had folded the antenna of my telemetry radio into my pack at the initial contact. It was a good move; it was difficult enough getting through the woods with the bear and cubs without having to drag gangly items.

After leapfrogging for about an hour, we came to the edge

9

of a wetland. The mother bear moved to the base of a nearby hemlock tree, propped her back against it, and nursed her cubs for ten minutes. For the first seven minutes, the cubs vocalized incessantly while they nursed. The remainder of the bout they nursed silently while their mother groomed them, licking the tops of their heads.

Finished nursing, the bears moved on to the top of a ridge and came upon a hunters' blind. The mother stood on her hind legs, her front paws resting on the side of the blind, rocking it back and forth while huffing through a small portal. The cubs all raised up on their hind feet and mimicked her, but their twenty pounds of weight against the blind hadn't nearly the effect of their mother's. After a few minutes, the cubs got bored and headed off down a game trail. The mother bear dropped to all fours and started after them with a stiff-legged walk, punching her feet into the ground. Then all of a sudden, as if a light went on in her head, she did an abrupt about-face and came back at me. With her ears back, her upper lip curled and slightly extended, making direct eye contact, she walked straight at me. From a distance of about thirty feet, in an explosive burst of energy, she performed a double-lunge charge, in which she lunged forward, both front paws slamming the ground simultaneously, along with a synchronized forceful exhalation of air—blowing. On this occasion, she performed two in a row. It is a pretty intimidating exhibition, particularly when you are not sure the bear is going to stop. I was not all that concerned, however. I had been told by experts that these displays were just blustery attempts at intimidation. I believed she knew I was not a threat to her or the cubs and possibly even recognized me as a benefactor. I had never made a move without what I felt was her approval. She had no reason to distrust me. Besides, if she really wanted to get me, she could. I interpreted this display as a message of sorts. Had she associated me in some way with the blind's former occupant? Was she relating to the cubs the danger of being near the blind?

10

Bears also exhibit variations of this blustery behavior. Sometimes lunges are performed with only one paw swatting the ground, sometimes paw swats may occur accompanied by blowing or huffing without the lunge. I have also seen bears incorporate a sapling or shrub into the routine, knocking it over with their chest or swatting it with a paw while charging by huffing and blowing, only to stop short of the target of their intimidation. The additional noise and motion, the result of incorporating the object into the display, gives it a more threatening, larger-than-life appearance. I am almost certain that that is why it is done. It may also give bears something on which to act out the display, providing an object on which to redirect their aggression rather than making direct contact with the real target. I have heard these displays termed *bluff charges*, and while that may be an apt description of their outcome, I'm uncertain that bluffing is in the bear's mind at the outset. It is quite possible that such charges are intended to evoke a response, the outcome depending on that response—stand pat, it's a bluff; waver and run, it's a rout.

I have never heard black bears growl, and I don't believe they actually make that sound. They do, however, make a low moaning sound from their throat, which starts out low and slow and then breaks into a series of *wa wa wa wha wha wha wa wa* sounds that increase in tempo and pitch and then trail off. Bears make this sound when they are highly agitated. I have seen two bears face-off while making this vocalization and move in a slow circle around each other with their heads down, necks extended, and ears back. In most instances this results in one of the bears being swatted, bitten, or chased by the other. It is usually the last sound preceding direct contact. But it is apparent to me that when bears engage in these ritualized threatening displays, they do not necessarily want to make contact. They just want their way. On only one other occasion, in six years of walking with bears, did a bear display threatening behavior toward me. On that occasion, I was at fault. I was rude and attempted to take food away from the bear—bears do not tolerate rude behavior well.

After the encounter with the blind, we did not go much farther on that first walk. But I did not want to reinforce the notion that the mother bear could intimidate me, so I continued to follow them for a while, albeit at a greater distance. I did not want to push it; I would continue to take the slow approach and let the bears be bears. My first bear walk! It was enough for me.

Shortly after that walk, I named the mother bear Carmen, after Carmen Miranda, the dancer—because of the stiff-legged dancelike motions she made when punching her feet into the ground and twisting them. By early June I was able to travel the forest with the bears for several hours at a time. In years to come, the walks lengthened, sometimes exceeding fifteen hours, lasting from light to dark. And eventually, I was able to discontinue bringing Carmen doughnuts on a regular basis. But on that day in May, as on many to follow, when I walked out of the woods, I felt euphoric. I asked myself how many other people in the world had walked with a bear family through the forest? Or had watched cubs nursing in such an intimate family scene? I liked the answer.

కావ

It has been six years since those first tentative steps with bears. Now here I sit observing Carmen's daughter and granddaughter outside their den waking from their winter's sleep, and I contemplate my first steps with a third generation of bears. While I have accompanied bears about their home ranges, logging mile after mile with them over the past years, they know their home range in infinitely more detail than I ever will, even after examining all types of maps of their territories, including Landsat satellite images and color infrared photos. Yet I want to know it better. I want to know and understand just what it takes to make optimum bear habitat. What habitat or combination of habitats is most important to bears? How do bears maneuver within a specific habitat type, and how do they get from one habitat type to another in the forest landscape? What difference does it make when roads are built across their travel routes? All of these are unanswered questions.

What I do know is that it takes a considerable amount of territory to support something as large and far ranging as a bear. Adult mother bears use an area of about ten to fifteen square miles as they travel about the forest—up to twenty-five square miles during breeding years. Adult male bears may use an area four or five times that size. Bears are relatively long-lived mammals. They are intelligent and have long memories. They are seasonal exploiters of habitats, and as such, they may travel quite a distance to take advantage of seasonally available foods.

Bears' knowledge of their home range makes them efficient in accumulating the calories necessary to overwinter and is of particular advantage in years of food scarcity. I wonder, as I sit here, if bears have a sort of cognitive map[2] of their home ranges in their heads, possessing the ability to move to any point in that range whenever they wish, and if they might select den sites in familiar areas so that upon emergence in spring they can more efficiently exploit available resources. This would make sense, though it's not proven.

The whole phenomenon of bears passing the winter in a den is fascinating. As I learn more about bears, it is their physiology that intrigues me most. Ralph A. Nelson of the Mayo Clinic, who has conducted extensive research on bear physiology, calls them "metabolic marvels." Denning or hibernation is thought to have been practiced by bear ancestors over 10 million years ago, probably as a means of adapting to seasonally available food supplies. Some folks maintain that bears are not true hibernators like marmots, ground squirrels, and bats.

They prefer to call the physiological state in which bears pass the winter something akin to winter sleep. This is because a bear's body temperature does not fall to near ambient levels, as do the body temperatures of true hibernators. By slowing their heart rate, termed *bradycardia*, and reducing blood flow to their extremities, bears are able to maintain their "core-temperature" (in heart, lungs, and brain) at a level only a few degrees (five to nine) below their normal level of 98 to 99°F. This adaptation not only conserves precious energy but also enables bears to become aroused more quickly while in their dens, a definite survival advantage when coexisting with predators larger than oneself.[3] Bears are surprisingly regenerative while in this reduced state of physiology: yearlings grow their permanent set of canine teeth while denned; mothers give birth to cubs; and all bears sluff off the keratinized layer of tissue on their paw pads, which then grows anew. As is the case in true hibernators, bears' respiration and heart rates fall to low levels. But unlike true hibernators, bears neither get up to feed from food caches nor drink while denning. And, as a rule, they are thought not to urinate or defecate while denned. I have on occasion, however, discovered scats in the dens of female black bears while conducting winter den checks. I guess the bears didn't know about rules. (Also, I witnessed one occasion—and observed sign in the snow indicating two others—on which a female bear emerged from her den in February to take a bite of snow at the den entrance and then reentered the den, not to emerge again until April.)

Some folks make a distinction between denning and hibernating, the distinction being that hibernation is a physiological state, while denning is the act of taking refuge. Hibernation thus evolved as a mechanism for circumventing food shortages and inclement weather, and denning as a means of preventing predation while in the reduced physiological state of hibernation. Whatever we choose to call it, the phenomenon of passing the winter in a den is to most people uniquely bearish.

Female bears are almost unmatched in their ability to carry out a pregnancy while in a state of starvation. Other than cetaceans—whales, for example—no other mammals do that. Only bears, some cetaceans, and pinnipeds such as seals and walruses, fast through all or part of their lactation. Bears are induced ovulaters, the female requiring the physical act of breeding to stimulate the release of her eggs. Bears normally mate from late May through July, but the fertile egg undergoes a delayed implantation, like that of the mink and some weasels. When the egg and sperm join, they form a zygote. The single-cell zygote enters the oviduct and travels to the uterus, developing into a hollow ball of cells, the blastocyst, as it goes. In the uterus, the blastocyst floats free and does not implant into the uterine wall. Implantation is delayed until about the time the female bear enters her den in the fall. Once implanted, the blastocyst develops rapidly, and cubs are born about ten weeks later. Whether or not the blastocyst develops into a cub is thought to depend on the nutritional status of the female. If she does not achieve a certain body weight (or perhaps percent of body fat), or some critical physiological state, she will abort the pregnancy and reabsorb the blastocyst or give birth to nonviable offspring. Black bear cubs are born nearly hairless, blind (their eyes will not open for forty days), and with only fleshy protuberances for ears. Their mother eats their afterbirth and licks the birth fluids from their bodies. She will also clean up after them when they void body fluids (an act that may require the stimulation of the mother's tongue). These activities provide a source of fluid nutrition for the mother, as well as serving to keep the den free of odors that might attract predators. Because both sexes of bears are promiscuous, the cubs in a litter may be from the same father or from different fathers.

When born, black bear cubs are only about eight inches long and weigh only about ten ounces, about as much as a bag of marshmallows. Among mammals, only marsupials are born smaller in proportion to the mother. Among nonmarsupial mammals, the gross weight of offspring in a litter is usually scaled precisely to the weight of the mother. This is true for all nonmarsupial mammals from tiny shrews to huge baleen whales with only one exception: bears. According to that ratio, mother bears give birth to offspring that are less than 1/10 the size that would be predicted. Newborn bear cubs are less than 1/300 their mother's weight. (Human babies are about 1/20 their mother's weight. Porcupines, at 1/15 their mother's weight, are even larger, while dogs and cats weigh up to 1/5 their mother's weight.)

If cubs were born at weights around ten to fifteen pounds, they would require more milk than could be provided by a slumbering mother. Producing small cubs at birth ensures more manageable needs. If we think of the den as an extension of the womb, cubs on emergence in spring are near the size predicted by the ratio.

∽∘∾

I watch Carmen's granddaughter climb through the maze of roots in the overturned aspen that formed the ceiling and facade of the den, using her teeth for climbing. Hanging on to a root with her teeth, she shifts her weight and swings to the next root in the lattice. She then claws her way to the pinnacle. It is a method used by all cubs in the litters I have observed, and I have witnessed it in adult bears as well. The cub then descends and begins forcing her attentions on her slumbering mother, whom I've named Nettie (after my wife Annette). Cubs, almost invariably, initiate the nursing sequence. At first Nettie rolls over in an effort to conceal her mammae. I have witnessed Carmen using this tactic; when nursing triplets, she splayed herself belly down on small tussocks in an effort to stave off the relentless efforts of her litter to nurse. But Nettie, a first-time mother, lacks Carmen's experience and after some encouragement by the cub, she gives in to the cub's demands. Nettie takes a few steps toward a nearby refuge tree as the cub scurries between her legs trying to get hold of a mammae. At the tree, she flops over, exposing her three pairs of mammae to the cub. She then shifts her body around until her back is toward the tree and she is resting in a slight depression. Her curled body position brings the mammae closer together. She proceeds to groom the top of the cub's head as it begins nursing.

I watch, coding in the activity as NV (nursing with vocalizations) on my data collector. Having gone high tech the year before, I am now using a portable global positioning system (GPS), carried in my pack, to record the bear's activities. This provides the advantage of allowing me to record their activities at intervals as frequent as one second, and while doing that, my location is positioned in the background by a constellation of satellites some eleven thousand miles in space. This positioning yields a nearly exact location of where the activity takes place. Back home, in the evening, I will download the data from the recorder onto my computer and overlay it on other maps I have developed. I can then analyze the location of each activity relative to attributes such as habitat type, elevation, slope and aspect, distance from streams, and the nearest road, among other things.

Nursing bouts vary in length throughout the year. And, as one might expect, they become shorter and less frequent as cubs get older. Some bouts last only a few seconds if Carmen or Nettie is disturbed or feels uncomfortable for some reason. But I have witnessed nursing events that lasted as long as twelve minutes. Initially, all nursing bouts are characterized by vocalizations from the cubs. And they can be loud. The first time I heard nursing cubs vocalizing, I started looking around for a helicopter in the distance. The sound might be described as a cooing-chuckle or hum. But it has a staccato, pulsating rhythm to it: I am sure it is a contented sound. And this cub is content.

The first litter of Carmen's that I walked with (which, as it turns out from interpreting the width of cementum layers in thin sections shaved from her teeth, was not her first) comprised three siblings, Nettie and her two brothers. A small male was the runt of the litter, and Nettie was the next biggest. In her next litter, Carmen produced two males. The following contained two females and a male. Nettie is a first-time mother and has produced only a single female cub. Of six bears in the study whose first age of reproduction was known, only one other gave birth to a single cub in the first litter; all others gave birth to initial litters of two or three cubs.

I wonder how life will be for this cub I am watching now. She will have no siblings to play with, no littermates on whom to test the tactile moves that have not only developmental utility but survival benefits as well. But then she won't have a dominant male sibling horning in on her meals, either. Perhaps it will be an even trade in the scheme of things. Seven minutes into this nursing bout, the cub stops vocalizing and begins alternating between mammae, switching top to bottom and side to side on all sets of mammae. I punch NK (nurse cub) into the data recorder. I know the lack of vocalization and switching mammae are signs that this nursing bout is coming to a close. If this were a litter of two or three, this would be the point that cubs start crawling around the stomach of their mother, checking to see if a sibling has missed anything. They often bite the mammae a little too hard or claw a sensitive spot in their zeal, bringing an abrupt end to the bout. When Carmen's nursing cubs reach this stage, she will simply brush them off and blow, sending them retreating up the refuge tree.

Nettie, however, is inexperienced. She has gotten up and is trying to walk away, the cub still hanging from her nipple and biting it as she is dragged along the forest floor between Nettie's legs. This cannot be very comfortable for Nettie. Nettie's solution for ending the bout is to trot for a few steps, which dislodges the cub. She is going to have to improve on this maneuver, or I will have to develop a new activity code.

Now the dislodged cub is left sitting about five yards from the refuge tree and has become intent on my presence. She is somewhat closer to me than is comfortable. The cub bawls. Nettie turns in my direction but looks right by me. She is alert that the cub may have detected approaching danger, but apparently she doesn't associate it with me. Walking to the cub, Nettie licks her head, and they play briefly, the cub lying on her back, swatting and biting at Nettie's face as she nuzzles her. I am pleased that Nettie does not view my presence as a threat to her cub. I have known Nettie since she was a cub and have walked with her over the last two years as she came into her own. It seems that once the bears accept my presence, they will look right through and beyond me for signs of danger. It's as if there is a sphere of influence, and if I am inside it and the bears are sure of my location and actions, then they don't consider me in their response to other stimuli in the woods. Constantly talking to the bears has paid off. They know my voice, and if we are briefly out of each other's sight when traveling through thick vegetation, they can pinpoint me by the sound of my voice. They then don't feel threatened by any noise coming from my location. A bear's biggest concern in the woods, I believe, is another bear. Unable to discern the source of a noise, they take no chances and bolt, either to a refuge tree or on a flat-out run.

My biggest concern on this day is to keep the cub from viewing me as a threat. Her mother accepts me, but the cub was born with an innate fear of strangers. I have to allay that fear yet not conquer it. It is a delicate balance.

I have put in enough time for the day and don't want to stress the cub, so I pack up my gear, say good-byes all around, and head for the truck, talking all the way: "See ya, Nettie, thanks, good to see ya, see ya, bye" until I think I am out of their hearing. I plan to go see the cub's grandmother, Carmen, today. She was with her two yearling males down along the east branch of the Whitefish River when I left her yesterday. I wonder where I will find her today. Probably not far from where I left her.

༄ঞ৹

After making my way through a hardwood stand where last year's beech leaves cling golden and rustling in the sun, I find my guess is close. The bears are along the shore of the Whitefish close to where I broke off with them yesterday but on the opposite bank of the river. Runoff has swollen the river, and ice is wedged here and there along its frozen banks, but it is neither uniform nor solid enough for me to cross on. I hadn't anticipated this and did not pack waders. Crossing ground this time of the year is always a challenge. I still have to pack and wear snowshoes while following the bears, or I might break through crusted snow to my knees while the bears scoot right over it. I'm already burdened with telemetry equipment, cameras and lenses, data logger and GPS unit, and a video camera. On any given day, I would be a lucky find for a mugger. Many times it occurs to me that I feel safer in the woods in the company of bears than I could ever feel walking big-city streets. Statistically, a person is ninety thousand times more likely to be the victim of a homicide than to be killed by a bear. Here, on bear walks, the biggest danger is getting a stick in the eye, banged shins, or following the bears into a nest of angry bald-faced hornets.

But my problem now is not muggers or insects but rather wide cold water that may be flowing too fast for me to stand up in it. I decide to head upstream a half mile or so. I know the river is wider there and has a solid limestone bed; it should not be more than a foot or two deep. When I arrive at the spot, it looks promising. The water moves slower and less ice juts from shore to hamper entrance or exit. I keep a few garbage bags in my pack to protect my gear from rain. I put everything in my pack into one of the plastic bags just in case I should go under. I tie my snowshoes onto the back of the pack. Then I remove my boots, lace them together, and sling them over my shoulder. I put a bag on each foot, truss them to my belt, swing my feet over the bank, stand up, and head across. It works fairly well until I spring a leak near the far shore. The water is brisk, but I am close enough to the other side to toss my boots onto the snow-covered bank. I have only a few more slippery steps to take when the current catches the small tear in the bag and rips it wide open. Not much else to do now. I make a dive for shore. (I knew I should have gotten the three-mil thickness.) I have a dry pair of socks in the pack, but my pants and long johns are wet to my knees. The air temperature is 40 degrees. At least my boots will be dry. I home in on Carmen & Company and move toward them quickly, attempting to get up some speed to take off the chill.

As I move the half mile south along the river valley to their location, I notice a few sets of deer tracks, the first I've observed in the study area since December. Deer migrating north is a sure sign that the temperature is on the rise and real spring is not far behind.

Carmen and her two yearling males wear radio collars. During the past two winters I have collared yearling males in their mothers' dens in an effort to determine when they disperse from their natal areas. The three radio signals sound strong and close together. I know they are near, so I start talking, hoping that if they heard the commotion upriver, hearing my even-tempered tone of voice will reassure them.

Females with yearlings exit their dens earlier than females with newborns. And not being anchored by newborns, they range farther. This time of year, the bears tend to be standoffish during my first few visits, as I have not made direct contact with them since denning last fall, some six months earlier. I have always tried to spend some time at den sites in late March and early April just prior to emergence, talking softly to them as they awaken, but even so, it takes time to get reacquainted.

This year, Carmen's den is located under the root system of a wind-thrown tree. Last fall, she dug into the cavity formed by the uplifted roots and gathered leaves and ferns and sticks and twigs from the surrounding area to form a nest in the center of the void. Judging by the size of the bed she constructed inside, it must have required numerous trips in and out for materials.

I am not sure what a "typical" bear den is, but the one that Carmen and her yearlings occupy this year is similar to a fourth of the nearly one hundred dens I have observed during the study. It consists of a semi-excavated hole at the base of an overturned tree, fallen log, or clump of brush. Almost always there is gathered bedding material or pieces of bark scraped from surrounding trees or the unearthed overhead roots to form a nest within the cavity.

About 50 percent of the dens I encounter are located under brush piles. Piles of tree tops and limbs are common in the numerous clear-cuts and pine plantings located throughout the study area. The bears appear to select brush piles as den sites opportunistically. Brush-pile dens are typically larger than other types of dens and are seldom augmented with excavation. Leaves and sticks present under the piles are normally raked together and formed into an oval nest, on which the bears sleep. Mothers accompanied by cubs of the year den in brush piles more often than pregnant females or lone bears, perhaps because the group is better accommodated by brush piles. Although they are roomier and require less energy for bears to construct, they are probably less thermally efficient than semi-excavated and dug dens. While bears do not normally share dens with other than immediate family members, on one occasion I observed a subadult mother bear denned with a porcupine and attribute the association to the roominess of the brush-pile den, in which the bear had constructed three nests of twigs and ferns.

The other 25 percent of the dens are the classic excavated or "dug" den. Usually dug at the base of a tree or stump or beneath a fallen log, the excavated chamber is totally earthen and normally is not lined with appreciable bedding materials.

One of the most perfect bear dens I ever crawled into was chosen and constructed by Nettie for herself and the two cubs of her second litter. It was semi-excavated under the roots of a three-trunked white cedar that leaned out over a small stream. There she shaped a bed of grasses and ferns and bits of cedar clawed from the hollow bole of one of the trunks. The nest rested six inches above the ground and was surrounded by the protective cedar. That winter, on a cold and windy day, I checked her den, accompanied by a small group of friends and fellow researchers, and was treated to as pretty a sight as could be hoped for. Inside the cedar den, which was as warm and aromatic as any sauna, the accumulated breaths of the bears had condensed and formed a halo of intertwining fingers of ice shards around the inside of the hollow trunk a few feet above the slumbering mother bear. When I stuck my head into the den entrance after tunneling through a foot or two of snow, I saw two perfect bear cubs poised motionless just below the crystalline structure, ready to make an escape up through the icy ring. It was one of those moments that lasts only an instant but you wish it would last forever because you know you have been treated to something more than special that can never be duplicated. Selfishly, I took no pictures and spent more time than usual inside the den pretending to work.

In fall, bears enter their dens earlier than most people might expect. And there seems to be a chronology to it. In our area, pregnant females are the first to enter dens in the fall and, on average, are in dens by October 10. Subadult females are the next to enter, an average of nine days later. Females with cubs den last, around October 22. It is likely that availability of abundant natural fall foods delays the onset of denning for all bears. In 1994, when natural fall foods (beechnuts) were abundant in the study area, Carmen and Nettie and other female bears entered dens an average of fourteen days later than in other years.

Pregnant females spend the greatest amount of time in dens, emerging with their cubs after 178 days on average. Subadults fall in the middle, spending, on average, 169 days in their dens. And females entering dens with cubs of the year exit dens (with yearlings) after spending the least amount of time in them, averaging only 160 days. (The longest duration of denning I observed for any bear was that of a pregnant female, in normal physical condition, that denned for 206 days, from September 14, 1995, to April 9, 1996—nearly seven months.)

Upon emerging from their dens in spring (usually late March through early April), bears often make day beds at or near the entrance. Day beds are typically constructed of sticks and twigs and the bark and boughs of whatever species of trees are in close proximity. Bears lie in the day beds on top of the snow on warm sunny days, retreating to the den during inclement weather and in the evening. As they awaken from hibernation, bears seem apathetic about food and foraging and lie around for a week or two while their bodies gin up. Sitting near a den, talking to the bears, allowing them to become reacquainted with my presence while I absorb the sounds and scents of another freshening of spring is a sure cure for cabin fever.

Last week I spent nearly three days posted next to Carmen & Company's den in an attempt to hasten our reassociation. I observed day beds outside the den and three sets of tracks in the snow at the entrance, evidence that the bears were spending at least some time outside the den during the day and were awake and able to hear me. So I sat and in my most comforting voice beckoned to the bears: "It's OK, it's just me, come to see ya, what ya doing, I'm a friend." But it was in vain, for the bears were long gone from the den. Yesterday, the fourth day of my visits, I discovered three sets of tracks exiting the rear of the den, which in the patch-worked snow, I had failed to detect earlier. The family of bears was miles from the den when I discovered my mistake. If I had used the radiotelemetry equipment to check, I would have known that. When I finally located the bears, they were in a thick stand of balsam fir saplings resting in day beds constructed from the bitten-off tops and broken branches of the conifers.

Today, as I approach the bears' signal, I find bloody bear footprints in the snow. I stand talking in the direction of a different stand of balsams. I have an idea of what is going on. I can hear the bears blowing lightly in discontent at my approach. I close the final one hundred yards from upwind of them so they will know it is me. Bear tracks lead off toward the northeast and then return from the same direction. Carmen and the yearlings are making trips from their newly constructed day beds to the carcass of a winter-killed white-tailed deer about one hundred yards distant. I presume that feeding on deer will be the name of the game today.

∽๑∾

Winter-killed deer can be a feast or famine proposition for bears. This year, I will observe Carmen & Company feeding on the carcasses of only two winterkills. In other years, she has been fortunate to locate as many as seven. Bears consume nearly every speck of meat on a winterkill before abandoning the carcass. Nearly all the offal, except for any vegetative matter in the stomach, is eaten. Bones are crushed and the red gelatinous substance that was formerly fat-enriched marrow is licked clean from the interior. Later, the bones and fragments of hide are used as play objects, occupying the bears' attention during idle times. A newfound deer carcass can dictate bear habitat use and movement for days. Frequently, the bears will drag the carcass to a preferred location such as the base of a refuge tree. Later, the find might be covered with sticks, twigs, and leaves for concealment between scavenges. But, for whatever reason, I have never observed bears concealing a carcass while appreciable snow cover blanketed the woods.

During winters of extremely deep snow cover and cold weather, well over 100,000 deer may starve to death in the Upper Peninsula. Much of this starvation takes place in or near "deer yards," areas where deer seek the refuge of thermal cover. Acting out learned behavior, they travel for fifty miles or more to these traditional yarding areas. In years of deep snow, migration takes place on traditional routes used for decades by generations of deer. Often these migration trails run parallel to drainages. Several major migration trails meander along the Whitefish River as it crisscrosses Carmen's and Nettie's home ranges. Deer are trapped there by intense December blizzards during their southward migration, providing an opportunity for the bears and their offspring, upon den emergence in early spring, to scavenge their carcasses. However, in years when rapidly decreasing November temperatures are unaccompanied by deep snow, deer might migrate right through the home ranges of bears in the central peninsula, few dying en route. In those years, carcasses tend to be concentrated near the southern yards, miles from the border of Carmen's or Nettie's home range. The few carcasses available to scavenge are of deer that perish in the spring as they migrate through the bears' home ranges on the return trip north. It has always seemed ironic to me that a deer would survive the ravages of an entire winter only to expire on the last leg of the trip. The deer's misfortune, however, is the bear's banquet. The protein from those scavenged deer provides a significant source of nourishment for a bear newly emerged from a winter den.

∽o∾

I follow as the family makes the trip to the remains of the deer. Carmen's yearling males, Corduroy and Aster, lead the way. A matched pair at birth, they remained so throughout much of the year—Corduroy's eighty-seven-pound March den weight only slightly besting Aster's eighty-two pounds. But that consistent, albeit slight, advantage, coupled with his bold approach, allowed Corduroy to win out in most of the contests between the siblings. Nudging each other, side by side, the pair now ambles ahead. Their glistening black coats contrast with the receding snow. The bears are able to pad across the crusted snow, but I am not. I break through to my knees, my snowshoes still strapped to the back of my pack. But the shoes would probably not have done me much good, even if I had put them on. The noise they would make would surely frighten the bears, and it is unlikely they would have let me follow them very far without running off. This time of the year is a difficult one for keeping up with bears. As I pick my way from patch to patch of open ground I watch the bears steadily outdistancing me. The carcass (which I determine to be a yearling buck) is nearly picked clean when the bears and I arrive. Gray jays flitter about in the pole-size aspens surrounding the carcass, which lies atop a patch of snow. A jay pecks at a scrap of tallow saddle-bagged over a limb in a nearby aspen. I lean into an aspen about ten yards from the site as the yearlings rummage the remains. Carmen, her back to me, occupies herself with a previously gnawed portion of a femur. The bears do not dawdle long at the site. Finding little profit here, they set off in a northeasterly direction.

I follow them into a cedar swamp where they locate some swamp thistle in a snowless area and begin feeding on it. Swamp thistle is consumed by first biting off the prickly basal whorl, then gnawing out the tender core. It is the most frequently consumed herb in the late-winter–early-spring diet of the bears. I watch as the bears each eat several over a half-hour period. As Carmen moves about locating the thistles, I notice the new growth of short fur on her ankles and feet. When we handled her in the den, we treated her for a slight case of mange. Now the fur is growing back but is still much shorter than the rest of her fur. She looks as if she's been barbered by the Jed Clampett school, obtained by putting a bowl over the head and cropping everything below.

I am chilled from working up a sweat following the bears into the swamp. The sun does not penetrate the thick canopy of the cedars, and my legs are becoming cold as my pant legs freeze while I stand here. Evening is approaching, and while I am enjoying the increasing day length, we are still two months away from our longest day. I decide to fold up my gear and say good-bye to the bears, allowing time for a daylight trip out. I have a river to cross.

Spring

It is hard to say exactly what any animal is **doing.** It is impossible
to know when or where an event in an animal's life begins or ends.
And our human senses confine us to realms that may contain only
a small part of the information produced in an event. Something
critical could be missing and we would not know.

—Barry Lopez

I am surprised on my next visit to Nettie's den to find that
she has moved. I did not think I needed to check her telemetry signal before going in on her and the cub. It is, after
all, only mid April, and normally females with cubs are still anchored solidly to the den site. Typically, female bears with cubs
vacate dens about the same time other bears do, in early April,
but, in contrast to other bears, they do not usually move far
from the den site until late April or early May, when their cubs

are older and better able to travel. Yet female bears have been known to abandon dens prematurely and move their cubs to alternate sites as the result of a number of natural causes, such as den caving, flooding, and disturbance at den sites by other wild animals. Bear cubs have sometimes died of such causes. In my study, bears were more fortunate. For example, in the spring of 1992, following unseasonably early rains, a female bear successfully moved her three cubs a distance of one hundred yards to an upland site after an ill-chosen den flooded. On other occasions, evidence in the snow at the entrance to dens occupied by female bears and their cubs told one story of a bobcat peering into a den and another of a coyote crouching near a den's entrance. Perhaps they anticipated a meal of newborn bear cubs, but to no avail.

Not all disturbances at dens are from natural causes or predators, however. This spring, Nettie's den abandonment is the direct result of human disturbance. Last fall, she selected her den site in the relative security provided by a stand of northern hardwood sawtimber within a vehicle-excluded area. The area is one of few in the Hiawatha National Forest that are off-limits year-round to motorized vehicles. Nettie excavated her den at the base of a root mass within a few yards of an abandoned logging road. She entered the den pregnant in early October. Later that fall, hunters walked the logging road, oblivious to her nearby hibernation. During winter, snowmobilers illegally traversed the road. Yet Nettie, with her newborn cub, remained secure under her cloak of protective snow. But this spring, a joy-ridden ATV twisted, plowed, and caterwauled its way past the den twice in the same day, forcing her to abandon the site. With the cub dangling from her jaws, she moved three hundred yards deeper into the forest, pausing twice en route to rest and adjust her hold on the cub, on her way to a more distant, yet more exposed nest site. I pieced the events together from telltale signs in broken snow. The culprit and stench of machinery were long gone.

At first glance, the Upper Peninsula, with its extensive wood-lands and rugged beauty, can conjure up surreal images of wilderness in the mind's eye of the unacquainted. The distinc-tion between romance and reality is often blurred, and here the geography of the heart clashes mightily with the geography of reality. Familiarization with the forests exposes just how badly they are carved up by roads, despite their relative solitude and seeming remoteness.

Roads. Many people still believe, with erring faith, that what is national or state forest cannot be despoiled. Yet people are permitted to drive some type of vehicle nearly anywhere they desire within the one-hundred-square-mile study area. The Upper Peninsula, by default, is wide open to off-road ve-hicles (ORVs). The Michigan Department of Natural Resources (MDNR) has an "open unless posted closed" policy for ORVs throughout the peninsula. What this means is that unless a trail is posted "closed," ORVs have free range: as though forests should be as accessible as downtown Detroit. I know from developing the geographic information system (GIS), incorpo-rating digital road maps into it, and analyzing available habi-tat relative to the web of roads that less than one-quarter of the study area is farther than one-half mile from a driveable road. Currently, there are in fact precious few areas where bears can roam even partially isolated from the influences of roads. De-spite that, some people persist in violating the sanctity of even those few places. It is my belief that anytime the incidence of intersection between man and bear is increased, it inevitably results in the demise of the bear. Roads do just that. And on av-erage, like bears, I rate them less than desirable.

Nettie remains at the surrogate den site for a week, anchored by the cub's inability to negotiate the forest floor. I visit her only once, not wanting to cause undue stress to her or the cub at this less than opportune location. It is hard to tell how the cub's habituation is progressing because she sleeps high up a refuge tree for most of the session. Nettie, as always, is tolerant of my presence and at one point walks off for a quarter hour, leaving me with my back to a hemlock alone with the sleeping cub. I consider following her but think it better to remain seated and familiarize the cub with my presence. It sleeps the whole time I'm there. I leave the bears in mid afternoon, with Nettie resting alert at the base of the refuge tree, the cub asleep above, cradled in the fork of a branch. While talking to the bears on my way back to the Jeep, I decide to name the cub June.

On my next several visits to Nettie and June after they leave the surrogate den site I focus on conditioning June to my presence. I hope that soon she will feel comfortable enough to leave the refuge tree and walk with Nettie and eventually allow me to follow along for short distances. My strategy is to break off the visits at the first sign of June becoming stressed. Each day I try to lengthen the duration of my stay, intending to make the process a gradual one. When the visits lengthen to several hours and June becomes more accepting of my presence, I begin the process of collecting data.

∽ο∾

4/28/94

Nettie has moved June east across the Rapid River Truck Trail. The truck trail is a well-used gravel road that runs north-south through the study area and bisects Nettie's and Carmen's home ranges. It is graded by the local road commission twice a year whether it's needed or not. During early spring the truck trail is best driven in early morning before its ruts and muddy potholes thaw into an impassable quagmire.

I locate the bears in an area of lowland conifers mixed with "pine islands." The pine islands rest on sandy soils only a few feet above the seasonal water table. Among their upland vegetation are large hemlocks and white pines that have escaped the ax and saw. The islands make the perfect refuge spot for a

female bear and her cub. On my way through the lowland conifers, I discover a deer carcass. It is only a few hundred yards
from the refuge tree, and I am surprised Nettie has not yet
spotted it. When I reach the bears, June is asleep far up a white
pine thirty inches in diameter. Nettie, resting at the base, alternates sitting and lying down. She raises herself to look up the
tree once in a while and yawns frequently, her long tongue
nearly curling in on itself. Occasionally, she meanders around
the tree sniffing objects but eats nothing. I notice few buds
swelling yet on saplings. Nettie clunks her jaws to June, and
June starts down, her tiny claws surprisingly noisy on the
tree's bark. When she spies me, she halts, then with an over-
the-shoulder look cautiously continues the descent. The bears
join at the base of the refuge tree and sniff faces. June takes a
few tentative steps, then pauses with front paw poised in midair looking directly at me. I say, "It's OK, June." Uncertain, she
edges back to the refuge tree, where she hesitates, then makes
a break and races to Nettie. She immediately goes partway up
another white pine. Nettie clunks to her again, and she descends. This time I let them walk off along the edge of the pine
island alone. I feel this is progress—at least she had confidence
to come down while I was close to the refuge tree.

5/1/94

The bears hang tight to the pine islands. Again June is up a
white pine when I approach. She moves around and wants to
come down but is wary of me. Nettie climbs about thirty feet
to reassure her. Nettie uses her teeth to pull herself up and to position herself during the ascent. She breaks many small branches
in the process. She rests a short time on a branch beneath June,
then begins her descent, tongue-clicking to June. On her way
down, Nettie makes a bad choice about the soundness of a
branch she grasps with her teeth, and it breaks when she places
her entire weight on it. Out of position, she begins falling but
is able to stop by slamming her front paws back into the tree,

raking deep grooves in the bark of the pine as she recovers from the slide. At the bottom, she sits with her head cocked at an upward angle to sniff the air. In a few minutes, June descends umphing and huffing lightly. I tell her, "It's OK, June," but even though Nettie is right there, she is reluctant to leave the refuge tree. She takes eight minutes to descend the final ten feet. As she stretches around the tree to peek at me, I note how rapid her growth has been. She weighed four pounds, ten ounces, in early March during the den checks; I estimate that her weight has tripled in the last two months. Once June is down, Nettie immediately moves away from the refuge tree, and June moves with her, hugging every tree as she goes. I follow—our first little walk. June scampers from tree to tree, and after a few hundred yards, I let them go on alone, talking to them as they move out of sight into the surrounding lowlands.

5/5/94

I feel I've made good progress with Nettie and June and decide to spend a day with Carmen. I catch up with the bears south of "bear-track bend" along the east bank of the Whitefish River. I have given this area that name because almost without fail I encounter fresh bear tracks whenever I come here. The macrohabitat is predominately white cedar mixed with a few aspen in the overstory. There is scant midstory vegetation, and upon entering the stand, I feel as if I am under a roof. Beneath the overhead lattice of cedar bows, organic soils are covered with river sediment and struggling vegetation. In places, the soil remains flooded. All three bears are nosing about, investigating a beaver lodge in a small backwater of the river. Having investigated the beaver lodge thoroughly, we meander off down an old river bed into an area of predominately white cedar overstory, which then grades into bigger aspens mixed with lowland conifers. Here the bears begin to feed on aspen catkins and willow leaves. Intermittently while foraging, Carmen plays with her yearlings, pawing and nipping their ears, but for the most part the yearling males play among themselves. Carmen meanders to an aspen-spruce lowland and then back to the shore of the Whitefish. The bears all drink from the river, then sniff around another beaver lodge. Bears obtain water from the vegetation and berries they eat, but they also drink from depressions in the upland forest floor, from all types of forested wetlands, from streams and rivers, and from holes in bogs. Water is ubiquitous in the bear's world, and never have I observed a bear making a trip to obtain it, other than to swim or cool itself. Carmen climbs partway up a white cedar then back down (I have no idea what this is about). Aster joins her at the base, and they play. There is not much going on in the woods yet—in terms of food—and the bears are hard-pressed to make a living. They appear slightly bored. Carmen meanders to an aspen–lowland conifer stand where there is a lot of standing water. Here my footfalls make a sucking sound. Keenly aware of my presence, Corduroy saunters back toward me. Standing on hind legs, one paw resting on a white birch, he blows and then swats at me with the other paw. I talk to calm him down while Carmen, sitting and scratching, begins to groom herself while watching us.

∽∘∾

As cubs, the males in Carmen's litters have remained more or less aloof. Once they are yearlings, they periodically attempt to reinforce their higher standing over me—my rank as runt of the litter having been established by default—more than female yearlings do. In the spring of their second year, the individual males of a litter sometimes mosey back toward me as I trail the family through the forest and try to intimidate me with tentative posturing and displays. My biggest concern during these tests is that Carmen will mistake me for an aggressor and return to deal with me herself. When tests happen in open woods and

Carmen can clearly see that I am not a threat to the yearling, she just continues her activities, leaving the yearling and me to work it out. Invariably, I back down and give them a wide berth. In closed woods, such as thick patches of balsams and dense cedars, Carmen might come near to investigate, satisfying herself that nothing poses an eminent danger to the yearling. In those situations, she sometimes sniffs the yearling or gazes directly at me, and I talk to her calmly, saying, "It's OK, Carmen, it's not me," or something to that effect, perhaps backing up a little, or maneuvering to place a small shrub or fallen tree between us while I talk. I find that inserting an object, such as a shrub, into the equation gives the yearlings something to display on. They'll always choose to act out any hostility on the object rather than confronting me directly. Afterward we travel on, my place in the pecking order once again made clear to all.

Once on a walk with Carmen and her first litter, in May of 1992, the scene played out somewhat differently. The dominant male yearling halted and stood directly in my path on a game trail. Somewhat apprehensively, he moved to block my route on each of several attempts to go around. Finally, I just stood still in anticipation of his demonstration. He raised up on his hind feet and blew at me to see if I would retreat. I always had before. However, I had recently been wondering if it was a good idea to be as submissive toward these subadult males as I had been. They would be dispersing from Carmen's territory in a short while, and might they not mistakenly employ this aggressive tactic on a hiker or camper sometime with a less favorable result? In a split second, I decided that what might be the most valuable lesson for this bear is that humans, under any circumstance, can be neither intimidated nor trusted. So, while his eighty-pound frame loomed large in my path, I kicked some duff from the forest floor into his exposed belly. His reaction was immediate and welcomed. He dropped to all fours and retreated, bawling all the way to Carmen. Alerted, Carmen rose to full height on her hind feet, looking in the direction of the approaching yearling, her upper torso and front legs twisted in the opposite direction, ready to bolt. But detecting no danger, and not suspecting I was the culprit, she lowered to all fours and resumed foraging. Never again was I tested by that yearling male.

5/5/94

Nettie and June are still at the pine islands. June is high up a hemlock. When she descends, she is reluctant to cross in front of me to reach Nettie, but I feel we are far enough along in the habituation process to remain in position and wait her out. There follows a round of descending and ascending the refuge tree. Finally, she peeks around the refuge tree to eyeball me and bawls to Nettie. Bawling cubs normally bring the mother on the run, but seeing there is no immediate threat, Nettie pays her little attention and moves off, forcing June to decide—up or down. She descends and follows Nettie. We move toward the edge of an old beaver meadow where there must be a sandhill crane's nest nearby—I can hear a pair rattling unison calls. We circumnavigate the beaver meadow just inside a line of sur-rounding lowland hardwood trees. Here both Nettie and June pause to feed on springtails located in small pools of water and on top of the wet leaves—licking up several large swirling masses of these tiny, wingless insects.

This time of year, the bears frequently find springtails within the fallen twigs and leaf litter, under bark and in decaying wood, and on the surface of water and snow. When found on the surface of snow, they give it the appearance of someone having seasoned it with ground pepper. Although less than an eighth of an inch long, springtails are capable of outstanding jumps, sometimes propelling themselves distances of two or three inches, a remarkable feat for so tiny an insect. A forked jumping organ (furcula), folded forward under the abdomen when springtails are resting, is suddenly and forcefully thrust downward when they are disturbed, enabling them literally to catapult themselves into the air. They are so small and so quick that it is difficult to see them both spring and land. It never ceases to amaze me that something as large as a bear can make a living off something so small as a springtail. And I wonder if the bears are drawn to them as much out of curiosity as appetite. The morning sun is warming, but the wind is chilly and begins to whistle through the swaying tops of the hardwoods. I notice buds are beginning to swell, and I halt here, allowing the bears to move on alone. We have traveled the last few hundred yards without trepidation on June's part, and I feel now is a good time to break off from them.

5/7/94

Carmen and her yearlings are down along the Whitefish again today in a stand of lowland conifers, predominately white cedar. Carmen meanders into a stand of aspen pole timber and spends time investigating the roots of wind-thrown trees. I lose sight of the bears twice in a thick stand of conifers but am able to follow and rejoin them by sound (a distinct advantage when walking with bears on less windy days). We enter a cattail marsh, but there is no feeding here. Carmen weaves us along the edge of the marsh and then in and out of a stand of aspens mixed with lowland conifers. Here, they feed briefly on willow catkins. Sitting on their rumps, the bears pull the stems down with little effort and steady them between their claws as they bite the catkins from the branchlets. Moving from shrub to shrub, Carmen comes upon the decomposed carcass of a winter-killed deer (a six-point buck). All the bears mill around the site, and the yearlings crush a few bones in their jaws and crunch the skull. After rummaging the site for a quarter hour, Carmen selects a clump of nearby cedars and rests while the yearlings continue moving around the remains. I leave them here.

Checking on Nettie and June, I am pleased to find that Nettie has managed to shepherd June back across the truck trail and into the gated, vehicle-excluded area once again. Even though she was forced from her den here, I feel that the area offers more security than any other. It certainly appears to offer more in the way of food. I stand on a stump near the den Nettie used as a two year old waving the antenna to pinpoint the location of her collar's signal and then move in that direction. I come upon the bears at the edge of a clear-cut in which several large brush piles are scattered about. Open water stands in small pools in low-lying areas of the cutting. June is up a hemlock at the cutting's edge, and Nettie sits alert at the base as I approach. Talking softly to Nettie, I move slowly and sit in the sun on the edge of the clear-cut, my back to a big sugar maple a few yards away. Having checked out the intrusion, Nettie resumes resting recumbent at the base of the cub tree. About ten minutes later she stands and stretches, then begins a forage meander through the cutting, feeding on grasses. When June climbs down to join her, she seems less apprehensive of me, although she still bawls weakly a few times during her descent and I must remain seated before she will leave the security of the refuge tree and start toward Nettie. Nettie stands and watches, habitually tongue-clicking reassurances to June.

More vegetation has begun growing here than in the lowland conifers, probably because of increased available sunlight and richer soils. As the bears meander along the edge of the cut area, June stands on her hind legs and rests her twenty-pound frame with front paws on Nettie's rump whenever the opportunity arises. My footsteps crunch through the dried leaves, and I fear I am making too much noise. June pads along behind Nettie sniffing briars and leaves. Near the southwest corner of the cut, the bears walk along a log out into a small emergent wetland and begin feeding on vegetation (mainly swamp thistle) near the perimeter. From here we move through the hardwoods toward a small opening. Nettie stops once along the way to stand on her hind legs and work her way around a sugar maple licking its sap—something I have never witnessed on a bear walk before.

Upon entering the opening, Nettie walks directly to a tree on the periphery. Here she stands on hind legs with a front paw resting on the tree and intensely sniffs it. It is a pole-sized white pine, broken off about six feet above the ground (I recognize the tree as one that I have been at with Carmen several times). As Nettie stands and sniffs the tree, I fully expect her to mark it as territory. I punch MT-SA-2L-WP (mark territory–standing–two legs–white pine) into the data logger in anticipation of the forthcoming display.

∞∞

Both Carmen and Nettie mark their territory with regularity as they travel about. Several different methods, alone or in combination, are employed with varying degrees of intensity. The different marking techniques probably communicate distinct signals to other bears that encounter them and perhaps express the temperament of the marker as well. They may also serve as navigational aids and reference points for the bears. In addition, while such trees are located throughout bears' home ranges, many exist or are established near the borders and perhaps serve to roughly define boundaries. Potential signals communicated are visual (such as bite marks and broken tree limbs) or chemical (such as scent from the deposition of saliva, hair, urine, and feces). The bears mark coniferous and deciduous trees, a variety of small shrubs, saplings, logs, and humanmade objects including hunting blinds, cabins, and power poles.

Trees on which such markings occur are fittingly referred to as "mark trees."[1] They are marked most often in a manner I describe as "arched-back rubbing," which is often combined with tree biting. The bears stand on their hind feet, their backs toward the tree, and vigorously rub and twist their upper torso against the tree in an up-down and side-to-side motion. Tree limbs are often broken in the process. Frequently, the bears will reach around the tree with either forepaw to steady themselves while gyrating. Often, while grasping the tree in this fashion, the bears turn their head and shoulders and bite into the tree, sometimes biting off the tops of smaller trees in the process. Hair from the bears' back, neck, face, (and on fresh markings, saliva) remains embedded on the tree. In addition to the mark tree itself, each site is typically distinguished by a set of bear foot "impressions" extending a half-dozen steps or so in either direction from the tree. These impressions are the result of the bears repeatedly punching their feet into the same spots, either on their approach to the tree or as they walk away after marking. With each placement of a front foot, the footpads are stomped and twisted into the ground. Bare spots (some the size of pie plates and a few inches deep) are sometimes worn into the ground. I also observe this form of marking without the foot punching, by both Carmen and Nettie during spring and summer when in the company of yearlings or cubs. A less vigorous form of the foot punching is occasionally performed after urination or defecation by adult females and by both sexes of their cubs and yearlings. Mark trees are revisited over the course of a year and remarked, and I have witnessed Carmen and Nettie (as a yearling and adult) both marking the same tree during the same year. An arched-back rub occurs typically on sapling or pole-sized conifers and less often on similar-sized deciduous trees. It may occur on large-diameter trees as well, but those are more difficult to bite. Arched-back rubbing seems to happen most during the breeding season along game trails, which Carmen and Nettie frequent at that time. It also occurs in summer and fall at favorite swimming holes in bogs or near concentrated food sources such as hunters' baits. While the exact function(s) of mark trees may remain known only to bears, I theorize that the bears use them to communicate their whereabouts, particularly during breeding season (late May into July), and that they also serve as an aid to the bears in navigation, perhaps as part of an individual cognitive map. I often

41

find myself reorientated upon encountering a known mark tree and think it reasonable to assume that bears might use them similarly.

The most common form of marking by the bears is what I term "straddle-marking." Both Carmen and Nettie perform this activity throughout the year as they traverse their home ranges. Female black bears have distended vulva hair, which is usually moist and occasionally dripping wet with urine (especially in summer when they are feeding heavily on berries and may void three to four gallons per day). As the bears travel about, they often straddle small bushes and saplings, leaving urine and hair on them. On numerous occasions while following the bears, I detected a sweet, musky odor at straddle-markings that I immediately recognized as coming from the bears. In time, I was even able to detect a subtle difference between the scents of the two bears, Carmen's seeming more intense and musky. (In a side-by-side comparison, I do not claim to be able to distinguish their scents, however, only to say that both are from a bear.) Straddle-marking also takes place following urination and defecation throughout the year, most frequently during the breeding season. During the breeding season, the activity seems almost habitual, as the bears frequently perform it while foraging on vegetation. Also during the breeding season, Carmen and Nettie straddle logs and rub their stomachs and vulva on them, sometimes quite vigorously. I am unsure if this latter activity is marking or simply scratching, although I have witnessed it only occasionally outside of the breeding season.

Another form of marking behavior consists mainly of head-rubbing, which takes place on almost any newfound human-made object the bears encounter in their territory, such as the corners of hunting blinds and cabins and the support posts for decks and porches at camps, as well as on trees and snags. The bears stand on their hind feet facing the object, with front limbs encircling it to steady themselves, and lean in and rub the top of their head and muzzle against it. Quite often the bears head-rub national forest boundary markers (posts), which they might also mark with bites, leaving a permanent visual signal. Vigorous head-rubbing sometimes grades into arched-back rubbing, and all of the marking methods are used in combination on occasion.

The bears also rub their flanks and rears against all types of trees simply to scratch themselves. When the bears are finished, the tree's bark is often discolored, and large clumps of hair remain embedded in it or on the ground nearby. Yet I believe this activity is more for scratching or grooming than marking.

Undoubtedly, the most dramatic type of bear marking behavior I have witnessed involves the dismembering and truncation of cedar trees. Although I have yet to witness this behavior by Nettie, I have seen Carmen perform it on half a dozen separate occasions when she has failed to overtake an interloping bear that she is trailing. She appears to release her frustrations in this ostentatious display of agonistic behavior.

Climbing a pole-sized cedar tree (I theorize that she uses cedars because of their relatively brittle limbs), Carmen very deliberately (using jaws and feet) breaks off nearly every limb on one side of the tree during her ascent. Upon nearing the top (some trees I estimate at more than thirty feet in height), she braces her hind feet on the uppermost branches, rises to full height, and clasps her jaws around the tree as near its top as possible. Then, hanging by her jaws, she begins tugging at the tree top until it snaps under her weight. (On the several occasions when I observed this behavior, I found myself standing literally knee-deep in branches at the base of the tree while it was going on.) Standing back and looking up after Carmen has finished her work, it seems to me that her message to the interloper is clear: If you can top this, I'll go. If not, then maybe you should! (Undoubtedly, my interpretation greatly oversimplifies the complexities of this form of marking, but it does provide a plausible explanation.)

∽⚬∾

Today, however, Nettie does not mark territory here. Rather, after sniffing the tree for forty seconds, she drops to all fours and begins foraging. She feeds on the tender shoots of grass in the small forest opening by pawing away sticks and clumps of old vegetation to get at them. June rests securely up a white cedar eighteen inches in diameter on the edge of the opening.

During spring, bears seek out and use forest openings, where they feed on newly emerging grasses and clovers as well as orange hawkweed, dandelion, and yellow goatsbeard. They seem to prefer small openings with close-by refuge trees around their perimeters when with cubs. (On a later walk this is confirmed when Carmen refuses to lead her two male cubs into a knee-high red pine planting that lacks secure refuge, skirting it instead because an unidentified bear trails behind.) Forest managers would do well to leave clumps of refuge trees in larger cuttings for female bears with cubs.

After about a half hour of foraging in the small opening, Nettie climbs the cedar refuge tree to rest with June, and I decide to call it a day. We have had a satisfactory walk, and I am pleased that June trusted me enough to move from her refuge tree while Nettie was at a distance. Next time I will stay longer. As always, I talk to the bears as I exit the area.

5/9/94

Nettie and June are at the gated area in a northern hardwood stand. June stays on the ground as I come in—this is good progress. Nettie continues feeding on vegetation and soon allows June to nurse while she feeds. This is accomplished in a weird position, June half hanging underneath—different! Both bears walk a leaning maple out to near its end, and Nettie begins to feed on the leaves of an ironwood tree growing alongside. She pulls in the branches of surrounding saplings with her paws while sitting, but scant foliage is available yet. The bears move to an aspen clear-cut and forage on grass. June nurses again (on the ground and in the classic position this time) in a clump of sapling aspens. After a brief rest and some grooming, Nettie walks about sniffing and pawing at stumps but obtains nothing for her effort. We work our way to a small opening where June goes up a big sugar maple. I recognize it as the same refuge tree that Carmen once joined her cubs in when she was spooked by a group of deer. Nettie "Carmendances" in the opening while forage-meandering for vegetation. (This seems to be her day to do two things at once.) There is a lot of sniffing of stumps and other objects in the area. Nettie spooks and trots at one point—I think maybe she smelled another bear. Then she sits and scratches. June comes down the refuge tree and bounds across the opening to her, and they both run into the hardwoods. We move through the hardwoods and down a south-facing slope toward a lowland conifer stand. Both bears run down the slope. (Typically, bears run or trot downhill. I don't know if that is because there is so much bulk in their powerfully built rear legs that going downhill is awkward, or if the longer length of their rear legs forces them to run or go head over heels.) At the bottom, Nettie feeds on ground vegetation in a shrub swamp amid the conifer stand. After only a few bites, she runs, and I lose sight of her. I think they have had enough for the day and decide to end the walk here. The wind is picking up, and they've been acting antsy ever since we entered the opening.

5/10/94

Today I catch up with Carmen and the yearlings in a stand of aspen-sawtimber. I wing them a few treats to break the ice.

The bears are becoming testy, as there is little food for them throughout the forest. (The winter-killed buck we came upon a few days before was picked over when I returned to it a day later and, judging by its condition, had provided little sustenance for the bears.) It does not take long for the treats to disappear. The yearlings test me for more, but I show them my empty crossed hands (a signal we have worked out earlier) and satisfied that I am not holding out on them, we are off. Carmen leads the way, forage-meandering, sniffing stumps and logs. The bears meander into a stand of white cedars mixed with red maples and black ash trees where they spend several minutes sniffing the ground at one location. When Carmen moves off, the yearlings linger, intent on examining the site. When the yearlings move away, I walk over to the spot and discover a hunting knife in its sheath. While the bears are not watching, I pick it up and slip it into my pack. The trio appear to be spending an inordinate amount of time sniffing the ground and smelling other objects in this stand. I can see nothing of food value in the vicinity, and while I am hoping their investigations will lead to another souvenir, I begin to suspect that they are detecting something else—probably the scent of another bear.

I am correct. A large male bear approaches us only minutes later as we make our way through the cedar swamp. A few large aspens are scattered among the cedars, and one has fallen over, taking a neighbor along with it. The fallen aspens lie crossed, their tops resting at an obtuse angle eight to ten feet above the ground. I sense the approach of the male bear only after the yearlings become huffy and the bears run for the throw of aspens. Up until now, I have been with Carmen only when she chased other bears, never when she has run from one. Not knowing what to expect from this intruder, I decide to join the bears up the blown-down trees, but because I expect that my presence at such close quarters will not be welcome under the current circumstances, I wait until the bears have chosen their aspen stem and moved near its end before I go up the other (mine is inclined at a considerably less favorable angle for mounting).

But my run to the leaning aspen perturbs the yearlings and they blow at me as much as at the intruding male. When I crouch low on the tree and peer beneath the limbs of the surrounding cedars, I can glimpse the interloping bear for brief periods. He remains about twenty-five yards from our position and circles us. I begin to think that I should not have reacted to the situation the way I did. I know that male bears coming in on us pose little threat to me, and I think I should have waited it out on the ground. Carmen is not yet in estrus and should not favor advances by a male. Any male bear would likely be on his way once satisfied that Carmen is not yet amenable to breeding. This male has more than likely been shadowing us for most of the morning and has only now chosen to get close enough to test Carmen's condition. The commotion I made getting up the leaning aspen has only made the situation worse. To my credit, I am not blocking Carmen & Company's most likely exit route, but I certainly have fouled up this bear walk, and the bears let me know it. Things calm down after about five minutes, and I presume the male has withdrawn from the area. Carmen and the yearlings climb down a larger branch of their aspen and drop to the ground rather than walk down the trunk that crosses near me. On the ground, Carmen does a brief dance, and the trio move off at a ninety-degree angle from where I last saw the male. They are not in a good mood, and I think it best to leave them to themselves. I stand in the leaning aspen saying good-bye to them as they walk away. I go spend some time with Nettie and June, where I hope things are calmer.

I hook up with them back at the interface of hardwoods and a clear-cut (the same spot as on May 7). Nettie feeds on grass along the east slope of the hardwoods at the clear-cut's boundary. She defecates and then meanders again toward the small opening in the hardwoods, weaving in and out of the hardwood–clear-cut area as she goes. In the opening, she checks out the mark tree, then Carmen-dances away from it urinating a stream. She settles in to feed on grass in the opening.

June is sliding around on her belly, propelling herself with her back feet over the grass and clover slick with morning dew—big fun! She runs to Nettie, and they play, after which, Nettie rests alert while June does some more gymnastics. June runs around a lot, grabs a stick and plays with it, then runs back to Nettie and flops down. Nettie bats at her with a paw, then there is rambunctious play for several minutes. Both bears stop to feed on vegetation briefly. Today is the first time I have observed June feeding on solids (I have observed other cubs feeding on vegetation as early as May 2). More play. This time Nettie is on her back batting at June with both front paws, and June runs circles around her. In the background, I hear the low-pitch-trail-off drumming of a pileated woodpecker. The setting is so fresh with the advent of spring, I fully expect a turkey to gobble—but turkeys do not fare well here in the deep snows of winter. Nettie rolls over and begins feeding on vegetation while on her belly, elbowing her way around the opening. June ascends the same white cedar as on May 7 and, tired from the intense play, sleeps cradled by several crisscrossing branches. Below, Nettie continues to feed on vegetation. About half an hour later, June comes down, and we leave the opening. Nettie turns to eye the mark tree as she passes but does not mark it. We move east across the aspen clear-cut, and Nettie pauses to drink from a pool in a low spot, then feeds on swamp thistle and cattail roots from scattered pools in the cutting. Exiting the clear-cut, both bears run across a bordering two-track and into a lowland conifer stand where I briefly lose sight of them. As I catch up, Nettie is sitting at the cub tree and June is descending. We walk-meander a hundred yards, then June goes up a white cedar and both bears rest. Nettie (at the bottom of the refuge tree) has an extended grooming session, which lasts fourteen minutes. Lying on her back, with a front paw stiff-armed into the air, she bites and licks at it, alternately twisting her torso to bite and lick her back. She is still roly-poly enough to look comical as she performs the activity. Intermittently during the grooming session, she clunks her jaws to June. Finished grooming, she rests alert at the base of the cedar. Shortly, she stands and begins to forage-meander, feeding on species of grasses that I can't identify. She pauses to drink from a depression, then returns to again rest alert at the base of the cub tree. An hour later, June descends. She falls the final five feet and lands on her back, then walks over and lies down next to Nettie. She appears unharmed by the fall. I say my good-byes and leave them resting.

5/13/94

Carmen and the yearlings are north today, and I locate them in an aspen-sawtimber stand near the north-central border of their range. Carmen spends much time sniffing the ground and standing on logs and just looking. There is no feeding until we get to a small forest opening, an old decking area, where all the bears feed on grasses. Log landings, or "decking areas," as I refer to them, remain open for years following logging operations because of the heavy disturbance and extensive soil compaction they receive while logs are staged and loaded by heavy equipment. Because of the relatively small size of such areas and the consequent proximity of refuge trees, female bears with cubs feel secure foraging in them once they revegetate. Early in the revegetation process, grasses and clovers, along with hawkweed and dandelion and yellow goatsbeard, invade the areas, and bears make use of those plants in early spring. In later years, raspberries and blackberries begin to fill in the borders of the decking areas, and in summer the bears use them as well as the Juneberry and hazelnut bushes that come after them. These smaller forest openings mimic those made by natural forest disturbances such as wind-throw and lightning strikes, and they can provide bears with food nearly year-around. The bears seem to prefer these smaller openings compared to the larger humanmade "wildlife-openings," which are created mainly for white-tailed deer, because the larger areas generally lack secure refuge trees close by. And also because the ripening of the planted vegetation (predominately rye and bird's-foot trefoil) coincides with that of many other natural herbs and grasses that are available in more secure settings.

Carmen sits and scratches, still looking very fat. We meander through an adjoining ash swamp, but there is no feeding here, and we move to an aspen clear-cut where all the bears again feed on grasses. On the edge of the cutting, Carmen encounters a porcupine and backs away from it. The yearlings do not react to it at all that I can detect and continue walking logs and ground through the cutting. We move south into an aspen–white birch–lowland conifer stand, where there is much sniffing of the ground and objects by the bears, and I see that there is other bear sign here. Carmen "pops" her jaws while sniffing a fresh bear scat. We then walk to a lowland conifer stand where Carmen plays with both yearlings. She sits and scratches, then stands to drink from a shallow depression. Corduroy walks toward me as I lean against a cedar and tests me by blowing and swatting halfheartedly in my direction. I calmly talk him down. Carmen appears agitated, and I cannot tell if it is because of the other bear sign, my interaction with the yearling, or the overall scant availability of food in the forest. I leave them resting at the base of a cedar and move on to locate Nettie and June.

I find them in the same general area as on my last visit. The forest is now noticeably greener, and I hear and see more wildlife than on just days before, especially birds. The bears continue to forage in the clear-cut for grasses and in a smaller opening for grasses and white clover. While meandering to the small opening, Nettie rips apart a decaying log and feeds on several wood borer grubs. June joins in and gets her first real scolding, a cuff and nip, from the heretofore indulgent Nettie for getting underfoot during the digging process. After, they rest under a refuge tree, and Nettie nurses June twice for just under six minutes each time. The nursing bouts occur only thirteen minutes apart, and I wonder if the unusual frequency is significant. Rested, Nettie makes her way north through a stand of hardwood-sawtimber and into a stand of selectively cut hardwoods of like size. The soils here are rich, and increased sunlight reaches the forest floor. I watch as Nettie takes her first few bites of sweet cicely for the year.

5/17/94

Early spring is by far the best time for walking with bears. The forest is open, and I am able to anticipate upcoming obstacles and see the bears clearly. The walks are leisurely, as cubs are not yet able to travel very fast. Biting insects are few, and temperatures are usually comfortable in the sixties. The bears seem comfortable, too. This day, when I join Nettie and June at midmorning, Nettie forages about on sweet cicely. While en route, June investigates things, tugging at the overwintered fronds of sensitive ferns and biting the newly emerging growth on sapling spruce and fir. Objects are tested for taste—she spits out those that are unsavory—as well as for their utility as playthings.

She discovers a leatherwood (locally called moosewood) bush, a slow-growing shrub that branches like a dwarf tree and rarely achieves a height of more than four feet. The rubberlike bark of the leatherwood was used by Native Americans as bowstring, as webbing for snowshoes and thongs, and in basket making because of its resilience. The soft and pliable stem of the plant gives way and springs back, and cubs like to bowl them over. June swaggers up to the bush, then lunges at it, straddling it and knocking it over with her chest, each conquest bolstering her confidence.

What initially seems to attract cubs to the leatherwoods are its yellow flowers, among the first to blossom in spring. Bears supposedly have poor eyesight, and, compared to their keen sense of smell and acute hearing, I agree that a bear's vision is *relatively* poor. Nonetheless, although somewhat myopic, I believe bears have good vision. It is known that they see colors, which enables them to recognize and differentiate edible plants, fruits, and nuts. I often notice cubs attracted to do battle with leatherwoods from quite a distance—even from upwind. Whether initially attracted by sight or smell, June appears intent on conquering the pliable leatherwood—which appears just as intent at springing upright. After pinning it a final time, she struts off to join Nettie.

In the hardwoods, Nettie forages exclusively and for as much as fifteen minutes at a time on sweet cicely, which when crushed emits a fragrance like that of anise, and I can smell it now underfoot. The plant is consumed by bears most often from mid May to mid June before leaves form in the overhead canopy and it grows from one to six inches high; the bears graze for hours on this shade-intolerant plant.[2]

☙❧

A year before, I was with Carmen and her cubs Corduroy and Aster, when they were just about as old as June is, while Carmen foraged on sweet cicely in this same hardwood stand, just a stone's throw from our location. I had just positioned myself to take the consummate photo of Carmen nipping off a sweet cicely top when suddenly there was a commotion, a cub crisis. The cubs were vying for possession of an unidentified object. Carmen, foraging with her head down, responded with an umph to their vocalizations and immediately ran toward them. The cubs were in a tug of war, but Carmen quickly quelled the ruckus by snatching the object and trotting away with it. The cubs in hot pursuit issued woeful bawls at being robbed of the find. As I moved closer to the stir, I recognized the object as the dried and shriveled carcass of a red squirrel—which each member of the bear family wanted. The cubs yanked at either end of the squirrel carcass, which protruded from the sides of Carmen's mouth. She began moving through the open woods at an increasing gate, but the cubs would not relinquish their hold and were dragged for short distances as they tried to wrangle the carcass from Carmen's mouth. At last, in an ostensibly magnanimous gesture (surely sensing she could no longer elude the cubs), Carmen flopped over on her back and assumed the classic nursing posture, exposing her mammae to the badgering cubs. The ploy produced the desired effect; the cubs capitalized on the opportunity for a sure thing, giving up on the dead squirrel. Carmen, her head tipped back (to keep from dangling the squirrel carcass in front of them) chewed and swallowed the fetid remains as the cubs worked her mammae contentedly. Crisis resolved.

Observing Nettie foraging, I marvel at how efficient she is. With agile lips and a prehensile-like tongue, she seems to inhale the sweet cicely plants, her head moving in a constant up-down manner as she bites them off at ground line. Occasionally, she uses her curved claws to elevate or steady a plant as she eats it. June joins in, although with less proficiency. Watching June as we move between the patches of sweet cicely, I notice that her hindquarters seem to sway and wobble as she surmounts obstacles on the forest floor. I wonder if perhaps she has a congenital defect or has suffered an injury from a fall in my absence.

Bears, it seems, are much better suited to their world than we are to ours. They are born with an array of assets that enable them to negotiate and exploit their world far better than infants of our species. Cubs, for example, seem to be born with what I refer to as the "up gene." No matter how early I arrive at a den site in spring, cubs, when startled, have hugged the nearest tree and quickly bounded up it—even upon first emergence from the den, when they look as if they could not possibly climb anything higher than their mother's back. Cubs use two principal methods for climbing unlimbed trees. The technique used most often in threatening situations is to run toward the base of the refuge tree, vault onto it with front limbs splayed while bringing the hind feet upward and centered almost under the body. Then, with hind feet moving in unison for propulsion and upper limbs used essentially as guides and for some slight upward pull, they hop up the tree, often huffing as they do so. Another method, used on more leisurely ascents, is to walk up the tree, moving opposite limbs (front and rear) in unison. During these leisurely climbs, the bears' front limbs appear to grasp farther around the tree than in hurried ascents, and the hind legs are used more for leveraging than for thrust. It is in this fashion that bears climb smaller-diameter, smooth-barked trees. To go down, they use the reverse order of this walking motion, for a head-up descent. If they are in a hurry, however, they use a reverse of the threatened ascent. On certain occasions, such as when a cub hears the sound of a sibling suckling below, they'll rush down the tree in almost a free fall. The up gene is a good one to have if you are a bear cub in an inhospitable world. Yet despite possessing excellent climbing skills, cubs occasionally make mistakes.

Early one spring, I watched one of Carmen's cubs plummet from tree top to frozen earth, the result of a misstep. The cub tried to swing under a dead branch in an effort to outmaneuver a sibling. The bark broke loose, and the cub fell, splayed-out backwards, flailing to the ground thirty feet below. I wondered, Would Carmen abandon the dead cub or might she eat it? Would she mind if I picked it up and put it in my pack to examine later? But my consideration proved premature. When the cub hit the ground, the loud noise sent Carmen running for a nearby tree. However, the sound had hardly dissipated when the cub, having landed on its back, sat upright for a few moments, regained its composure, and ran for the tree in which Carmen had taken refuge—apparently as surprised as everyone by what had just happened. Two weeks later I watched the same cub fall from a height of fifteen feet while playing in a hemlock. The cub suffered no discernible lingering effects from either fall.

Still, I am concerned now about June's weak hindquarters and her lack of coordination when negotiating even rather ordinary obstacles. I leave the bears at evening, resting near the edge of a vernal pool.

5/18/94

I locate the bears near where they were yesterday. June is standing on a leaning yellow birch, and Nettie remains on the ground underneath. Both bears look in my direction, and after confirming that it is only me approaching, they resume their activities. June begins walking the length of the birch, digging at its bark, while Nettie forages on sweet cicely. The bears move south across a two-track, through a strip of hardwoods, and into a sedge meadow. June spends time digging and biting a decaying log, then jumps off and bounds over to Nettie, who lies grooming. They begin playing, June alternately resting atop and biting at Nettie's back. They both cease playing to listen (nearby birds continue singing, so I am not too concerned), but their attention is not held long. As Nettie begins grooming again, June rolls off her back and runs to climb a maple at the edge of the meadow, digging at the bark of its high branches and mouthing its red buds. She maneuvers herself into several precarious positions while pirouetting thirty-five feet above the meadow. When she descends, there is more play. Nettie walks off into the surrounding hardwoods and begins to forage on sweet cicely. June goes up a thirty-six-inch-diameter hemlock and rests while Nettie returns to the edge of the meadow to drink from a pool, then walks to the refuge tree, where she sits and scratches herself. Then she pulls down a sapling ironwood growing near the base of the refuge tree and first taste-tests its buds, then eats some.

Ironwood gets its name deservedly, and many a sawyer maintains that it will actually throw sparks when being cut with a chain saw. Stiff-trunked and unbending, ironwoods are worth the investment to bears, for their newly developing leaves contain as much as 7-percent nitrogen, equivalent to about 40 percent protein.

Abandoning the ironwood, Nettie rolls onto her stomach and turns a decaying log over and casually claws at it. She is acting bored, and I feel that we are both waiting for June to grow and endure extended walks. Later, June descends the refuge tree and stands on her hind legs to sniff and taste the buds Nettie mouthed earlier. She attempts to nurse, but Nettie walks away to dissuade her. Nettie bowls over a sapling beech with her chest and nibbles at its buds while straddling it. Finished, she walks off and drinks briefly from a shallow depression, then leads the way back to the sedge meadow, where she and June begin another session of play. Afterward, Nettie walks over to an ironwood sapling growing on the edge of the meadow and stands on hind legs to reach and eat a few buds and unfurling leaves. June climbs the ironwood while Nettie holds it partially bent over. When Nettie releases it, the sapling springs upright, flinging June about and this proves great fun for both of them. Nettie stands on her hind feet batting at June, who tries to out-maneuver her in the branches of the sapling. They play like this for some time, and when they are finished, the top of the iron-wood is bent and broken. It could easily be mistaken for a mark tree, considering all the outward sign and bear hair that remains. Nettie crosses the meadow and stands with her front legs resting on a fallen log and canvasses the surrounding hardwoods for a long while. Then she sits and alternately rests alert on the log. June joins her, and they play, taking turns backing each other to an end of the log. Finished playing, Nettie straddles the log with all fours and rests lengthwise, her chin flat against it.

The blackflies are increasing with the heat of day, and as I film Nettie resting, one gets caught in the video camera, grinding it to a halt. It will not be long before the bloodsucking female deerflies will be here in great numbers. These rival even the yellow flies of the South in inflicting painful and lasting bites. But both have the satisfying quality of lacking speed. Some say there are only three seasons in the U.P.: mosquito, blackfly, and winter, but there are four if one considers deerflies.

Nettie stands and begins walking the log; June follows close behind, and when Nettie stops, June rises on her hind feet and stands with her front paws resting on Nettie's rump. The shiny black of Nettie's coat contrasts with the brownish hue of June's and accentuates the patches of light brown fur behind June's ears, a trait shared by all of Carmen's and Nettie's cubs. The ear spots become less conspicuous as the cubs grow and usually disappear by August. I am unsure of the purpose, if any, of these marks, but in bears' practical world there is little room for frills. One likely function may be as an aid to mother bears in locating cubs amid the growth of the forest floor. The movement of the spots is most often what I notice initially when returning my gaze to a cub partially obscured in ground vegetation. Other mammals, such as lions, also have ear patches, but the lion's is retained throughout its life, along with the black tip of its tail, which contrasts with the tawny color of its coat and the surrounding vegetation.

When the bears step off the log into the hardwoods, June bounds up a large sugar maple and rests, splayed over the crotch of the first branch. Nettie begins foraging around the base of the tree, feeding on sweet cicely and digging rotting logs, from which she obtains a few beetle larvae. She roams about for several more minutes sniffing objects, then returns to the refuge tree to check on June. She stands with front paws resting on the tree and sniffs. Satisfied, she moves off a short distance and begins feeding on the buds of an ironwood sapling. I sit twenty yards from June's refuge tree in plain view of Nettie and watch as she goes about the task. I can hear her footfalls crunching leaves as she walks away from the ironwood, and it reminds me that we need rain. Eventually, Nettie forages toward me, pausing only a few feet away. She stands and stares at me, then begins curling her lip, as if I am in her way or have done something wrong. A slightly curled upper lip is a preliminary signal of agitation. I wonder what the problem is and begin talking to her calmly. She blows at me lightly, thus escalating the face-off a notch. To this point, I have never had a confrontation of any sort with Nettie, and at a distance of five feet even her light blow is intimidating. Then I spot a patch of sweet cicely alongside my stump. Standing slowly, talking to her as I rise, I back cautiously away from the spot. She moves in for a few quick nips of the herb, then sits and scratches while clunking to June. All is now OK. Behind me I can hear June's tiny claws on the bark of the sugar maple, and I do not have to look around to know that she is climbing down. She comes to Nettie and attempts nursing, but Nettie again walks off to avoid it. Walking to the top of a slope, she stands and looks for a long time before heading down. June follows, and they both run to the bottom. I let them settle down before following. I have found that following too closely as bears go up or down hills seems to make them uneasy (perhaps they feel that they are being chased), and they will run or turn to confront the threat. I let them range ahead, then speedily make up the distance, talking steadily as I advance. At the bottom of the hill, Nettie drinks from a depression at the side of an abandoned logging road. The cut ends of "corduroy logs" protrude from the old roadbed. When I catch up to them, we move toward a stand of cedars. We walk a narrow game trail that is familiar to us all. The scents of balsam and cedar permeate the air. All across the forest floor, last year's fallen leaves are being pushed up by newly emerging forbs and herbs to form thousands of miniature pup tents.

Spring

The whole scene, so full of the stuff of spring, reminds me of a walk I took with Carmen when Nettie was just a yearling.

సోం

My gaze was fixed on a solitary black morel growing near where Carmen sat scratching her jaw with the claws of her rear foot. I logged SISC (sit scratch) into the data recorder. Most scratching takes place in the sitting position, although bears sometimes stand on three legs or lean against trees to scratch their flanks with a rear foot. Periodically, SISCs can turn into full-blown grooming (GM) sessions, some lasting up to forty-five minutes. GMs are more intense sessions involving licking, parting of belly hairs with claws, biting at ticks, and all types of scratching, and they take place most often when the bear is prostrate or sitting with its back propped against a tree or hum-mock. SISCs are shorter and confined mainly to scratching, occur more often, and, especially when they are accompanied by a bear's nervous yawn, appear to be an ersatz for knowing what to do next.

Anticipating a lengthy grooming session, I leaned into the nearby trunk of an aspen and immediately began to scan the area for more morels. We were three hours into our morning walk, and the temperature had climbed into the mid seventies. The bears had been foraging on sweet cicely and the unfurling buds of beech and ironwood saplings in an adjoining hardwood stand. We had just descended a fairly steep hardwood slope on the western boundary of the stand. At the bottom of the slope, the bears ran across an abandoned logging road. I recognized the spot and believed we were heading for a refuge tree in the coolness of a cedar stand.

It was late May, and we were halted in a small stand of as-pens mixed with white birch, spruce, and a few dead elms (killed by Dutch elm disease, a fungus carried by the European elm bark beetle and brought to bear country by humans). Wet sands overtopped shallow limestone bedrock. Here and there the ground was pocked with voids left by the roots of wind-blown balsam firs, which were elevated above the floor of the forest by their embedded and decaying limbs. The stand was only a few acres in size, a little spur off a neighboring clear-cut stand of lowland hardwoods, itself now overgrown with balsam poplar seedlings, and its pungent odor hung rank in the air. This stand had probably escaped being clear-cut by virtue of its wet soils, its rocky substrate, and the overall poor quality of its trees. Many of the aspens showed the rough, blackened wounds of hypoxylon canker, which rendered them unacceptable as pulp wood. Despite its shortcomings for the mill, the stand proved perfect for morels.

Morel mushrooms are the spring sentinels of the forest. A fleshy fungus, the morel is the fruiting body of the underground portion of the plant (the mycelium). Unlike green plants, however, morels contain no chlorophyll. They alter and destroy compounds to achieve their growth rather than manufacturing them from the raw materials of sunlight, water, and minerals. While all the specific requirements for morel production are not yet known, sufficient moisture is essential, and the warm seasonal rains of May make it the month for morels in northern Michigan. Easily recognizable by their cone-shaped, brown, pitted surface, morels are edible and choice. By walking slowly and vigilantly, you can sneak up on a morel, catching it unawares. If you maintain direct eye contact and exercise an unwavering approach upon first spying a morel, it will remain fixed by your gaze long enough to be collected—but break eye contact, turn your back, waver in the least, and it will disappear in an instant. Then you must stand still and watch a long while for its reappearance.

Carmen's runt yearling pressed in close to her flank and eyed me from his safe haven while Carmen scratched. The yearling's body vibrated with each motion of Carmen's leg. His littermates explored a short distance away, pausing now and then to check Carmen's whereabouts as they tugged at the flowers of violets that had poked their way through the dry surface leaves. The woods were quiet, except for the drone of blackflies. I could see a swarm of them around Carmen's head, which she shook vigorously, warding them off. I spied another morel near the base of the tree I was leaning on, and it was close enough to gather. I took a couple of short steps, talking to Carmen and the runt as I stooped to collect it, "It's OK, it's just me, making noise, it's OK, guys." Abruptly, Carmen stood and walked on. I fumbled with the mushroom as I punched WM (walking meander) into the field computer and followed. We resumed our heading for the stand of mature white cedars only a hundred yards distant. I grabbed the morel near where Carmen had been scratching herself as I walked by. As we neared the cedars, I had collected four morels, all reasonably large and moist, considering the lack of rain. Carmen stopped to scratch again. The yearlings foraged about, tasting the flowers of violets. It struck me that we had just walked through a patch of edible mushrooms and the bears had not eaten any. Without giving it further thought, I tossed the handful of mushrooms among the yearlings. They quickly mouthed them, then spat them out. Carmen noticed the motion and moved in to investigate. She sniffed the pieces, then turned and walked into the cedars. So much for bears enjoying my taste for morels. I can't say it bothered me either, I could live without the competition, although it would have been nice to be introduced by the bears to prime patches of them. I spend a fair amount of time in May searching for morels and good spots are hard to find. And over the years, I have found that beneath mature aspens in the vicinity of dead elms situated on wet sandy soils make excellent locations to search. To date, the highest and best use to which I have put modern soil surveys, is hunting morels.

Carmen led the way through the cedar swamp, stopping now and then to feed on golden saxifrage. The bears waded into small muddy pools to consume the inconspicuous green leaves and prostrate creeping stems of the plants that formed mats on the surface of the pools. No sooner had we stopped than I noticed that we had left quite a few blackflies behind. The cedars were probably ten degrees cooler than the hardwoods, and that change was also welcomed. Finished with the saxifrage, the bears walked on. I followed, cultivating my technique for maneuvering from one bit of solid ground to the next. We moved at a brisk pace, and I punched WD (walk direct) into the computer. The yearlings were ahead of Carmen and began bounding as we approached a familiar rest site. I recognized the spot as one we had been to two days prior but from a different direction. The yearlings vaulted up the cedar refuge tree, the clawing of bark and breaking of branches making considerable noise. Carmen flopped at its base and began grooming. I reconnoitered, found a cedar growing at suitable elevation above the damp floor, and sat down with my back to it watching the bears.

Fifteen minutes into her grooming session, Carmen sat alert and began blowing. The yearlings began huffing. Carmen then huffed too, as she climbed the cedar and stood on a branch just below the yearlings. Now they were all blowing and huffing, and the commotion was reminiscent of earlier "unwelcomes" I had received. I was sure something was about—why else would the bears behave in such a manner? Up to this point, our walk had gone very well, the bears scarcely acknowledging my presence. I sat and waited, but nothing happened, and the bears continued their fussing. After a few minutes, I still could not tell whether the bears were perturbed about my proximity or something else. Not wanting to add stress to the situation, I packed up my gear, circled the refuge tree, and talked softly to the bears, saying my good-byes. I continued talking as I walked away until I felt I was out of their hearing. I retraced our route through the cedars and back to the aspen stand, where I spent the better part of an hour hunting morels.

When I had picked several dozen, I headed west along the corduroy two-track toward the Jeep. I was about midway along the edge of the two-track parallel to the clear-cut when I heard something running toward me through the clear-cut. I stood still, fully expecting to surprise a deer, as the wind was right for it. What I saw more than surprised me. Out of the cutting bounded a pair of wolves. For a split second, I thought coyotes, but no, these were unmistakably wolves. They immediately sensed my presence and halted. We stood eyeballing each other across a scant few yards. I tried to take in every nuance of the encounter, but it ended in a few seconds when I started to unzip my fanny pack to remove my camera. At the sound, the pair turned and bounded back the way they came. I heard others retreating ahead of them as I rushed to catch a final glimpse. A *pack* of wolves! Picture or no, the sight was etched in memory.

∽०∾

I follow Nettie into the cedars, and she flops down near a clump of fourteen-inch-diameter white cedars and begins playing with June. She begins dragging June around by her ear—I wonder how much fun this can be for June. Nettie's play often seems rough to me. Soon the bears stop to rest and fall asleep, and, tired myself, I leave them at the base of the cedars and walk back to the Jeep on the same two-track on which I had seen the wolves that previous spring.

5/19/94

I decide to pay a visit to Carmen & Company, as I have not been with them for nearly a week. I feel I am neglecting them. Normally, my near daily visits to the bears are determined by roll of dice. During the past week, my intended appointments with Carmen all fell on windy days, so I made no attempt at contact with her. Although I accompany the bears in all types of weather, they appear most ill at ease when the wind exceeds twenty miles per hour, and I rarely initiate visits under such conditions. When it becomes windy during a walk, the bears allow me to continue walking with them, but their behavior seems to change. They become uneasy, and unable to discern noises easily they sit more often, looking about, testing the wind, and listening. Carmen will tip her nose straight up in the air and inhale deeply for several minutes at a time. The wind is said to be a bear's newspaper, and I wonder if high-speed and variable winds provide bears with additional useful information or, like a fat Sunday paper, they simply require more time to filter through the superfluous news.

On windy days the bears are often startled by unfamiliar sounds, and will bolt for short distances when an unannounced branch comes crashing down. With cubs, this can have a snowball effect, the cubs bolting past one another until the whole litter is in perpetual motion. Occasionally under such circumstances, particularly when cubs are older, Carmen will follow the cubs' lead, not taking the time to identify the cause. In that event, the fiasco will eventually end at a refuge tree, where things are sorted out. Sometimes, the bears will simply find an acceptable spot, lie down, and wait it out. I try to fit in on windy days by talking more often to reassure the bears of my whereabouts as we negotiate the forest. But if I feel that I am adding to the confusion, I drop out and call it quits for the day.

Today I am accompanied by Richard P. Smith, an outdoor writer and photographer from Marquette, Michigan, who has shared many bear walks with me. We are in the Jeep, pointed south on the truck trail, headed for Carmen's home range.

Early in the project, I asked Richard to try making contact with Carmen alone, in order to determine whether she would abide others following her when I was not present. Richard has plenty of experience with bears, and Carmen knew him from his frequent visits with me. We reasoned that if anyone would be able to make and maintain contact with her in my absence, it would be him. But on each of several attempts by Richard to initiate contact, Carmen and her cubs (or yearlings) ran from him. Other times, I tried dropping out of walks, leaving fellow researchers to continue walking with the bears. Carmen would not accept that either and would simply run away. It seemed Carmen was a one-man bear, and secretly I could not have been happier.

The day is a fine one. The wind is calm, and the woods are wide open as leaf-out is not yet upon us. It is the perfect spring day for a bear walk. The Jeep rattles and spits gravel as we pull to a stop at a favorite spot from which to locate Carmen. Bingo! The pulse of her radio collar immediately sounds loud and clear as I raise the antenna and hold the receiver to my ear. We are lucky—normally, after a day of not contacting the bears I have to spend an hour or two locating them. I pull the Jeep off the truck trail and down to the end of a Forest Service road. Richard and I saddle-up our gear and head in on the bears.

We hustle through the hardwood on an abandoned logging road, both talking to the bears as we approach. Northern hardwoods in mid May have an aroma all their own—it's clean and refreshing. Soil organisms (actinomycete) are becoming active, and they emit an odor in spring that I regard as unmatched in signaling revitalization of the forest. Carmen is fortunate by birthright, her home range consists of soils that are richer, more fertile, and less drought prone than those of the female bears on the east side of the study area. In the ten thousand years since the last glaciation, the soil parent material in Carmen's home range has developed into a mosaic of rich substrates, perfect for the patchwork of highly interspersed cover types essential to quality bear habitat. Having carved out about fifteen square miles of some of the best, Carmen is able to garrison it for herself and her daughters until they are capable of fending for themselves. The richer soils of the area have probably enabled her clan, on average, to develop larger body size, reproduce at an earlier age, and produce more offspring with a corre-spondingly higher survival rate than clans of females with home ranges on less fertile earth. Of more than twenty female bears monitored during the study, only Carmen and Nettie and a daughter from Carmen's third litter, Bows, are known to have reproduced at age three. All others gave birth for the first time at age four or five. The fertile hardwoods among which Richard and I walk are in a portion of Carmen's home range that over-laps with Nettie's. I consider it prime bear habitat.

As we approach the trio of bears, Richard is first to spot them. They are sitting near a vernal pool, aware of our pend-ing arrival. Carmen walks a log out into the pool and stoops to lap water. The bolder of the two yearling males approaches us, testing Richard's scent. When everyone is familiarized, Carmen having reassessed Richard with a stiff gaze, we are underway. We head south, at a good pace, toward where I had been with Nettie and her cub the day before. I toggle the keys of the data logger and enter WD. Today, I sense at the outset that Carmen is on a mission.

We come into a small forest opening where the yearlings feed on vegetation while Carmen sniffs a balsam poplar sapling and dances while popping her jaws. From here, we cross a clear-cut stand of aspens and move to an adjoining hardwoods where Carmen arched-back rubs a sugar maple sapling. The bears proceed south through the hardwoods, and Carmen straddle-marks two shrubs en route. Along the way, the yearlings loiter to play a game of sorts involving a hollow log. Taking turns, each one sticks his head in the hollow end of the log while his littermate climbs atop and then pounces on his brother from above. Richard and I watch, hoping to capture the sequence on film. Carmen, preoccupied, does not join in. She is busying her-self with sniffing twigs and buds, not for any potential food value but rather for the lingering olfactory clues they hold. Her lungs pull air across tiny receptors located in the epithelium (surface membrane) lining the turbinal bones in her nasal cavity. She is taking a good hard look but doing it with her nose. I have an idea what might be commanding her attention.

Moving south, we enter a small sedge meadow surrounded by hardwoods, the remains of an ancient beaver flooding. The soil here is moist but not inundated and surprisingly dry for this time of year. I was here with Nettie and June less than a day ago, as they lounged among the clumps of sedge in the warmth of a midmorning sun. Carmen dances at the edge of the meadow upon entering it. Then she begins moving from one clump of sedge to the next, sniffing each with great concentration. I suspect she is smelling her granddaughter for the first time. I punch SO (sniff objects) into the data logger.

When the bears sniff objects, it can be performed either casually or with great intensity. The more intense inspections are distinguished by upper lip curling; sometimes a twig or stem is cradled between lip and nose while the bear inhales deeply. Should an object be too large to sample in this fashion, the bears will often move around it, sniffing it from multiple directions. Occasionally, the force of the inhalations and exhalations is so great that smaller objects actually get moved about. Bears might also lick their noses, which I suspect prolongs the retention of scent molecules, enabling them to better sort through the clues. During these more intense scenting sessions, the bears seem to draw air through their mouths as well as their noses, possibly a form of retro nasal olfaction—sampling from the mouth, much like a connoisseur of fine wines. It is also possible that the vomeronasal gland (Jacobson's organ), a chemoreceptor important in pheromone communication, is being used to detect intraspecific chemical *pheromonal* clues. Richard and I agree that Carmen does not seem agitated as she inspects the exact spots I know Nettie and June to have been at the day before; she just seems intensely curious, spending an inordinate amount of time scenting each site.

Meanwhile, the yearlings, apparently uninterested in the prior presence of kin, have climbed a huge maple snag. The snag is spottily covered with loose bark, and the yearlings are struggling for good footing on which to stand for a mock battle. The short carol-like song of a scarlet tanager sounds from the top of a balsam spire as we watch the yearlings from below it. Their battle is similar to king of the mountain, a game acted out on children's playgrounds everywhere, although for the yearlings the exercise is far more critical than child's play. Skills are being honed for use in serious future contests. The present contest is decided quickly, the runt yearling dominated by his larger sibling, who is also bolder and more cocksure.

Throughout the yearlings' competition, Carmen remains intent on her scenting activities. Oddly enough, she has not visited the nearby ironwood that Nettie and June broke down while playing. Apparently finished with her inspection of the meadow, she meanders off toward the southwest, straddle-marking a few bushes as she exits the area. Richard and I follow. The yearlings, seeing Carmen leaving, quickly descend the maple and move to join their mother, taking a circuitous route around Richard and me to fall in line behind her. We move through a large patch of aspens and into a shrub lowland where we find ourselves flanking a beaver pond. Brown tannic waters flow over the dam and foam in the stream below.

If any animal has a major impact on the form and function of the landscape, it must certainly be the beaver. Beaver floodings and dams dot the study area, and I skirt and traverse them regularly while traveling with the bears. Not far to the north, on Grand Island in Lake Superior, researchers have found evidence of an ancient beaver flooding, one that may be the largest ever known in North America—if not the world. Its dam is said to be at least eight hundred years old. The shallow fringes of beaver floodings, flush with succulent vegetation, make excellent foraging spots for bears, but the tender shoots and roots of cattails and other herbs on which bears feed have yet to appear here, and the bears do not tarry. As we round the downstream end of the dam, above the babbling of the impounded side stream, I can hear a torrent of water and realize that we are nearing the Whitefish River.

We move southerly along the east shore of the river, through stands of large white cedars from which the waters of snow-melt have now receded leaving a conspicuous high-water line where ice has scored their trunks. The stand is mostly open underneath, and the soil is mucky. We have ceased "moving direct," the bears now resting and playing briefly in patches of sun, as we progress southward. The yearlings discover the remains of a boat hull sunken in layers of mud and begin exploring it. They bite and claw at it, and for what, I wondered. This time of year, the presence of mycelium under the bark of decaying logs seems to interest bears, and frequently cubs and yearlings will lick at it as if to summon up a more substantial reward. I wonder if that is what interests them in the boat. They soon tire of it, however, and, having substantially decreased its half-life, move downstream toward where Carmen explores the lodge of a bank beaver. En route Corduroy stumbles onto the decaying remains of a steelhead trout lying along the shore of the river. There is not much left of the carcass, and he claims it all for himself. Seeing his preoccupation with the carcass, Carmen moves in to commandeer it. But the year ling blows at Carmen (a bold move, Richard and I agree) and hustles away with the remains of the fish. I recount the story of the squirrel carcass to Richard and remark that Carmen, no longer lactating (having nursed the cubs for a final time in late fall), will be unable to charm the yearling out of his find in the same manner. The loss of the fish leaves Carmen in a bad mood.

Yes, bears do get moody. I believe they have good and bad days just like people do, and like people, they seem to get over some things sooner than others. The inability to garner nearby food always seems to bring out the worst in Carmen; she registers her displeasure with her yearling by approaching Richard and lightly blowing at him. Richard, experienced in bear

communication and body language, does the correct thing—
he stands his ground and shows no sign of intimidation at the
mild threat. After all, he has done nothing wrong, and Carmen
knows it. Almost simultaneously, we both begin talking to Carmen in an effort to calm her. We wonder aloud in soothing tones
how she can blame one of us for losing a meal to her yearling.
This seems to do some good, but until the fish is gone and for-
gotten, we all have to stand and listen to the Whitefish rumble
by, while Richard suffers the brunt of Carmen's agitation.

To lighten the sober mood, I recall for Richard the only other
time I observed the bears eating fish. It was the spring of 1992,
as I followed Carmen and her yearlings through a lowland
scrub–shrub swamp, the bottom of which was unseasonally dry.
The area consisted mostly of red osier dogwood shrubs, but
there were also small isolated patches of cedars and balsams
scattered about. I estimated the overall patch size at 160 acres,
and we were on a narrow game trail about midpatch, making
a direct crossing. I punched WD-GT (walking direct–game trail)
into the field computer. The trail passed near one of the cedar
patches, which contained a large snag. In the broken-off top of
the snag, about sixty feet up, was the nest of an osprey, and I
could see a bird sitting on the nest. Ospreys usually nest along
the shores of lakes or waterways, and I suspected that the pair
was fishing the Whitefish and a nearby lake. Not too long ago,
high levels of pesticides seeping into surface waters and ab-
sorbed by fish depleted North American populations of ospreys.
They are now staging a comeback of sorts, along with bald
eagles, both of which are not uncommon in the study area.

Carmen led, as usual, and as she passed by the nest tree,
she showed no particular interest. Her yearling female (Nettie),
however, started to climb it. This immediately elicited some re-
marks from the nesting osprey. As Nettie climbed higher, the
bird took flight from the nest, calling a shrill *chewk-chewk*. In the
distant sky I saw its mate approaching, a fish clenched in its
talons. The distressed bird circled the nest, where it was joined

70

by its mate. By this time, Nettie had abandoned her ascent and was shuffling downward as both ospreys continued calling overhead. For some reason, the fish-toting osprey dropped the catch, and it plummeted to earth on a path intersecting Carmen's. Struggling to remove my camera from my pack, I watched as sunlight glistened off the sides of the fish during its fall. The fish hit the ground with a *thwack* about two steps in front of Carmen, who immediately gulped it down, barely breaking stride. When I arrived at the spot, all that remained of the fish was part of the caudal fin, not even enough to identify it.

During the recounting of the fish tale to Richard, Carmen is able to panhandle a morsel of fish from the yearling, and it seems to mollify her. When she finishes her fragment, the bears revisit the boat and the beaver lodge, as if repeating the sequence might somehow produce another fish. Finding nothing, they continue down the shore of the river.

As we travel south, Carmen's outward agitation is ameliorated, and she now appears to want to interact with the yearlings. Family breakup is only a short time off, and I wonder aloud to Richard whether her behavior has anything to do with that, or she is just making amends for her recent belligerent behavior—or if it matters at all to her.

We follow the bears to a stand of mature cedars, where they rest. They all begin grooming and lounging. When Aster attempts to suckle Carmen, we are surprised that she allows it. We know that Carmen is not lactating, and we wonder why and for how long she will tolerate the activity. The sound of nursing always seems to attract littermates, and the yearling's efforts are rebuffed in less than a minute when his brother attempts to join in. As Carmen blows loudly and rolls onto her stomach, both yearlings abandon the effort.

The grooming resumes, and the bears settle in. We watch as, one by one, the bears fall asleep. We begin recounting the events of the day, and I suddenly realize it is my birthday. There are few other places I would rather be at this moment than with Richard in the company of bears in the Upper Peninsula of Michigan, although I do not say it aloud. I believe Richard feels the same. For us, there will always be something special about being with bears, regardless of being bug-bitten, sweaty, and muddy to one's knees.

I always welcome Richard's company on bear walks. His vast experience with bears and his understanding of their behavior are definite assets. There is little that transpires during our bear walks that the two of us don't analyze and draw conclusions about regarding the bears' behavior. There will always be the nagging question of what has transpired prior to our arrival, and how that affects the bears' present behavior, as well as the question of what will take place in their lives after we depart. For us, however, the pursuit is the reward; finding out is a bonus.

An hour later, after reaching several hypotheses regarding Carmen's scenting activities and the yearling's attempt at nursing, and after I reassured Richard that Carmen's behavior toward him at the river was not personal, we leave the bears at rest. Carmen raises her head slightly as we talk our way out, saying, "See ya, Carmen. Thanks, guys. Good to see ya again. Bye." "Don't get pissed next time," Richard intones.

5/21/94

I again join Nettie and June in the hardwoods in the vicinity of the small clearing. They are hanging tight to this area. We move to a vernal pool, and Nettie investigates emerging plants while June slogs around and drapes herself playfully over moss-covered logs. A tanager sings overhead. June mouths the fronds of a fern and slips headfirst off the log she is sprawled across. As early as late May but most often in early June, the bears move to stands of northern hardwoods that contain vernal pools, undoubtedly one of the most preferred spring habitats that Carmen and Nettie exploit, especially when they have cubs. Vernal pools exist as small (usually less than a quarter acre), shallow depressions on the forest floor where seasonally pooled surface water temporarily gathers; over time, the periodic inundations and favorable pH characteristics of the soil provide suitable conditions for the growth of wetland plants. Among the bears' favorites are wild calla, water plantain, water parsnip, spotted touch-me-not, and pickerelweed. Most of these species flourish in the partial shade provided by the surrounding canopy, benefiting from reduced desiccation. Removing a significant portion of the canopy will likely result in the encroachment of less valuable, shade-intolerant, "weedy" aggressive species such as speckled alder, which in time will crowd out the wetland herbs that bears so enjoy. Vernal pools do not appear on forest stand maps, but even if they did, the likelihood of detecting their use by bears with conventional telemetry methods would be slight, given their small size and the inaccuracies of telemetry. Had I not the advantage of walking with bears and witnessing firsthand their extensive use of these tiny wetlands sprinkled among the hardwoods, I would never have guessed their value. Another reason vernal pools make perfect spots for female bears with cubs during spring is that they are bordered by potential cub-refuge trees, which allow the mothers to forage in the nearby wetlands unencumbered by their cubs.

We move to a clear-cut, and Nettie feeds on ironwood leaves (the cutting appears even greener than only a few days ago). Next, Nettie moves us to an aspen stand mixed with lowland conifers. When she stops to groom, June tries to nurse, but Nettie is unaccommodating. June then climbs up a white cedar and comes right back down. I leave them both resting at the base of a cedar as the wind picks up.

5/23/94

Yesterday was a windy day. A cold front moved down from the northeast, and high winds (more than thirty miles per hour)

73

buffeted the study area. The roads are strewn with fallen trees and branches. I always carry a chain saw in the back of the Jeep, never knowing when I will find a tree across the road. This morning I am forced to use it more times than I want.

On my walk in to the bears, once familiar game trails are obscured by windfalls. Both Nettie and June are up a huge leaning cedar and are testy when I approach (they probably could not distinguish my voice clearly over the rumbling sounds of a nearby creek—I must talk louder in the future). They climb down, however, and we move off toward the creek. As we approach the creek, Nettie feeds briefly on swamp thistle, then sits and listens for a long time. Walking on, both bears feed on catkins in a windblown aspen. June lowers herself to the ground through its branches and hustles to join Nettie, who has moved off and begun feeding on beetle larvae in a decaying log. As Nettie moves from the log, June moves in and discovers a little meal in the disintegrated wood. Finished at the log, June ascends a white cedar refuge tree and climbs up very near the top. Nettie forage-meanders, feeding on sweet cicely and grasses. She again stands and listens for a long time (I think I hear voices but decide I am probably hearing just the stream murmuring past). After walking to the edge of the stream for a drink, Nettie forages her way to the refuge tree and sniffs it vigorously, acting as if she forgot which tree June is in. She climbs to the very top and sniffs June, then descends, using her teeth at times to lower herself between branches. I end the watch with Nettie at the base of the refuge tree.

∽o∽

Only twice, when I was present, have the bears ever encountered other people. Bears' senses are acute, and while I cannot be certain, I suspect that most often they are able to steer clear of such encounters well in advance. On the first occurrence, I

74

was with Carmen and Corduroy and Aster, then cubs, on a nice, quiet day in early May. We were resting in an aspen stand next to an opening in the forest. The cubs slept partway up a medium-sized cedar tree about ten feet from the edge of the opening. Carmen, lying on the ground between me and the cubs, was about fifteen yards distant. The cubs were about ten yards beyond her. Suddenly, Carmen sat alert, her ears perked. After holding the position a few moments, she walked over to the cub-tree and huffed to the cubs, sending them higher up the tree. Then she returned to where she had been and resumed sitting alert. I thought another bear was coming, which was not unusual, but I could see or hear none. We sat awhile. Then, on the other side of the clearing, I saw something tawny-brown moving—I thought it might be the flank of a deer. (I hoped to see a cougar, as their presence here remains highly debated.) Casually, Carmen walked off about fifty yards behind me (away from the cubs and the clearing) and lay down. She remained very alert, looking toward the opening. It was then that I recognized the tawny-brown movement as that of the legs of a man dressed in khaki pants. He walked directly toward the cubs and me, right along the edge of the opening, coming within fifteen feet of the cubs. The cubs were quiet, and Carmen did not make a move. The man walked right on by, oblivious of the bears. About half an hour later Carmen remained in her alert resting position. I turned to watch the cubs, now asleep in the top of the cedar, and thought, "Come on, Carmen, he's gone. Let's go do some bear stuff," when I heard brush breaking about fifty yards away. A quick check revealed Carmen had not moved. She was still lying there watching in an alert position. Then I heard a man's voice: "Honey, where are you?" A woman's voice responded, "Over here, dear." The man then proceeded to walk right between me and the cubs. I crouched behind the windblown stump that I had previously had my back against. For some reason, it was all I could do to keep from laughing. The man passed only ten yards from the cubs and never had a clue they were there. What is more important, Carmen did nothing but watch throughout the incident. The couple walked off. About fifteen minutes later, Carmen stood, walked past me to the cub tree, and umphed and tongue-clicked to the cubs. They immediately scaled down and joined her at the base. Then the three bears, with me following, walked off in the opposite direction of the couple.

Not a bear tale to make headlines, to be sure, but I suspect that for every time someone has a negative encounter with a black bear, my story is acted out thousands of times. I believe it is largely untrue that female bears aggressively defend their cubs regardless of the consequences. Quite often the opposite is true. For example, in order to determine cub survival in the study area, I used telemetry equipment to sneak in on females and their cubs during spring and summer. I attempted to get close enough to count cubs and determine if and when any were missing. On twenty-seven of fifty-two attempts at sneaking in (under conditions chosen to provide me the most advantage), the bear families detected my approach and fled before I was able to make visual contact. On the other occasions, I was able to approach the families to within fifty yards and then rush them, sending the cubs up nearby refuge trees so I could count them. Although I surprised the females and their cubs at very close range, on every one of those occasions, the females abandoned their cubs and fled the area. During August this tactic was less successful because the cubs by then were big enough to run off with the fleeing female. The point is, we should not fear black bears for this or any other reason. We should respect them and give them space. We should also educate ourselves about bears and learn to do what is necessary to get along with them. After all, aren't we the big-brained species? Should we not make some effort at getting along? Bears try to avoid us, and on nearly all occasions are successful without us even realizing it. There is little question that bears can and will do their part. Will we do ours?

It should go without saying that bears are a part of the forest. And they belong there. So do people, I believe. What a pity that through our own insecurity, we tend to eliminate wild things like bears from our wild lands. Are we not removing the very things that serve to stir our souls? A forest is most assuredly a hollow place without the awesome presence of the black bear. And something I find hard to imagine.

5/25/94

It rained yesterday. I join Nettie and June in the hardwoods at the north end of the gated area. Overhead the maples are leafing-out, and the forest floor is noticeably greener. The bears are again feeding on sweet cicely. Nettie meanders through a grove of maple saplings and bends a stem to check a bird's nest near its top. It proves empty and when she releases the sapling, it springs upright, the force partially dislodging the nest. Nettie leads the way to an area of mature overstory, and here she begins feeding on the unfurling leaves of beech and ironwood. June parks herself up a nearby hemlock and immediately falls asleep. Nettie feeds virtually nonstop on vegetation, mostly the tender leaves of beech saplings. She strips off mouthfuls while sitting, steadying the bent branches with the claws and pads of her front feet. Sometimes she stands on her hind legs and grasps a sapling in her teeth to pull it down, pinning it under her weight while she feeds. Other times she bowls the saplings over with her chest and lies on top of them gathering the branches in with her front paws. As she sits on her rear end and strips branch after branch of their leaves, I think that if she had a wide white stripe around her middle and a little white fur on her face, she could pass for a panda, the most herbivorous of all the bears.

Even though black bears are 90 percent herbivorous, their digestive systems lack the complexity of a true herbivore's. A bear's digestive tract is relatively short—only 40 percent the length that would be expected for a herbivore of equal size. A herbivore's digestive tract may be twenty-five times its body length, while a bear's digestive system is only five to eight times the length of its body. (It is interesting to note that the panda, the most herbivorous of all bears, has the shortest digestive system—equivalent in length to that of a comparably sized carnivore. The panda is able to digest little more than one-fifth of the bamboo it eats, as opposed to the 60 percent digestive efficiency of ruminants. Because of its inefficient digestion, the panda must consume 12–15 percent of its body weight in bamboo every day, sometimes feeding for fifteen hours a day to meet its energy requirements.) The foods Nettie eats, however, contain an average of three times more digestible energy than bamboo does. Therefore, she has less trouble meeting her daily energy requirements.

Bears' simple stomachs allow a more rapid passage of food. Bears are set up to glean the cream of the crop from seasonally abundant resources. They gulp in berries, lick up insect pupae whole, and in general, take little time to masticate food. Because their teeth are not well suited to grinding and breaking down vegetation, they depend instead on a strong pylorus, or stomach muscle, to grind foods and a low stomach pH (3.5) to dissolve available nutrients from the vegetation they eat.[1] Their digestive tracts have evolved to capitalize on readily available energy while allowing unusable cellulose and lignin to pass through their system relatively quickly, thus making room available for the more easily digested foods. Foraging on spring vegetation, the bears never seem to gain weight. Regardless of how much time Nettie and Carmen spend foraging, they continue to lose weight well into summer, until the advent of ripe berries; this is especially true when they are with cubs.

Nettie spends most of this day feeding on the leaves and buds of beech and ironwood saplings. She has an extended play session with June at the base of the hemlock refuge tree, which lasts twenty-two minutes. Later, she climbs and nurses June while in the tree. It proves to be an interesting maneuver, as both bears balance delicately on wavering branches, after which they play and rest in the tree, both falling asleep cradled in its branches. The blackflies are bad today, and I leave the bears, not altogether unhappy to make my getaway.

5/27/94

I locate Nettie and June in a northern hardwood stand not far from their May 25 location. Nettie drinks from a vernal pool and digs and eats the roots of an unidentifiable fern before moving into the hardwoods and sniffing a large rock. Climbing atop it, she rests alert. Later, she walks off the rock, sits and scratches, plays with June, grooms, and feeds on grasses and beech leaves. She sniffs the ground and a few objects and then walks a log out into the wetland to check vegetation. While she is standing on the log, something bites her on the rump, and she jumps and looks back. I am glad I'm not too close—at my distance she knows it wasn't me. June feeds on grass in the vernal pool, then hones her stalking skills on a caterpillar. She walks the log on which I am sitting and makes a little bluff charge at me! This is probably serious, but I can't help snickering. Nettie looks our way, and I tell her it's OK and she goes back to her task. June eases around on the log and walks its mossy surface back into the hardwoods (satisfied, I guess, that she showed me). Nettie moves to the hardwoods and feeds on beech leaves. June joins her, and they play and alternately feed on beech leaves. Nettie meanders to an adjacent vernal pool, where the bears lounge in the water and appear to wash their faces. When Nettie faces me, I can see that an engorged tick, previously noticeable above her right eyebrow, has been dislodged. Then both bears wallow on a particular clump of submerged vegetation. (I wonder if this can be bearnip, but I am unable to locate it on a return visit.) Nettie meanders to a stand of large-diameter hemlocks, and when she is under their canopy, she starts running. Both bears climb trees partway up, then drop back down and run through the stand, playing what appears to be tag. Then they rest recumbent at the base of a hemlock, where Nettie nurses June for several minutes. Later, following a long bout of play, I see that June has managed to get a porcupine quill stuck in her ear. Nettie, continuing the play session, drags her around by her other ear—not much June can do. Tiring of all the fun, Nettie grooms her chest and belly, then meanders back to the vernal pool for a drink and to feed on vegetation. She moves back to the refuge tree, where June tries to nurse, but Nettie blows at her and then walks off—her maneuver for discouraging and ending nursing bouts is much improved. Both bears wade for a while in the vernal pool, then Nettie moves through hardwoods to an old logging road and feeds on vegetation. She spends a lot of time sniffing objects along the edge of the logging road, her actions signaling to me the recent presence of another bear. She straddle-marks a small shrub and urinates a stream, then stops to feed on grass before turning around and walking back the way she came. She appears nervous. Near an old log decking area, she stands on hind legs sniffing a hollow hemlock that is broken off about fifteen feet above ground. June climbs it and plays inside, seemingly oblivious to Nettie's concerned demeanor. Nettie walks the logging road and sniffs the end of a culvert protruding from under the road. She moves into the hardwoods and digs the stump of an unknown species of tree but gets nothing from it. Next, she moves to a vernal pool but does not forage in it, and she urinates a stream as she exits. Meandering back into the hardwoods, she climbs into the top of a windblown beech that is still attached to the trunk about fifteen feet above the ground. June climbs the trunk and then out onto the limbs. But she has trouble climbing down—she does not know whether to go headfirst or backward down the smooth-barked, steeply sloping limbs. Nettie descends the limbs headfirst but must brace herself to keep from sliding headlong down. June ends up sliding down the branches sideways, then, hanging by her front feet, she drops the final three feet to the ground. Nettie meanders back to the logging road, where she feeds on clovers and grasses. After standing and sniffing a raspberry cane for a long while, she becomes fidgety, huffing lightly. June presses into her side, and they both stand and look into the hardwoods. Nettie bolts a short distance down the logging road, then stops. I run to catch up. Both bears run ahead again and then stop. Something has disturbed Nettie—she runs again. I decide to let them sort it out for themselves and say good-bye before this very good day comes apart. They stand and watch me as I go, then begin to run.

5/28/94

I locate Carmen in a northern hardwood stand less than a quarter mile from where I was with Nettie and June yesterday. She is separated from her yearlings and is accompanied by a large male bear. The big male (I estimate him at 350 pounds) stands on his hind feet as I approach. He is obviously anxious about Carmen's failure to flee upon my approach (other males have had this same problem), but he is reluctant to leave her. I anticipated finding Carmen with a male today, having checked her radio signal earlier and learning that she was nearly a mile from the yearlings. Just in case things should get out of hand, I have brought along my walking stick. (Often a loud noise, such as a stick striking the side of a tree, will give a black bear pause and a chance to rethink his actions.) The stick is ironwood and a veteran of other encounters with male bears. I continue to run a steady stream of chatter to Carmen as I approach. The male bounds off when I am fifty yards distant. I walk to Carmen, re-move my pack, and toss her a few treats. They are summarily inhaled. The male rises to his hind legs seventy-five yards away. He stands a moment looking at me, then drops to all fours and begins straddle-marking beech saplings and then Carmen-dances, forcefully punching his feet into the ground. He walks very deliberately back and forth several times as Carmen watches. He then straddle-marks a good-sized beech sapling and sits watching us. Out of habit I begin talking to him. Carmen stands watching me, and when I show her my open, crossed, palms-up hands, she walks in the direction of the male, and they mosey off, more or less side by side.

Carmen and the male walk up a side hill in the hardwoods, where they lie down about ten yards apart. After a few minutes, Carmen walks off, and the male walks over to where she has lain and sniffs the spot. When she stops to rest again, this time nearer the top of the hill, the male again rests about ten yards below her. The bears repeat the routine a third time, then both walk off and disappear over the hill. When I reach the hilltop, they are resting in a hollow at the base of the hill, lying only a few feet apart. Carmen wiggles around a little bit, nuzzling toward the male, then drapes herself over a nearby log. After only minutes, she is up again and bellying around near the male. Neither now appears the least bit concerned with my presence only twenty-five yards from then.

I am videotaping the bears but must confess that being around a strange male bear is initially disquieting and takes some getting used to. My association with Carmen and Nettie is now built on hundreds of hours of experiences. We have to come to anticipate, if not trust to some degree, how one another will respond in a given situation. Should things go awry, I know (and believe the bears do, too) that there are no devious intentions. Not so for me and strange male bears. While to a large degree bears are predictable, that predictability is achieved only after coming to know the bear as an individual. I have found strange males to be much less predictable, often bolder, and I am unsure of how they perceive my presence. So I am careful to avoid any testy situations.

Both bears are in the shade of the hardwoods below, and Carmen periodically continues her wiggling action. I squint my left eye as I look through the viewfinder of the camera with my right. Out of the corner of that eye, I catch movement. Something black. Another (bigger) male walks over the hill only fifteen yards from where I stand. I am sure that he is unaware of me—his attention is fixed on the bears below. I feel the need to make him aware of my presence but do not want to surprise him at this close distance. Carmen and the first male are now standing below watching the interloper. The original suitor paces back and forth Carmen-dancing. The interloper continues his downhill approach. When he is halfway down the hill, I begin talking to him. He stops and wheels around, blowing. This puts everybody (including me) in motion. The second male has no interest in me once he is satisfied that I am not a bear, and he follows Carmen and her original suitor up and over the top of the next hill. I rationalize that this is a good time to discontinue the bear walk, not wanting to disrupt things further or to contend with two unfamiliar males at once.

I am glad to see Carmen with the males today but am disappointed that I was not there when she and the yearlings broke up this year. I suspected it was eminent.

&oo&

Several years ago, on the day preceding the breakup of Carmen's family, I witnessed an intimate scene. The four bears—Carmen and her three yearlings—rested near the base of a large-diameter aspen. It was midday, and they had just finished digging and eating cattail roots from a nearby wetland. Carmen was trying to rest, but the yearlings appeared restless. The dominant male of the litter was going from resting bear to resting bear nudging them with his shoulder trying to evoke a response. He nudged into Carmen and then flopped down next to her. Carmen, resting on her side in the leaves, rolled onto her belly and began grooming the yearling. Bears frequently groom themselves and occasionally each other. It was more common for Carmen to groom her cubs than to groom her yearlings. Today, her grooming consisted of biting at ticks on the neck and ears of the male. After a few minutes of this, she rested a paw on his back and initiated a protracted grooming of his entire body. Finished with his head and back, she rolled him over and began grooming his underside in a meticulous manner. The yearling resisted this and tried to wiggle free. Carmen, insistent on grooming him, pinned him down with her paw, disregarding his disgruntled vocalizations. I perceived the event as having overtones of incestuousness as Carmen sniffed and licked the yearling's genitals. After nearly forty-five minutes of this intensive grooming, the male was allowed to walk away. In less than forty-eight hours the family was split apart.

I wondered then and do now if the grooming was coincidental or if I had witnessed a farewell ritual of sorts. Was Carmen perhaps trying to familiarize herself indelibly with her male offspring in an effort to prevent some future chance of inbreeding? While female bears are ceded a part of their mother's territory, males are shunned by their mothers and, if unwilling to separate voluntarily, may be forcefully driven off. Close inbreeding is thus less likely. However, the phenomenon of male dispersal has proved to be somewhat plastic and operates differently among male offspring.

The next day, the day Carmen and her three yearlings parted ways, started like any other, at least for me. It was a calm May day, the Friday before Memorial Day, and the bears' telemetry signals indicated that they were together in a northern hardwood stand just south of an area I had labeled the blow-downs, a dense stand of windblown aspens resulting from a 1990 wind spout. Traversing the blow-downs was difficult, and I avoided it if possible. But today the stand lay in the path of my most direct route to the bears, and, anxious to join them, I decided to venture a crossing. I traveled quickly, gaining poise as I went, hopping from log to log about four feet above ground. I had learned the year before, while watching Carmen and her cubs, that this approach, walking atop the logs, rather than below,

84

was the most efficient way to travel this woods. I paused periodically to regain the bear's signals and stay on course through the stand. I began talking to the bears as always when I neared, but I was breaking more brush than usual as I negotiated the maze of logs. When I finally made it to the far edge of the blowdowns, I was standing on a good-sized log, and I spied Carmen sitting about a hundred yards into the hardwoods. As I silently congratulated myself on my newfound skill as a blow-down navigator, the bark of the log on which I was standing gave way. I suddenly found myself straddling the log unceremoniously, and instantly I fell off onto the sodden ground, assuming a fetal posture. Somewhere a hidden memory link recollected the pain of straddling the crossbar on my first boy's bike. (Loose bark may be of serious consequence to both man and bear.) Out of the corner of my eye I saw Carmen bolt a short distance then sit. With some reluctance, I gathered up my fallen equipment. The camera I keep stuffed in my shirt between the second and third buttons had fallen out and was going to need a new film-advance lever. Otherwise, things were disheveled but mostly intact. Carmen sat watching as I hobbled toward her. I considered bagging the walk for the day but afterward was forever glad that I did not.

I had expected to find the bears feeding on sweet cicely, as this hardwood stand contained particularly plentiful patches of the herb and the time of year was right for it. But the yearlings were nowhere to be seen. I thought perhaps they had spooked during my noisy approach, but then I glimpsed a bear behind Carmen, then another and another. The yearlings were there, but why were they holding back? Probably I had made too much noise. I reminded myself to be more careful on future approaches so that the bears would hear my voice before they heard my commotion and would not take flight. I tossed Carmen a couple of treats, which she mouthed uninterestedly; she then headed off toward the yearlings, who had now begun moving eastward. Carmen began trotting after them, and I had to run to keep up with her. Up to this point, I had never really *run* through the forest with the bears. As I reached behind my back to locate the cinches on my pack, I hoped, in my present condition, that the run would not last long. We soon came to a halt near the yearlings. I began taking off my pack, expecting the entire family now to demand treats, but the yearlings still held back, all hugging the bases of separate trees. Carmen immediately walked off toward a cedar swamp north and east of our rendezvous site. She was clunking her jaws as I have heard her do before when locating lost cubs or when out of sight of the refuge tree. I would have to follow her and leave the yearlings. After all, she was the main focus of my research, and to date, whatever moves she made dictated those of the litter. So I saddled up and took off after her. En route, she sniffed bushes and twigs and straddle-marked small conifers and shrubs. After covering a distance of a few hundred yards, she met another bear; they nuzzled, and he (I presumed it a he) mounted her. They began the motion of copulation, but upon spotting me over his shoulder, the male blew, dismounted, and ran off, all in one motion. Carmen, left alone, meandered back toward the yearlings. I followed. We joined them not far from where we had left them, but upon our approach, the yearlings all seemed to evade Carmen. Again they hugged trees, this time with their upper lips extended, and they huffed ever so lightly as Carmen tried to reassociate with them. It took nearly forty-five minutes for the family members to warm to each other and begin moving through the forest as a unit once more. All through this reassociation period, the yearling female (Nettie) acted as the reconciliator, going to each of her brothers and nuzzling and mingling with them and tongue-clicking and umphing to them as I often witnessed Carmen doing when regrouping with them. I wondered if it was maternal instinct.

We meandered through the forest, the bears eating some sweet cicely as we went, but the union had an edge to it, and the family seemed unsettled. As we continued, I considered whether my presence might be affecting the outcome of certain events, interrupting Carmen's breeding the way I apparently had. I did not want to miss anything in the lives of the bears, especially something as important as breeding. Yet if my presence was a hindrance, the right thing to do would be to abandon this walk and forgo future ones until the end of breeding season, whenever that was. But on second thought, I concluded that if the bears really wanted to get away from me, they could do so at any time. They could just move off and leave me in their dust. So I reasoned that they must not. And I continued following.

We arrived at an abandoned log-decking area via an old logging railroad grade. The grade was overgrown with ironwood saplings and tag alder brush but had a well-worn game trail in it. The bears fed on the tops of dandelions, hawkweed, and grasses that had reclaimed the area. Carmen arched-back rubbed a broken-off balsam fir sapling at a spot where the grade joined the opening, a spot where I had watched her do that before.

Watching Carmen marking territory and the yearlings foraging, I wondered if the yearlings' reluctance to reassociate with her was a response to atypical behavior on her part or perhaps the lingering scent of the foreign male on her coat. Up until now, it had been my understanding that it was the adult female who shuns her offspring, occasionally driving them from her range. What I had just witnessed was the opposite: it was the yearlings who reacted with apprehension when she returned from her encounter with the male. A bear family's breakup now appeared more complex than I had thought.

The bears traveled southwest from the decking area through a hardwood stand and then south along the limestone banks of the Whitefish River. We crossed the Whitefish while heading west at a point I knew to be an outside corner of Carmen's home range. Was she expanding her territory? More likely this spot was new only to me and perhaps the yearlings. Carmen stopped at several spots to mark territory using arched-back rubs, and the little female emulated her behavior at every site. As I watched Carmen and then the yearling female marking territory, I realized that Carmen had participated in more marking behavior with, and had directed more attention toward, the yearling female than the males since den emergence. In later years, it would become apparent that, when accompanied by yearling litters that contained females, Carmen increased the size of her spring range—as if showing the young females around new territory. If clues found during these excursions indicate that an adjacent territory is occupied, perhaps the young females confine their dispersal; if no such clues are found, then perhaps they spread out into those voided areas. It was also apparent to me that all the yearlings were learning some valuable lessons in foraging during this final spring with Carmen, benefits they would have lacked if orphaned or estranged earlier.

Finished marking territory, the bears resumed their westerly heading. We were at the confluence of two branches of the Whitefish, and the ground there was low and mucky. When we reached the near shore of the west branch, I decided to call it a day. It was about a two-mile circuitous route back to the Jeep, unless I intended to go through the blow-downs again. I knew of a series of game and logging trails that would take me around. I felt as though I had put in a good day with the bears and believed I had witnessed what were surely the first signs of family breakup. What I did not know is how rapidly that breakup would transpire, that the bear family would never again be together after that day.

The next day I attempted to locate the bears early in the morning, thinking that a shot of Carmen with a male would make a good picture. I was standing on the "pie-plate" road (a road named by our research group for an old dinner plate someone had nailed to a beech tree where the entrance to the road veered off the truck trail) at first light listening for the fa-

miliar *ping* of the bears' radio collars. The tone of t
collars told me they had turned back north and w
the hardwoods south of the blow-downs. The r
sounded exceptionally loud, while his brother's a
signals sounded muted, but all their signals seem..u to em-
anate from the same general area. When I tuned the receiver to
Carmen's frequency, she was nowhere to be found. I wondered
if she might be behind a hill or other obstruction and her collar shielded. That happened often, and sometimes I had to get
within a half mile of bears to pick up a signal, particularly
when they were in hilly country. I decided to proceed toward
the yearlings, believing I would detect Carmen's signal as I
approached.

I jumped back in the Jeep and drove five miles around, starting in on the bears' signals from the south. When I arrived, the
runt was high up a hemlock very near the top, which explained
the strength of his collar's signal. His siblings were in the vicinity but were separated from each other by a narrow strand of
cedar swamp. I said hi to the runt as I passed below, but he
huffed at me and retreated farther up the hemlock (as it turned
out, he spent the rest of the day there). I now felt some sense
of urgency to locate Carmen, concerned that something might
be amiss. (The preceding fall, a radio-collared female had been
killed illegally in the study area.) I spent the remainder of the
morning locating her. When I finally caught up to her, she was
almost five miles from the yearlings, near the northern border
of her home range, consorting with a male bear. She would be
with different males, off and on, over the next three weeks.

5/30/94

Nettie and June are still in the hardwoods at the gated area.
I am surprised to find them there, given the proximity of Carmen and her male suitors. They are moving when I catch up
with them, and they run into a vernal pool, where Nettie begins
to feed on water parsnip. June splashes along behind, slipping

and straddling her way along a mossy log. Things are starting to grow, the woods are alive, and it seems to me a perfect day for a cub to act like one. Nettie, her head down, feeds on wild calla along with the water parsnip. June runs through the water and climbs a pole-sized red maple. Then she descends and sniffs a balsam fir stump, digs it and licks at something (maybe ants), then sits and grooms while only a few feet from me. Nettie moves us away from the pool to an adjacent clear-cut and feeds on the tips and roots of cattails in wetter areas of the stand. She becomes interested in sniffing shrubs and objects, then stands on her hind legs looking and sniffing. June finishes her scratch and walks calmly into the cutting and begins feeding on willow leaves; then moving on, she locates some ants in a small log. It has been nearly two months, and June is finally acting confident around me. Nettie smells something on a shrub and then runs. She stops in the middle of the clear-cut and Carmen-dances, then sniffs the top of a moth mullein. Both bears meander about uneasily, feeding on grass and clover. Nettie sniffs more mullein tops, then Carmen-dances again. The wind picks up to twenty-plus miles per hour, and I end the walk as the bears move from the clear-cut to a stand of lowland conifers.

A short visit to Carmen confirms that she is with a male in the hardwoods at the gated area. I cannot tell for sure, but it looks like the original suitor from two days ago and not the late-coming larger male. But I can now clearly see a white chevron on this bear's chest, something I did not notice on either of the males two days ago.

∾

The breeding season for bears extends from late May until early July. In all years, Carmen has been the first female bear of those in the study to commence breeding activities (always beginning on Memorial Day weekend) and the first to complete them (by mid June). On June 1, 1992, Carmen was between mates and traveling the forest alone, while other females hadn't even separated from their yearlings, something I learned firsthand. When I joined Carmen that day, she was in a stand of red maples near the shore of a shallow marl lake. She was foraging on sweet cicely in what I considered a poor woods for it—the soils there were wet and cool, and there was only a patchy distribution of stunted sweet cicely. I knew of three or four more favorable patches of the herb within her range. (But she *is* the bear, after all, I acknowledged, and must know what she's doing.) She foraged east, came to a two-track, and walked it north some distance before reentering the woods and resuming her easterly heading. We walked into another red maple stand, where she began feeding on sweet cicely and an occasional jack-in-the-pulpit. She worked her way to a wetter part of the stand, where the previous May I had watched her and the cubs dig and eat the roots of dwarf ginseng. Now as she moved south through the stand, she began intensely sniffing objects. I immediately suspected a male bear and anticipated more breeding activities. I cinched my pack, ready to move. Carmen began trotting south, and I could make out the shape of a bear moving about a hundred yards ahead. I slowed, not wanting to run headlong into a strange male bear, but Carmen's pace quickened. I was a little more than fifty yards behind when she chased the bear up a twenty-four-inch-diameter sugar maple. The bear was smallish, and I was sure it was not one of her yearlings (I had located them some distance away just before joining her). Carmen began to sniff around the tree, then climbed up on it and blew. Dropping down, she meandered off a short distance to the south, all the while diligently sniffing the ground. I followed as she traveled in a small arc and returned to the treed bear. As she approached the tree, she bowled over a five-foot-high balsam fir with her chest and accompanied the display by blowing and swatting the ground.

As the small bear climbed higher in the tree, I noticed another bear perched above it and then noticed radio collars on both. Confused, I toggled the receiver to the frequencies of Carmen's yearlings. The check revealed that these were not her yearlings, but the yearlings of a bear named Sandy (named for the sandy soils in her home range). Carmen stood on her hind legs, her front legs braced against the tree, and blew, then quickly climbed the tree for a couple of body lengths, slapping it forcefully with both front paws and blowing as she did so. On cue, the yearlings simultaneously defecated. Carmen blew at them and descended and once again bowled over the balsam while forcefully exhaling air and swatting the ground. She then walked directly to the southernmost point of the arc she had traveled earlier and began scent trailing. The picture began to clear for me, and I punched Sandy's frequency into the receiver. She was straight ahead, and Carmen was now moving out of sight in her direction. Stowing all gear, I cinched my pack and followed.

Things began to go wrong from the start. Almost immediately, I ripped what had formerly been a rip-stop shirt as we bowled our way along a creek bottom through a windblown stand of pole-sized cedars. I could see Carmen's back as she climbed over the downed logs. She knew I was there but was not the least bit interested and was rapidly outdistancing me. I hooked the antenna and cable to the receiver, figuring I might need technology to stay in the chase. Next, I felt a trickle of blood from an ear. But there was no time to dress wounds, so I did my best to ignore it. I shortly lost sight of Carmen and began using the telemetry equipment to shadow her route. When the antenna cable snagged a limb and was torn loose from the receiver, I gave up the chase and began the long walk back. About two hours after it all began, I crossed under the tree in which Sandy's yearlings had sought refuge. The female yearling was gone, but for some reason, the male had stayed put. I counseled him to follow his sister's lead as I walked by, but he

I struggle to elevate the Runt's head prior to returning him to his den. He was one of only two of thirty-three study area males not to disperse from their natal areas as yearlings. The Runt was the only male of Carmen's to survive past age two. (Kevin Doran)

Author prepares to sedate a bear in its winter den by hand-injecting it using a jab-stick fitted with a hypodermic syringe. (Steve Harryman)

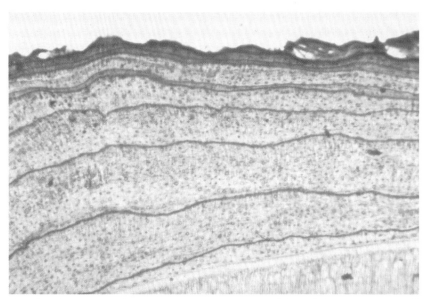

Annuli and cementum layers in the premolar of this eight-and-three-quarter-year-old female show that she produced cubs at ages five and seven.

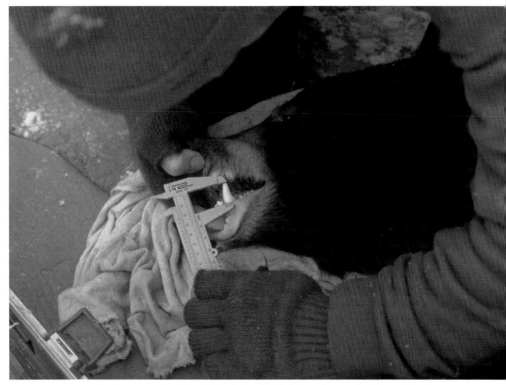

Author measuring female black bear's (Vicky) canine teeth. (Jiquan Chen)

This bear was probably injured by another bear in a dispute over food resources. (Terry D. DeBruyn)

Bottle Brush shaken from the comfort of his favorite barrel trap, June 1990. (Terry D. DeBruyn)

Brown phase yearling female grooms fat belly, Orr, Minnesota. (Terry D. DeBruyn)

The cinnamon or brown phase of the black bear is common in western states and comprises as much as 40 percent of some states' populations. (Terry D. DeBruyn)

Black yearling standing on hind legs looking up while brown phase sow and sibling forage. (Terry D. DeBruyn)

Close-up of a male black bear resting alert, Big Bay, Michigan. (Terry D. DeBruyn)

Nimble and dexterous paws are an aid when handling some foods, Orr, Minnesota. (Terry D. DeBruyn)

Carmen rests on a log in a lowland conifer stand, summer 1992. (Terry D. DeBruyn)

This cub uses its teeth to grip a limb while descending a refuge tree. Cubs and adults often use their teeth and strong jaws to advantage when climbing and descending trees. (Terry D. DeBruyn)

just hugged the tree more tightly. I attempted to collect the scats from the base of the tree but found them too dispersed.

Back at the Jeep I attached a new cable to the antenna and began tracking Carmen and Sandy by vehicle. By the time I caught up with Carmen, she was nearly two miles to the south and beyond the boundary of her territory. Sandy was approximately one mile from Carmen and two and a half miles from the former border of her home range. I did not know if Carmen had made contact with Sandy, but when I rejoined her later, she was foraging on jack-in-the-pulpit and bore no visible marks of a fight. Sandy returned to her home range by late the next day and was reunited with her yearlings. We never again documented Sandy or any of her offspring within the boundaries of Carmen's home range.

❧

6/2/94

I walk in on Nettie and June while they are at rest today. Nettie rests alert at the base of a hemlock as I approach and take my seat against a tree about ten yards from her. June is in the tree. Soon she climbs down and immediately initiates nursing. Nettie accommodates her while sitting with a front paw braced against the hemlock. When finished, June walks toward me, climbs partway up a small sugar maple near where I sit, and begins to blow at me. I talk to her, attempting to calm her, as she climbs the maple to a height of about fifteen feet and then shuffles back down. Nettie sits and watches. Then she stands, moves to rub her side against a beech tree, walks to a depression and drinks, and begins to feed on beech leaves. June loses interest in me and returns to the base of the hemlock. Nettie joins her there, and they play. Nettie interrupts the play to groom herself and then June. Following that, both bears rest recumbent at the base of the refuge tree, and I go in search of Carmen.

I locate Carmen resting on the edge of a clear-cut in the northwest corner of her home range. Although she appears to be alone, I situate myself in anticipation of a visit from a male bear. This time of year silhouettes of males often drift in and out of view as I rest with Carmen. The more anxious paramours sometimes make themselves known by trammeling an out-of-sight bush or two. Others march headlong into Carmen's resting spot only to do an about face upon detecting my presence. They'll just have to get used to me. After a while Carmen gets up and meanders around sniffing and digging stumps but obtains no ants. It is early yet for the insect's appearance. Near the edge of the cut, she dances, then rests under a white spruce. There is a lot of resting today, and four hours and no other bears later I leave.

6/3/94

9:04. Carmen is in a semi-open area about three miles from where I left her yesterday. She is feeding on a yellow goatsbeard and meanders into a stand of aspens mixed with balsams and defecates solids, stands on her hind legs to sniff an ironwood, then drops down and dances. We meander across a tamarack planting and into a soft maple stand, where she arched-back rubs an ironwood tree at the edge of the stand. She straddle-marks a leatherwood while we meander through the stand. She stops to feed on sweet cicely, then straddle-marks another leatherwood. She continually sniffs the ground and objects as we travel. She exits the maples onto a two-track, and we "walk direct" on the two-track. Carmen appears to be favoring her left rear leg, and I think it is probably breeding related. She meanders into a red pine planting, then back onto the road, and it appears to me that she is searching for males (10:00). She encounters and chases her runt yearling up a maple in a hardwood stand. She goes to the base of his refuge tree and starts up, then quits and comes back down. The male is huffing and blowing at us (10:11). Carmen discovers the fresh and partly consumed carcass of a fawn nearby. Surprisingly, she is uninterested, and after sniffing it, she walks away (10:15). She walks direct on a two-track, sniffing objects, then runs and trots a short distance (10:20). She arched-back rubs a sugar maple sapling alongside a grassy two-track (10:22). We walk north through a lowland conifer stand. She urinates a stream and dances in a small forest opening (11:13). She drinks from a puddle in the two-track (11:15). She runs on a game trail along an old railroad grade in the cedars (11:23). She trots along a game trail (11:40). She runs on a two-track (11:54). She feeds on sweet cicely in a soft maple stand and dances along the edge of the stand as she exits (12:03). She walks direct on a two-track and ducks under the entrance gate to posted property (12:18). She stops to sniff a bear bait, placed there before the legal date. The bait pail is empty. She enters a stand of "dog-hair" cedars and begins moving west (12:20). She clunks her jaws as we move through the cedars. I suspect that she is trailing and trying to overtake another bear, most likely a male (12:23). I am unable to keep pace and lose sight of her three times, the final time at 12:37.

Carmen used many roads today. We traveled through no less than twenty habitats and covered more than seven miles in approximately three and a half hours. Walking with bears can be infuriating and this is one of only two times I quit a bear walk because I had had enough.

❧

Without question, Carmen moved about her home range differently when unencumbered by cubs or yearlings. Today's walk reminded me of a walk I took with her a week after her family's breakup in 1992. On that day, as I tried to home in on her with the telemetry equipment for our initial rendezvous, she was moving away from me at a pace that if maintained would be hard to match. Rounding the corner of a clear-cut stand of aspens on a two-track, I was able to intersect her. She was not at all interested in me or my treats and conspicuously swung her head away, then straddle-marked a head-high aspen sapling. We moved directly onto an abandoned turn-of-the-century railroad grade that adjoined the two-track and bisected a broad cedar swamp. I caught on quickly that this would not be a leisurely stroll.

Carmen's objective was clear: increase the incidence of intersection with male bears. She traveled old railroad grades, abandoned logging roads, and well-worn game trails in an effort, I surmised, to cover as much ground as possible. Female bears, I have come to understand, are every bit the aggressors that male bears are. We crossed the Whitefish on an abandoned railroad trestle in the upper reaches of her home range. The trestle, now dilapidated and augmented by beavers, offered a picturesque setting, but we were traveling much too quickly for capturing anything other than a mental image. I was inspired by the setting, and it immediately conjured up images of stout loggers forging their way into undefiled territory. It certainly must have been different when mature forests covered the whole of upper Michigan. But then I dared not dawdle in thought because Carmen was disappearing from sight across the trestle. If she reached the dog-hair cedars too far ahead of me, I would lose sight of her.

Fortunately, when I arrived across the trestle, Carmen was moving south down a well-worn game trail on an adjoining grade overgrown with tag alder, and I easily made up the distance lost negotiating the trestle. As we approached the intersection of an east-west grade, Carmen straddle-marked a small balsam fir and stopped to arched-back rub a well-worn mark tree. We had traveled over a mile in half an hour. Continuing south, Carmen started to lope. I was braced for the worse when, unexpectedly, Carmen flipped herself head over heels onto her back, wiggled in the grass and sedges, righted herself, grabbed the end of a four-foot-long alder branch and began dragging it like a retriever puppy romping in play. Hard to believe—an adult bear, on her own, at the height of the breeding season, playing? I chalked it up to hormones. (That fall, I related the incident while giving a talk to a group who called themselves the Over-50s Club. We all had a good laugh when it was explained to me the freedom one feels when the weather is fine, hormone levels are still relatively high, and the kids have finally gotten the boot. I find that as plausible an explanation as any for Carmen's behavior on that day.) As we moved south on the grade, Carmen continued her *sans souci* jaunt, occasionally flipping herself over and acting playful. At one point, we intersected a two-track road that paralleled the Whitefish River, and she boldly ambled down it for a distance of a quarter mile even though it was midday. She did not seem worried about exposing herself. I suspect the business at hand was more important (at least in the short run) than concealment.

Somewhere along the railroad grade near the old trestle, I stumbled on something that went *clank* against the toe of my rubber-bottomed boots. I took a mental note of the spot and planned to return and investigate. As Carmen exited the two-track and moved into a lowland conifer stand, I decided it was a good time to abandon the day's walk and returned to the spot. What I discovered was a rusty length of chain attached to a grappling hook. As I pulled it from its bed on the old railroad grade, I made a wish for a Newhouse #5 bear trap. What I got was a half-dozen #4 Victor spring-steel coyote traps in reasonably good, albeit rusted, condition. They were probably left decades ago by a trapper who was either unable or unwilling to relocate them. It was a good find, a memento of an era gone by. I wonder how it would have been walking with bears before Europeans left their mark on the land.

Humankind has undoubtedly influenced the scheme of things for bears. For example, consider the effects of lumbering and railroads on Upper Peninsula forests and present-day bears. Even though railroads did not make an appearance in Upper Peninsula logging ventures much before 1880, by the turn of the century they were an essential component of all big lumbering companies.[3] Railroads aided and abetted the switch from the era of pine lumbering to that of hardwoods. The relatively dense hardwood logs, which could not be floated down inland watercourses as easily as the more buoyant pine logs, could be brought to mill by rail. In the lowland conifer forests of the eastern and central Upper Peninsula, railroads changed the seasonal nature of logging and also opened up areas that were formerly inaccessible. Prior to railroads, tramroads were constructed and teams of horses pulled logs from the forest. This usually took place only during the frozen months to avoid swampy conditions and sinkholes. However, with the advent of railroads and the construction of solid beds beneath them, spring and summer work in the forest became feasible. Whereas before, at the onset of spring, pine-era loggers stopped cutting to concentrate their efforts on floating winter-cut logs down rivers and streams in order to take advantage of spring melt-waters, railroads allowed year-round transportation of logs and the pace of deforestation was accelerated. Railroads also contributed to clear-cutting of the forests. With railways nearby, it was feasible and economical to remove even what were formerly considered cull logs from the forest floor and haul them to the mills. In some operations, eight-hundred-foot cables attached to railcars were used to winch fallen logs to the trains. The removal of treetops, for fuel wood and chemical uses, was now also economically feasible and contributed further to the devastation of the forest.

The patterns and scale of changes that humankind inflicts on forests are obviously different from those created by nature, which my friend John Frey refers to as the Great Lady. Openings caused by fires resulting from lightning strikes and wind-thrown trees are usually smaller and have irregular borders compared to the relatively large size and straight boundaries of clear-cuts. Our propensity to grid off the landscape with roads and trails certainly affords greater opportunity for humans to intersect with bears. This is especially true for hunters, both those who are responsible and those loathsome individuals less inclined to abide by the rules of "fair chase." But I wonder if, overall, things are better or worse for bears? My instinctive response is worse. But the truth will probably never be known.

While recovery from turn-of-the-century cutting is deemed responsible for the comeback of the white-tailed deer to upper Michigan, its impact on the bear remains largely unknown. Yet it is reasonable to assume from observing bears' use of openings that early successional stages of forest growth are of some value to bears. Certainly, we know that the shade-intolerant species of plants that provide the seasonally abundant berries on which bears fatten are benefited by a reduction in the forest canopy. For example, aspen clear-cuts. Aspens can grow from seed (a mature female tree produces several hundred thousand of the cottony seeds in spring), but because seeds are rather exacting in their site requirements—they must reach moist soil almost immediately, and the seedlings are highly shade intolerant—aspens most often regenerate as "sucker growth" on the roots of a common ancestor following fire or clear-cutting (mostly clear-cutting in recent times because of fire suppression). Tens of thousands of these same-sex "clones" will initially invade an acre of disturbed ground.

Bears make considerable use of such young stands. In the initial year or two following a clear-cutting, bears feed on the newly emerging grasses and clovers that appear. Then a year or two later when shade-intolerant soft mast like raspberry appear, bears forage extensively on them. Years later when the overhead canopy of saplings fills in (and the clones thin to several thousand stems per acre), the berries of shade-intolerant soft masts are no longer available to bears. But in clear-cut stands where sufficient stumps and downed woody materials remain after cutting (are not burned, roller-chopped, or chipped and removed), that material provides habitat for colonization by ants. Eventually, as the stand matures, the initial flush of food types wanes. However, in mature stands of aspen, bears are able to feed on the berries of sarsaparilla and Juneberries and eventually the nuts of hazel that will later grow there. In those mature stands, bears also feed on the buds and catkins of aspens that blow over or that they occasionally climb. As I walk the forest with the bears and observe the preferences that they display for these early stages of aspen regeneration, I continually wonder if the value of the stand to bears in the years immediately following the cutting outweighs the value of what was destroyed to create it.

I suspect the answer to the question of whether human beings' activities make things better or worse for bears depends for the most part on the temporal and spatial nature of those perturbations—and if, in the long run, manipulated stands (such as clear-cuts) provide as much in the way of life requirements of bears as the original cover type would have. For me, the knowledge we need to address this issue centers on the capability to delineate optimal bear habitat. What habitats, in what combinations, and in what proportions and arrangements in the landscape are optimal for bears? When we understand that, we will have a gauge with which to measure our manipulations. That knowledge proves elusive, and although there is much conjecture, to date I know of no definitive answers.

That evening, in front of the computer, I roughly charted the day's travels with Carmen. From the point where I intersected her near the aspen clear-cut, we traveled more than six miles in slightly less than three hours. She used roads, trails, and abandoned railroad grades during her peregrination. Knowing this, some might say bears are pragmatic. Perhaps. Still, I prefer my bear country unsullied by the paw prints of human beings.

6/3/94

I find Nettie and June in a fingerlike peninsula of hardwood and mixed conifers protruding into a quaking bog. Nettie is forage-meandering, sniffing stumps and various objects. She does a considerable amount of stump sniffing but little digging, although we are nearing the time for ants. She feeds on sapling beech leaves. We walk to the bog, and she drinks at the edge, then begins feeding on wild calla and pickerelweed. Finished, she moves back to the peninsula for rest. Later, she nurses June, and both rest at the base of a hemlock.

6/4/94

Nettie and June are on the peninsula in the quaking bog again. There are enough fresh scats around the hemlock refuge tree to make me believe they have stayed here overnight. June descends the refuge tree and nurses. (I video the entire scene.) Nettie, engrossed in nursing, has her head back, drifting to wherever female bears go in the throes of a nursing bout. At one point, she is lucid enough to hold out a paw so a pesky fly can land, then bites and swallows it. After a short sleep she stands and sniffs, then walks toward the bog defecating and urinating on the way. She drinks from the bog and feeds on vegetation, then walks back to the peninsula, pausing to sniff her scat. At the refuge tree, she rubs her flank against it, then plays with June for eight minutes. Finished playing, and with June up the tree, Nettie grooms for a while, then stands and sniffs and then runs to the bog (I wonder, why run?). At the bog's edge she feeds on calla and pickerelweed, then returns to the refuge tree to groom and play with June for ten minutes.

6/5/94

Today I locate Carmen at the edge of a tamarack planting. A large male bear stands at the far edge of the planting along a block of hardwoods. Carmen digs at stumps and feeds briefly on ants. She locates a few swamp thistles and some hawkweed, which she also eats. As I watch her maneuvering around stumps for the best angle to dig from, the male bear disappears into the hardwoods. Much of the tamarack planting lacks ground cover, and it is clear to me that the spraying of such plantings by logging companies eliminates much of the vegetation on which bears might feed. Carmen walks directly across the sparsely vegetated portion of the planting. On the edge of the hardwoods, where the male stood, she sits and scratches, then stands and looks into the hardwoods. She walks the edge of the hardwoods sniffing small bushes, then turns to earnestly sniff one (I wonder if she is getting direction or some type of clue). She enters the hardwoods at a point low in elevation, where she drinks from a depression and then straddle-marks a leatherwood bush. She meanders through the hardwoods, then across a two-track and into a semi-open area, where she digs a stump and feeds on ants and pupae. (I notice she is still limping on her rear leg as we cross the two-track.) She spends a few seconds rolling a log around in the open area but gets no ants or pupae. Meandering across the opening, she feeds on hawkweed and yellow goatsbeard. For the next quarter hour, she meanders through the semi-open area feeding on vegetation and a meager amount of ants obtained from a small logs. In the full sun I notice that her coat looks quite full and thick, but it appears that she has lost weight. On the periphery of an opening, she straddle-marks a pin cherry sapling, then meanders into hardwoods to the east, shaking her head to rid herself of mosquitoes as she goes. In the hardwoods she feeds on sweet cicely, then walk-meanders and sniffs an old den site. It is an earthen den dug at the base of a stump. Walking away from the site, she straddle-marks two leatherwood shrubs back to back, then flops down for a twelve-minute grooming session.

6/6/94

Larry Visser, Michigan Department of Natural Resources research biologist, is along for the walk today. Carmen is near a big clear-cut in the north-central part of her home range. She is moving north at a rapid pace, and initially we are unable to close the gap. When we finally make contact, I toss Carmen a few treats to draw her in and hold her in close proximity, allowing her to become familiar with Larry. We notice two male bears nearby. (I see the red ear tags we reserve for yearling males on one of the bears and fear that our walk may be cut short by one of Carmen's yearling males trying to reunite with her.) Carmen continues north on a game trail into a red maple stand, where she straddle-marks a shrub, then rubs her rump on a sapling. She takes a few bites of vegetation, then sniffs the ground and rolls a log to check it for ants. We skirt the corner of an aspen clear-cut, across which Carmen trots. She enters a mixed stand of red maples and lowland conifers and again rubs her rear on a maple sapling, then straddle-marks a balsam fir. Pressing on, we come upon an old railroad grade and enter a lowland conifer stand. (I have followed this route with Carmen before and believe she is trailing or looking for males.) She pauses to rub her rump on a white birch. Shortly, Larry and I notice a small male bear paralleling our course. Carmen stops and looks intently in its direction, then gives chase. It is the runt of her litter unwilling to sever ties with his mother. Carmen chases him up a leaning cedar. Huffing and blowing, she then walks off, defecating, and returns to the railroad grade and heads north again, leaving the yearling up the cedar huffing at us as we move out of hearing. A few minutes later we turn to see the yearling following us on the railroad grade as we follow Carmen. (Larry thinks it would be interesting to view the scene from the air—us with our "bear escort" front and rear.) The yearling follows for nearly a hundred yards before Carmen turns, walks past us, and gives chase again. We stay put on the grade this time and watch as she chases him out of sight, but we continue to hear the chase, the subsequent treeing, and plenty of huffing from both bears. Shortly, Carmen returns to the grade and again resumes her northerly heading. Near the

103

junction with an east-west grade, she stands on hind feet to reach a robin's nest in a spruce sapling. Stretching, she uses claws and teeth to bend the branch that holds the nest. Then uninterestedly, she bites and mouths the nestlings, killing one, which she does not eat. Ignoring the adults scolding overhead and leaving the dead chick with its nest mate on the ground next to it—breathing what I'm sure are its last few breaths—we turn our backs and press on. She stops to groom only a short distance from the destroyed nest, and Larry and I ponder the reason for the seemingly pointless annihilation. Carmen continues north on the grade, and coming upon a cedar mark tree, she stands to sniff it and then bites the tree while facing it and turns to arched-back rub it while turning her head and biting it some more. She sits near the mark tree and grooms, then stands to sniff a white cedar on the edge of the grade. We head west through dog-hair cedars on an adjoining grade and lose sight of her briefly. When we recontact her, she is sniffing the ground; then she drinks from a stream flowing through the grade. Heading to the west on a spur-grade, she crosses the Whitefish River at the site of an old railroad trestle. (This is the third time I have been this route with Carmen, and the spot on the river always looks to be good brook trout habitat, even with its sandy bottom.) Carmen makes the crossing ahead of us, and we again lose sight of her briefly but locate her sitting and scratching in the grade on the other side. She leads us off the grade and into the surrounding dog-haired cedars, where after a short distance she lies down to rest. After an hour or so of sitting and talking while waiting for Carmen to resume her movements, we decide to call it a day.

6/8/94

On the drive this morning, I see two snapping turtles laying eggs in freshly dug holes in the gravely bed of the truck trail at a creek crossing. I assume this to be the most suitable material around in which to deposit eggs, but I can hear in the distance a county road grader approaching from the south. Acting quickly, I grab each turtle by its tail (they hiss in ingratitude and the egg-laying muscles under their tails flex involuntarily) and toss them in the creek just as the grader rounds the bend in the road. Their eggs are graded, but the turtles will live on. One was steering wheel size.

Nettie and June are east of the truck trail and to the north. This is new territory for June. I can see why we're here the minute I arrive. Nettie stands in a vernal pool while June rests in a hemlock at its edge. It is a perfect day and a perfect spot. Nettie continues feeding on water parsnip as I talk my way in. Recognizing me, June climbs down the refuge tree and joins her, walking a fallen red maple out into the pool. The hardwoods grow to the very edge of the pool, and I notice the claw marks of other generations of bears on a few of the surrounding beech trees. Irises with their showy mauve and violet flowers bloom throughout the pool, a big patch of chest-high lady fern grows in the corner, and the whole scene—the bears standing on the log in the bright sunlight, a brilliant blue sky overhead, all set against the backdrop of northern hardwoods—makes me stop and gawk. There are days when I feel compelled to give thanks that I am alive. Most are related to the out-of-doors, and many come on bear walks. This is one such day. Things are alive and growing, and I can just feel the life all around. I am glad to have given June her name to remind me of the smells, sounds, and sights of this very fine June day.

Nettie exits the vernal pool and makes a swing through the surrounding hardwoods. June, hustling to join her, halts directly in front of an overturned tree root. She immediately begins swatting the ground in front of the root mass. Nettie approaches to urge her on, paying little attention to her interest with the roots. I tarry my usual few steps behind, watching. With some additional coaxing from Nettie, June reluctantly moves on. But then in apparent rebelliousness, she returns to deliver a final novice swat to the ground in front of the root mass. I follow, looking into the small grotto formed by the roots and observe the unmistakable barbed quills of a porcupine, its back exposed in defensive reaction to the danger.

Porcupines may carry upward of 30,000 quills on their backs and tails.[4] A quick lash of the tail can cause serious injury to a would-be predator. June was flirting with trouble. Cubs at this stage of life are full of character yet heedless of certain dangers. While they feel vulnerable to sudden or unusual noises, which send them hustling for trees, movement appears to intrigue them. The little bear would certainly have been no match for the painfully lethal quills of this animal; it is a good thing Mother intervened.

‹∾o∾›

The following spring I witnessed another interaction between a porcupine and the cubs of Carmen's third litter. While following the bears through a stand of mixed hardwoods, the biggest and boldest cub, a male, and his two sisters all run to the bottom of a red maple to investigate the movement, sound, and smell of a porcupine retreating noisily up the bole of the tree. The porcupine sounds a shrill bleat and rests on a branch, chomping its teeth at the cubs as one by one they climb partway up the tree to investigate. The cubs are all huffy, and Carmen successfully coaxes the female cubs from the tree with umphs and tongue-clicks. Dutifully, she returns a second and third time to the base of the tree in order to finally gather up the male cub and continue our walk. Some cubs simply require more convincing than others.

Spend enough time in the company of bears, and you will notice that from the time of den emergence as cubs, they are recognizable as individuals, not just by their physical markings, but by their behavior, temperament, and character. It is quite evident to me that June displays more independence than other cubs exhibit at this stage of life. She strays farther from Nettie as they move about the woods and, like Nettie when she was a cub, seems to investigate more plant foods than male cubs do. While male cubs always seem to show up for the big-ticket groceries like their mother's milk or clumps of beetle larvae, unlike female cubs, they appear relatively uninterested in (at least seeking out) less spectacular food items. After walking with six litters of cubs (eight males and six females), I am tempted to chalk it up to boys being boys. However, science deems this an expression of phenotypic variation on foraging behavior.

∽०∾

After the incident with the porcupine, Nettie turns northeast, and we travel to another vernal pool, where she feeds on water parsnip and water plantain. From here we again move north and east and into a stand of hardwood that has recently been selectively cut. By her cautious movements, constant scenting activity, and overall apprehensive demeanor, I presume this to be new country for Nettie. As the bears cross the cutting, the contrast of the requisites of their lifestyle with the fresh cut ends of felled beech trees (some marked with the ancient pugs, or claw marks, of bears) is striking. Nettie stands on her hind legs to bite and pull down a piece of blue flagging at the boundary of the cutting. June rubs her head on it and pushes it along the ground after Nettie drops it. Nettie continues to meander through the hardwoods, and we emerge at the edge of a spruce bog.

Nettie still acts tentatively while skirting the edge of the bog. She runs a little way out into the bog and stands on her hind feet to look around. Dropping down, she walks to a tamarack and standing on her hind feet, reaches up with a front limb and bends it, then begins to sniff the length of its stem. June stands on her hind feet and sniffs in an imitation of her mother and then climbs the tree as Nettie bends it further. When Nettie

107

releases the tree, June is nearly shaken off its trunk and drops down to join Nettie as both bound away. Nettie slows and walks to a hole in the bog. She wades in, then swims, while June remains at the edge. Bobbing in the murky water, Nettie bites and swallows a piece of sphagnum draped over her front paw. She paddles around and splashes, shaking her head, which she seems always to keep above the water. Upon exiting the water, she Carmen-dances and then straddle-marks a ten-foot-tall tamarack, bowling it over with little effort. Once she has marked the tree, she shakes, then turns around and marks it again, this time rubbing her underside back and forth on the branches and stem of the tree as she straddles it. Again, after leaving the mark tree, she performs the stiff-legged Carmen-dance. All Nettie's footfalls seem to have more force than usual as she continues walking through the bog. She approaches a sapling balsam fir, and, pulling it down to the height of her midsection, she stands on it with her front feet and rests like that, while looking around. I believe that she is incorporating a new piece of territory into her range and at this very moment is surveying her domain. The now upright balsam is still vibrating as both bears walk a fallen black spruce into the hardwoods on their exit from the bog.

Standing next to the fallen tree about midway along its length, I notice how big June is getting, especially her feet, as she walks by. Nettie maneuvers through the hardwoods and into a vernal pool, where she immediately begins feeding on jewelweed. Here, the herb is only a few inches tall and appears fresh and succulent. June is drawn to the many blossoms of a blue-flowered violet growing in a shaded portion of the vernal pool. She begins eating all flowers within sight. (I cannot be sure whether sight or smell has drawn her to feed on the flowers; I am certain, however, that the violets are a threatened species, and I think to myself that there could be no higher or better use for them.) Nettie's head bobs up and down like it is tied on with a slinky as she feeds on the jewelweed. Equisetum, fiddlehead ferns, and sedges also grow among the jewelweed, but she concentrates only on the latter. I take a seat on a log in a shaded portion of the wetland and watch Nettie and June foraging nonstop on the nutritious wetland. A cool breeze comes out of nowhere and feels good. It's been one of those near perfect days with the bears, and a half hour later, when the pair moves into the shade of the hardwoods, I let them continue the walk alone in the little daylight that remains. On the walk out, as I round a bend in a sandy road that skirts several bogs, I spot the remnants of turtle eggs dug up by a striped skunk. I follow its tracks in the road and come upon it in a short distance as it predates the eggs in a second turtle nest. I give it a wide berth as it goes about its task. A tough day for turtles all around.

6/9/94

Ed Rumbergs, a Northern Michigan University student assisting me with telemetry, is along for the walk today (students who perform competently are rewarded periodically throughout the field season with bear walks). We join Carmen at the edge of a two-track in a northern hardwood stand. She is moving and seems uninterested in treats when we catch up to her. She begins foraging on jack-in-the-pulpits.

Jack-in-the-pulpit has proven to be the most ubiquitously consumed herb in the forest by the bears. They eat the plants whenever and wherever found. They eat the cotyledons of newly emerging plants in spring, they eat the spathe and spadix and roots in summer, and they dig and eat the corms in fall. But never once have I observed the bears eating the bright red berries of jack-in-the-pulpit. Jack-in-the-pulpit (and its berries) contains calcium oxalate crystals (oxalate acid) and, unless stringently prepared by thorough drying, is poisonous to humans. Calcium oxalate crystals when ingested cause the precipitation of potassium and phosphorus from the blood. This results in a shrinking of tissue and consequent constriction in the throat, a potentially lethal effect. American Indians used the aged dried roots of jack-in-the-pulpit in a tea as a remedy for colds and coughs and externally for snake bites. In addition to jack-in-the-pulpit, bears are known to eat other food items that contain calcium oxalate, including wild calla and skunk cabbage, although the latter is an uncommon plant in the home ranges of Carmen and Nettie and one that I never saw them eat. I once taste-tested jack-in-the-pulpit by bruising a freshly dug corm between my fingers and then touching my fingers to my mouth. My lips and tongue burned for the rest of the day.

∽o∾

Carmen forages south, and Ed and I follow. After crossing a two-track, we enter a hardwoods and meander into a semi-open area (the same one I was at with her on June 5), and here she feeds on grasses and hawkweed and digs for ants in logs and stumps. Meandering south, she stops to drink upon entering a lowland conifer stand and then defecates. Ed collects the sample. While we are placing the sample into Ed's backpack, I spy the shed antler of probably an eight-point buck. Ed stows that in his pack as well. Following Carmen south and east, we cross a small creek before coming to the truck trail. After a nonchalant crossing, Carmen stops to paw at a fallen log near the edge of the road. I hope we will move from the road's edge quickly, as I feel we are too exposed here. Carmen obliges, and we move easterly into a vernal pool, where she begins feeding on wild calla. As we exit the pool, she stops just inside the bordering hardwoods and sits with a front paw resting on a red maple while scratching the underside of her front leg with her rear foot. The sound of nails against skin is loud, but she acts as though it feels quite good. She moves on, and we follow. As I come abreast of the tree where she rested to groom, there is a whirr, and a ruffed grouse bursts from its nest at the base of the maple. Carmen, meandering ahead, does not respond to the bird's flight—nor did she notice the bird as it sat tight on its nest right below her extended front leg while she scratched. Hard to believe. I guess the "hold-still" gene is useful at times. I stoop to count the eggs; there are eight in the clutch. We go no more than a few hundred yards in the hardwoods when Carmen locates a dead fawn. She drags it to a spot in the middle of several trees and begins to feed. I punch FOV (feed—*Odocoileus virginianus*) into the data logger as we look for a suitable location from which to observe. Carmen alternately rests and feeds on the fawn. She covers the carcass between feedings and sleeps atop it. After an hour, we leave her resting on the buried carcass. On our trip out, we retrace our steps and scout the area where she discovered the fawn. We look for any signs of a struggle but find none. We have no clue as to the cause of the fawn's death but feel the body has been put to good use.

6/12/94

Nettie and June are near the same location where I found them on June 8. The vernal pools continue to command their interest. Jan Schultz, an ecologist with the U.S. Forest Service, is along today to help me verify the identity of the myriad wetland plants Nettie is consuming in the vernal pools. We are not disappointed, as Nettie proceeds directly to a vernal pool and begins foraging on the tender herbs it contains. The situation is so perfect that Jan is able to sit on a log and enumerate the values of vernal pools while I video her with Nettie and June foraging in the background. It could not have worked better, except for the deerflies, which are ruthless. Nettie leads us from the vernal pool through the hardwoods, where June stalks a white plastic oil jug (thoughtlessly discarded by a sawyer), then bites and plays with it. We meander farther south through the stand, and the bears check several stumps for ants, but find no one home. As we begin our ascent of a hardwood slope, Nettie usurps the USFS claim on the land and asserts her own by thoroughly marking a boundary post. June stands on her hind feet and follows suit, rubbing her head and back on a small lathe stake near the marker. The wobble in June's hind legs is much better but still slightly visible as she pivots about the stake. As we crest the slope, I see June put her nose directly on a bedded white-tailed deer fawn. The fawn bleats and jumps. June instinctively gives a short chase, but the fawn flees right into Nettie, who chases and trips it. The fawn bleats while Nettie rests her foot on its neck and begins to feed.

Nettie proves herself to be a neophyte killer. (In all but a few of the more than dozen fawn kills that I witnessed over the years, it seems that both Carmen and Nettie were inept at finishing the kill and lacked a good move for it.) The fawn dies a slow death while being eaten. After some time, with the fawn still pinioned to the ground with her front paw, Nettie, panting and with a sanguinolent muzzle, drags the carcass off and covers it with duff near a refuge tree, where she nurses June before proceeding with the repast. Jan and I watch from seats on a fallen log. We agree that what we have witnessed is a dramatic and unparalleled wild scene.

∞∞

The black bear is often labeled an opportunistic omnivore. Many hastily interpret this to mean that bears will eat just about anything. In reality, they are selective about their diets when given a choice. They may prefer meat over other available dietary items, but they are not very efficient predators. Their bulky, thick-boned bodies are designed to carry the large amounts of fat on which they must overwinter. They are not set up to chase prey for any distance. Their plantigrade (on the soles of their feet) style of walking contrasts markedly with the more speed-efficient digitigrade (toe-walking) style of real predators. Yet bears are opportunistic and will prey on relatively immobile newborn fawns when they happen upon them, occasionally giving chase for short distances, when their predatory pursuit instincts are triggered by the fawn's fleeing prey behavior.

Bears' predatory behavior seems to originate as curiosity. I doubt that many instances of predation start out with a kill explicitly in mind. But rather, inquisitive by nature, bears are constantly exploring their environment for food—a meal being potentially present in nearly any situation. Probing with their nose, if something is exposed, stationary, and smells good to them, they invariably taste it. If it is concealed, they will likely force entry to expose it. If when probed, it runs, their predatory instincts kick in, and they pursue and attempt to capture it. Once captured, if it offers little resistance and they sense its ability to escape has been defeated, they begin to feed. If it stands its ground and offers resistance, however, they will likely pause to reassess the situation.

Fawns are pursued with neither anger nor malice—but rather because a bear can only be a bear. For a female bear, strapped with the chore of cub rearing, an opportunity to prey on a fawn renders a mighty source of protein at a time when little else of nutritional value is available. The Great Lady holds no grudge.

Summer

One learns of a landscape finally not by knowing
the name or identity of everything in it,
but by perceiving the relationships in it
—Barry Lopez

From the time of winter solstice through vernal equinox until summer solstice, the north half of the earth tilts toward the sun and the sun climbs higher and higher into northern skies. The heightening sun and consequent longer days warm the hemisphere. Life responds. Summer comes to the north woods. For those of us living by the calendar, it arrives on June 21. But bears and summer's bounty are ungoverned by such rigid calibrations. The ebb and flow of their comings and goings are tied to a broader arrangement of things: frost-free dates, growing-degree days, rainfall, soils—variable things. The harbingers of a bear's summer are ripe berries, and to a large degree their availability will dictate a bear's whereabouts in the summer forest. In our area, summer's first berries *normally* appear mid June, so my summer with the bears begins then. But no matter when summer arrives, it never seems soon enough for Carmen and Nettie, especially in the years they are mothering cubs. While spring provides the occasional find of a winter-killed deer and a measure of sustenance from greenery, overall it is a season of negative forage balance for all bears and more so for females with cubs. Regardless of the effort put forth to secure food, their weight steadily declines. Toward the end of spring, when they are taxed with growing cubs, protracted nursing bouts, the waning nutritional value of vegetation, and depleted fat reserves, they begin to show the strain. Their ribs protrude, and they appear haggard. Their dispositions also seem to change. They are noticeably less tolerant of cubs underfoot, especially at feeding sites. While the appearance of summer's ripening berries signals the onset of nutritional gain and easier times for bears, this year that time of relative plenty is still weeks away. For although we savored a mild spring, we lag behind normal rainfall and growing-degree days by two to three weeks. Vegetation (of waning value), the infrequent fawn, and colonies of ants must bridge the gap.

6/15/94

Over the next few weeks the research crew and I are trapping the project area to get a handle on the bear population. It is our second and final field season devoted to this task. We have placed nearly forty barrel traps and set an equal number of camera traps throughout the one-hundred-square-mile study area in the hopes that bears, both unmarked and marked, will allow us to capture them and their portraits. Afterward, through a string of mathematical formulas, we will approximate their number. It is a tall order. Bears do not hold still well, or for long, making both the capture of their image and the estimation of their number onerous. Jodi Helland, a Michigan Technological University graduate student, spearheads the activity. Upon initial capture of each bear, following tranquilization, we ear-tag any unmarked bears, and radio-collar any new females. Bears are weighed, have blood samples drawn, and have copious body measurements taken—our trapping adage is: "If it sticks out or goes in, we will measure how far or how deep." This effort requires portioning my time to include checking traps and handling captured bears—time I would rather spend walking with Carmen and Nettie. It also requires that if I handle any trapped bears, I expunge all trace odors before joining Carmen and Nettie. The scent of foreign bears is discomforting to them, and they act suspiciously.

∽○∽

Today, Carmen locates me! Or, more correctly, I believe, the sound of the Jeep. Some animals are adept at differentiating sounds. A decade or so ago, Annette and I lived at the end of an uphill, quarter-mile gravel road. Our beagle, Boots, was cooped in the barn and our spaniel, Britt, in a garage attached to the house. When an unfamiliar vehicle started onto the gravel road, Boots would sound off. If the approaching vehicle made it beyond the dead-end sign and into the yard, Britt would join her. But neither dog ever barked at the approach of our vehicles. It was a good warning system, and Annette and I wondered how the dogs could tell that strangers were coming and not one of us. After some experimentation (driving home in friends' vehicles and friends driving our vehicles home), we confirmed that the dogs had come to know the sounds peculiar to our vehicles.

Considering this and having used the Jeep on hundreds of approaches to Carmen, many inadvertently within close range, I was not surprised while trying pinpoint her location with telemetry equipment, to have her mosey in for a look-see. Like the dogs, Carmen approached only my Jeep. A bear's senses being what they are, she had probably come to know the racket of the Jeep better than I did. Now she circles purposefully through the sapling aspens while I hurry to pack my gear. Although her approach makes things easier (not having to assemble and dismantle telemetry equipment), I try to discourage the behavior by not acknowledging her presence. Instead, I walk off through the aspens, talking as always, and wait for her approach. She overtakes me near an ephemeral wetland on a hardwood ridge adjacent to a lowland conifer swamp. After our rendezvous, she walks to the lowland conifers, where she feeds on jewelweed and swamp thistle. She spends some time sniffing the ground and various objects. I neither see nor hear other bears as we travel the forest and believe the breeding season for her is past. She stops to drink twice within twelve minutes, which is unusually frequent, but today is our first day over 80°F. "Cotton" from aspens is everywhere. Whisked by air currents into tight little windrows, or lying in plate-sized globs on the forest floor, whichever air current and microtopography dictate, it surrounds us. Carmen lies down in the cool of a balsam fir thicket. She rests first alert then recumbent. Four hours and fifteen minutes later, she rolls onto her back and rubs her head and snout with both paws to rid them of mosquitoes, but she shows no sign of getting up.

6/16/94

Nettie is east of the truck trail today and in a stand of red and sugar maples mixed with yellow birch and hemlock. This is big timber. June is not with her, and Nettie is walk-meandering, clunking her jaws, and sniffing the bases of trees. She displays all the behavior of trying to signal a lost cub. I am a little concerned because earlier this morning, some two miles to the north, on the fringe of Nettie's range, I released a cub from a barrel trap unharmed and without handling. The cub,

118

like June, was untagged. I am sure if had been June I would have recognized her, and in any event Nettie would likely have remained near the trap. But still, I am hoping that I did not, through some colossal blunder, fail to recognize June and that because of it, Nettie is now two miles away searching for her.

Nettie stands still on my approach, then abruptly turns and defecates—a fine how-do-you-do. I collect the scat and store it in my pack for later analysis. Nettie meanders, clunking her jaws, for the first half hour of my visit. She then climbs up and back down a huge white spruce near our original rendezvous point. I hope this is the refuge tree but can detect June nowhere above. Nettie continues the meander and jaw clunking, sniffing objects as if searching for June. She makes a big loop to the south, and I lose sight of her for a while when for some reason she begins trotting. We end up back at the white spruce about forty-five minutes later. Nettie sits alert at the bottom of the tree, and in a hail of loose bark, June descends—in the tree the whole time. She obviously was not uncomfortable with being left behind as Nettie ranged nearly half a mile from the refuge tree.

Nettie stands and leads the way onto an old railroad grade, and we walk to the edge of a vernal pool, where both bears feed on vegetation. From the pool, Nettie meanders the hardwoods and stops to arched-back rub a USFS boundary marker. There are aged bite marks on the post, and I recognize it as a spot we have been at before. Nettie walks to a close-by hunting blind and begins to head-rub a corner of it. June mimics Nettie's behavior at the boundary marker and joins her at the hunting blind, climbing atop, on ever improving but still wobbly hind limbs, to play. Finished head-rubbing, Nettie walks to a nearby maple sapling, and, bracing all four feet, she leans into the sapling and begins rubbing her flank on it—hair flies. After a good scratch, we meander into a lowland conifer stand, where the bears feed on wild calla, jewelweed, and grasses. Nettie meanders back into the hardwoods and again rubs her flank on a sapling but this time less vigorously and playing with June as she does so. Continuing through the hardwoods, we come upon a huge, hollowed-out yellow birch that must be at least four feet in diameter. June scampers inside, and the bears play in and out of the birch's cavity, batting and nipping at each other, for forty-two minutes. This is big time play! I film the activity, the birch cavity affording a splendid setting, but I wish we were moving, as the deerflies are persistent and I am a sitting duck. After the rollick Nettie heads us west through the hardwoods, and we emerge onto a newly built gravel road where the coarse calls of overhead ravens mark our arrival. We are on national forest property, and many of the trees are splashed with blue and yellow paint, a sure sign that the stand is to be logged soon—the purpose of new road, the purpose. The ravens continue badgering us for some way as we move north on the road. Nettie moves hurriedly, June scrambling right behind. Pausing periodically to look back over her shoulder at me, Nettie seems more suspicious of my intent while on the open road. A hundred yards north, Nettie and June resume play in the road's cul-de-sac. After the play session, Nettie hustles into the hardwoods. Because the leaves are crunchy, I make more noise than usual, and Nettie turns to look back at me every so often. She leads the way to a vernal pool, where she begins feeding on vegetation. (Stumps from the road construction have been bulldozed into a portion of the pool, leaving its waters blackened and clouded.) June joins her there, wading and swimming in the murky pool. There is a film of scum on the pool's surface, and June parts it in a V as she makes her way toward the opposite side. There she shakes, goes up a hemlock, and immediately falls asleep. Nettie forage-meanders below and digs up a colony of ants from beneath a fallen and decaying balsam fir. There is much digging and licking, and occasionally blowing, as she expels inhaled duff from her nose. When she moves off, I drop a small transmitter to mark the ant-feeding site. She walk-meanders for a while, intermittently clunking and tongue-clicking to June. Then she returns to climb the refuge tree and rest on a branch just below her. I anticipate a lengthy snooze and pack up my gear and head for the Jeep, my pack noticeably heavier from the samples of scat collected during the walk.

෴

Biologists, as any honest one will admit, are infinitely more prolific at data collection than at their analysis. It's a nearly automatic response for me to collect a scat. I invert a handily kept zip-lock bag over my right hand, grasp the warm scat firmly and lift it, pull the bag forward over my clenched fingers, press it against my chest to void the air, zip it shut, and place it in my backpack. Given all the practice, I can almost accomplish the task without breaking stride. Later on, I label the sample and toss it in one of three freezers kept mainly, but not entirely, for storing scats.

Throughout the six years of walking with bears, I have had the love, support, and understanding of my wife, Annette. Traipsing around after bears has often caused me to miss family gatherings and social events, not to mention making a drastic change in our lifestyle. All of that Annette graciously accepted. The true test came when we had no available freezer space for a Thanksgiving turkey because every space was occupied with frozen bear scat. I knew then that it was time to begin data analysis.

Early in the project, a major dent was made in the store of scats by Yu Man Lee, who came to the U.P. bear project by way of New York City. Despite the fact that she had never driven a vehicle, having ridden subways all her life, she was seated behind the steering wheel of a Michigan DNR four-wheel-drive pickup truck and pointed north—she was barely able to see over the steering wheel. Sink or swim. She told me later that she suffered mild culture shock the first time she sat alone upon a white pine stump to eat her lunch amid the peace and quiet of the north woods. It is a testament to her never-give-up attitude that over the next two years, Yu Man showed herself to be the most enthusiastic, dedicated, and hardworking assistant on the project. Together, we were able to analyze an initial 132 bear scats in 1992. What we found gave new direction to the bear walks.

The stage was set for our discovery in 1990 when a May 10 snow squall dumped fourteen inches of heavy wet snow across the project area. Tree limbs gave way under the weight. Flowers and buds of soft-mast–producing shrubs were frozen and their crops decimated. That year, Yu Man's analysis revealed that the bears switched from a diet normally containing about 46 percent fruit, 41 percent vegetation, 3 percent animal matter, 4 percent ants, and 6 percent other, to one of 16 percent fruit, 59 percent vegetation, 5 percent animal matter, 8 percent ants, and 12 percent other.

The apparent doubling of the bear's ant feeding (myrmecophagy) stayed in the back of my mind over the next year. Perhaps, I thought, there is a way to actively manage ants so that in years of soft-mast failure more ants might be available to bears. If so, that would enable us, for the first time, to actively manage habitat for bears. Unlike that for white-tailed deer, hares, and other game species, the management of forests for bears is still more by default than by design. Only the killing of bears is managed (i.e., how many, where, and to some extent the sex). Bear habitat has never been managed, mainly because no one knows how. Perhaps by studying the relationship between ants and bears, we might discover something. We needed to know more.

In 1993, Laurie Johnson, a graduate student at Northern Michigan University, joined the project, and she spent the next two years studying bear myrmecophagy and its relationship to bear habitat use. To accomplish this, a study was designed whereby I collected a sample of the ants fed on by Carmen or Nettie, took a GPS location, and dropped a small transmitter at the site. After the bears vacated the area, Laurie located the transmitter and performed an inventory of the site. Various parameters were recorded including site description (i.e., stump, log, ground nest, or rock); species, size, and rate of decay of stump or log; habitat type; soil series; and species of ant. That information was then compared to information obtained by random sampling throughout Carmen's and Nettie's home ranges. The results indicated that patterns of habitat use were dictated by the bears' preference for certain ant species. Of more than thirty resident species of ants identified, the bears feed on only fifteen species; furthermore, more than 75 percent of Carmen's and Nettie's feeding sites contained one of four primary ant species.

∽o∾

6/19/94

Today we captured one of Carmen's yearling males in a trap set near the north boundary of her range. I released him unharmed at first light.

Richard P. Smith is along for the walk today, and we find Nettie and June in a hardwoods at the gated area. Nettie is not as accepting of strangers as Carmen is, and it takes awhile for her, and especially June, to warm to Richard. Eventually, she feels comfortable enough to lead the way to a small forest opening, where she feeds on hawkweed and clover while June remains up a white cedar refuge tree on the periphery. Finished in the clearing, Nettie calls June down, and we meander through the hardwoods to a stand of seedling and sapling aspens, where Nettie locates a colony of ants in a log. She rolls the log around, and, because of the way it has decayed, she is able to extract the intact heartwood and prey on the colony outside the log. She meanders to another stump and digs at its base, uncovering another colony of ants. June joins her in feeding, and when Nettie moves off, Richard and I hold back to allow June to eat her fill of the ant colony. June emerges from the feeding with her head covered in sawdust. We follow as the bears meander to an ecotone of hardwoods and aspens, where Nettie alternates between sniffing stumps and sniffing the ground. She moves into the hardwoods and rests at the base of a sugar maple and plays with June. Rested, the bears continue to meander along the ecotone of the two habitats. Suddenly, without warning, Nettie flushes a bedded fawn and quickly captures it. The commotion sends June running for a refuge tree. Nettie feeds briefly on the fawn, then walks toward the hardwood, clunking to June. Richard and I stay put near the fawn carcass, and eventually Nettie returns. Fresh from the kill, the cheeks of her muzzle crimson and her eyes appearing slightly glazed, she claims the carcass and drags it away from us to feed concealed by brambles. After consuming a portion of the kill, she partially covers the dead fawn with leaves and twigs and returns to June's refuge tree once again to check on her. We decide it will be best to leave the bears to themselves, lest our presence deprive June of the surfeit. Besides, as we have witnessed before, the fawn kill will dictate the bears' behavior for the remainder of the day. We decide we have plenty of daylight left in which to pay a visit to Carmen.

After some looking, Richard and I hook up with Carmen behind a camp in the west-central portion of her range. She frequents this area much more when alone than when with cubs or yearlings. She is feeding on jack-in-the-pulpit along a rick of stacked cordwood near the edge of a hardwoods. I can smell crushed leeks underfoot as we approach. Carmen feeds on jack-in-the-pulpit copiously for over forty minutes, then leads Richard and me into a neighboring stand of lowland conifers. It is a cool spot, and she rests on her back, rolling over occasionally to bite at pesky flies. We rest here with no sign of her moving on. The respite gives Richard and me an opportunity to discuss Nettie's taking of the fawn. Inevitably, we recall the first time that we witnessed a bear capture a fawn.

Carmen head-rubs a hunter's blind recently constructed in her home range, spring 1995. (Terry D. DeBruyn)

Carmen, her head tilted back, drifts wherever it is bears go while nursing her cubs in a cedar swamp, spring 1995. (Terry D. DeBruyn)

A sub-adult Nettie, fall 1993. (Terry D. DeBruyn)

Carmen and cubs rest in the Whitefish River after giving up the search in the lost cub episode, summer 199
(Terry D. DeBruyn)

Carmen's cub stands with needle-sharp claws on a tree, spring 1995. (Terry D. DeBruyn)

A Landsat view of the study area. Northern hardwoods show as red, open water as dark blue, wetland meadows as light blue, and lowland conifer swamps as green-gray.

This male has shed the long guard hairs of his winter coat. Black bears have pale skin beneath their coats; polar bears have black skin, which aids heat retention. (Terry D. DeBruyn)

Carmen maneuvers an energetic troop through open northern hardwoods, spring 1995. (Terry D. DeBruyn)

Carmen's cub resting in an aspen sapling after feeding on leaves, spring 1993. (Terry D. DeBruyn)

Carmen's cub gets his first glimpse of a new world from their 1993 den. The cub's blue eyes reflect the blue sky. Later they will turn brown. (Terry D. DeBruyn)

Carmen, Corduroy, and Aster play tag on a maple, spring 1993. (Terry D. DeBruyn)

Carmen stands to arched-back rub and bite an aspen mark tree. (Terry D. DeBruyn)

Nettie and June play tag in an ironwood sapling growing in a wetland meadow, spring 1994. (Terry D. DeBruyn

∾ↄ∾

It was on July 10, 1991, and Carmen was piloting her litter of three cubs through a stand of lowland aspens mixed with dead elms, both fallen and standing. Richard and I were bringing up the rear. In an opening, tall with sedges, Carmen was walking a log when suddenly she became more alert. She jumped off the log onto a bedded fawn, killing it with a bite to the back of its neck. It was over in less than thirty seconds, but not before the commotion and the fawn's vocalizations sent the litter-mates in different directions (the smallest cub hightailed it and did not return before Richard and I left, some four hours later). Carmen dragged the carcass into a thick clump of aspen saplings, and there she and the two remaining cubs fed on it. Later, she dragged the partially eaten carcass near a refuge tree, where she slept, drank, and nursed the cubs between scaveng-ing bouts while Richard and I watched wide-eyed.

Up to a certain stage it is possible to age a fawn by the length of its hoof growth. There is a contention that fawns are cap-tured by bears only during the first two weeks of life, that there-after they are able to avoid predation by bears. As a budding scientist, I wanted the hoof for aging. So while Carmen rested at the base of her refuge tree, the fawn lying midway between us fifteen yards away, I walked to the carcass, withdrew my knife, and began to sever the front leg. When Carmen arose and walked straight toward me, I talked calmly to her while continuing my task. At a distance of five yards, she "lunged" and swatted the ground with both front paws while forcefully exhaling. Her message clear, I dropped the fawn and retreated to my seat, offering apologies. Carmen grabbed the fawn by its rear leg and dragged it nearer the refuge tree, where she par-tially concealed it with duff from the forest floor. It was a boneheaded move on my part, and the first of two for which I was disciplined by Carmen. Both involved fawn carcasses; both were my fault; and both could have turned out worse.

Following those times, through a combination of good fortune and courteousness, and an inordinate measure of tolerance on the bear's part, I never again felt threatened while on our walks. The next morning when I visited the fawn-kill site, Carmen and her cubs were a quarter mile away feeding on raspberries. I collected a hoof from the skeleton and later approximated the fawn's age at twenty-seven days.

∽∘∾

Today's walk with Carmen proves to be somewhat less exciting, and a few hours later, while she snores, as she sometimes does, Richard and I call it a day. Carmen rises only slightly as we depart talking.

6/20/94

Carmen is resting alert in a stand of lowland conifers and sits up as I approach but lies back down when she recognizes me. About a half hour later she gets up and meanders to a black ash stand and rests recumbently there for an hour. She then arises and meanders into the conifers and becomes intensely interested in a small hummock among a thick patch of sapling white cedars. After sniffing around the hummock for several minutes, she moves on. I investigate the spot and find the nearly perfectly coiled skeletal remains of a small bear. Although it is quite decomposed, I estimate that it died this spring. I mentally mark the spot for revisiting and hurry to catch up with Carmen. She continues foraging in the stand, then rests again. An hour later, I leave her resting. Walking out of the swamp, I have the feeling that she is recuperating from the breeding season and awaiting the arrival of more plentiful food days.)

I return to the remains of the bear and as systematically as possible collect all visible bones and hair. I have learned—and it helps to have a bear show you—that the forest gives up few of its secrets and therefore little of its character to the hurried. Carefully inspecting the ground for any revealing evidence, I find the bear's baculum, or os penis—penis bone. Considering it, and judging by the size and dentition of the skull, I estimate the carcass to be that of a yearling male. (Interpretation of the cementum and annuli layers of a premolar from the skull later validates the estimate.) I can find no evidence of foul play, although I believe the bear's death to be connected to a newly constructed camp nearby, where several wildlife feeders hang suspended from cables strung among the trees.

If bears discover such a wildlife feeding site, they may consume a fair bit of the corn and grains there—foods that people intend for other animals like deer and birds. Some camp owners initially encourage the periodic visits of bears to their feeders, but what is at first an enjoyable novelty can quickly devolve into a costly and damaging experience as bears become emboldened and leave no stone unturned in their quest for the camp's food. The bear is then relegated to "nuisance" status as owners become afraid for property and person.

Approaching humans and their dwellings is not an inherent behavior of bears. They do it only because they have been rewarded for it. Just as they do with the abundant berry patch and the oak or beechnut grove, they remember the location of wildlife feeders and return. They will continue to return as long as they are rewarded and several times afterward just to make sure another "crop" does not appear. Fearful, some owners take resolution of the situation into their own hands and simply eliminate the bear, shooting it in the stomach so that it will run off and die where they don't have to deal with the carcass. Others accomplish the task by poisoning. In either case, the bear dies a painful death, a death that I believe is more common than most wildlife managers and law enforcement officers expect or will admit. A year later, while walking with Carmen and her third litter, Richard and I found another dead male bear near the same site.

6/21/94

Nettie and June are in a northern hardwood stand east of the truck trail. Nettie rubs her flank on a windblown yellow birch as I approach, then climbs upon it and watches me. She walks off the end of the log, then leads June and me off through the hardwood. As I close in behind them, it becomes quite apparent that one of the pair has had an encounter with a skunk. As we near the border of an aspen seedling and sapling stand, I flush a grouse that then dive-bombs Nettie as its chicks take unsteady flight and sail spread-winged onto surrounding aspens. The hen continues to "grouse" at us and makes another bombing run, but the bears pay her no mind. We move deeper into the aspen stand, where Nettie sniffs and digs stumps and feeds on ants. Later, we move into a bog, where she feeds on the roots and tips of cattails. When June is engrossed in feeding on a cattail root of her own, I move in close enough to verify that it is she and not Nettie who smells of skunk. Finished in the bog, Nettie walks to the bog-aspen ecotone, where she sniffs stumps, then it's back to the aspens for more stump sniffing but little ant feeding. When Nettie stops foraging, June walks to her, and they play. Then June climbs up a refuge tree, and Nettie walks to the base and rests. Nettie plays with a stick at the base of the tree for a while, then meanders around until she locates a large ant colony in the roots of an overturned yellow birch. After feeding, she sits and scratches, then grooms; then she meanders back to the refuge tree, where she rests.

6/22/94

Same location as yesterday. Nettie and June are in an aspen seedling and sapling stand sniffing stumps and logs for ants. June discovers the wings and bones of a grouse and lies looking right at me while crunching them. When she passes by me on her way to a refuge tree at the edge of the stand, I can still detect the faint odor of skunk. Nettie, finished sniffing and digging stumps and feeding on ants, meanders to a hardwood stand and rests at the base of a hemlock. Later, she leads us into a lowland conifer stand, where she locates the skull of porcupine. After gnawing at it for several minutes, she relinquishes it to June and moves off into thick brush. I watch June for a few moments and then attempt to move around her to follow Nettie, which causes her to abandon the skull. After I talk to her calmly and back up a few steps, she returns to the skull and I move past. Nettie is in a patch of scrub brush too thick for me to actually see what she is doing, but one good whiff of air heavy with the fetid odor of carrion is clue enough. I stand listening to the sound of bones crunching and take shallow breaths to stave off the overpowering foul odor. This, it seems, is our day for skulls and bones. I have seen a bear gag only once and wonder now if I will see it again. June comes from behind and gives me a wide berth as she joins in. The bears mill about for nearly half an hour and then abandon the site. When I move in, I cannot find even a drop of blood to give evidence of what was eaten, but the odor lingers heavy and repugnant. I presume it was a stillborn fawn. It is now unlikely that June will smell of skunk any longer. We cross a series of small streams and walk fallen cedars and balsams to get to a thick clump of sapling cedars. Nettie rests here on the ground with June near her side. I find a log on which to sit. After they have an hour of rest and a six-minute nursing bout followed by another hour of rest, I leave them and make my way back to the Jeep to locate Carmen.

Carmen is in a tag alder swamp near an old trapper's cabin on the Whitefish, feeding on wild calla. When I approach, she stands on hind legs to look my way, then eases down to resume feeding. We meander to a lowland conifer stand, then in and out of a soft maple–lowland conifer ecotone and back into the conifers. Carmen feeds for a while longer on calla in the conifers and then rests alongside a big moss-covered log. She throws a leg and forearm over the log and sleeps hugging it. We rest here an hour, until I leave. (Somehow, Carmen is able to sleep through a terse scolding by a winter wren—she has probably heard it before.)

✃∞✃

Circa 1912, Asopho "Acey" Helmer—with the help of a friend, Sam Hews—built the log cabin on the east shore of the White-fish River in the west-central portion of what is now Carmen's home range. Acey, like other U.P. residents of the time (called Yoopers), eked out a living the best he could from his sur-roundings. The camp was originally built to serve as a line shack for his trap line; he ended up living there until his death some twenty years later. In life, he was said to be a mild-man-nered individual. Only occasionally did he become upset, such as when someone pilfered a few brook trout he had caught and was keeping in a pool near the camp for later use. Good with his hands, he often whittled during conversations and con-cluded by handing the visitor a sculpted dog, cat, or Indian. He trapped for a living—mostly small mammals like muskrat, fox, and coyote, and occasionally bears. By all accounts, he was "a good man in the woods," a moniker not bandied about by Yoopers.

Acey's cabin, hewn from white pine and cedar, stands to-day. Its current use is as a way-point for canoeists paddling the upper reaches of the Whitefish River. I discovered Acey's Christian name from the scribes of George Webber, a neigh-boring landowner, in a log book maintained at the cabin. On occasion, I stop off there after a walk with Carmen or Nettie to read from the log's entries. Aside from the craftsmanship, what most impresses me about the cabin are the snakes.

Michigan has only one indigenous species of poisonous snake, the massasauga, a pit viper, and I have never encoun-tered one in the Upper Peninsula. So when walking with the bears, I feel safe sitting down anywhere without regard to poi-

130

sonous reptiles (or plants, for that matter; poison ivy, which I can catch even on the wind is virtually nonexistent). You can't do that everywhere; certainly not, for instance, if you were in Florida, where there are no less than nine species of poisonous snakes, including the aggressive pygmy rattler and the neuro-toxic coral snake. For this reason, I felt somewhat self-satisfied when walking with bears—I was already in the company of the "baddest" thing in the forest. I seldom encounter snakes in the north woods; only once while on a bear walk did Carmen and I encounter a snake.

On summer days when I approached the cabin, however, there might be a half dozen or more snakes basking in the sun near the south footing. Mostly present were eastern garter snakes; less common were the larger yellow-and-brown-spotted western fox snakes known locally as pine snakes.

One day in 1992, after the breakup of Carmen's first litter, Carmen and I were traveling the woods alone; her tolerance and trust had grown immeasurably. At early morning I hooked up with her in the south-central portion of her home range near a large beaver flooding. She held for me as I approached, and after a brief rendezvous she foraged ahead downstream of my position, as I chose to walk the beaver dam, where I would not sink so far into the mucky organic silt. Feeding on the tips of cattail fronds and here and there on jewelweed, Carmen worked her way westward along the foot of the dam. We crossed the Whitefish River at a spot where a bed of nonerodible limestone forced the down-cutting water to expand its banks instead. The water, only a few inches deep, rippled over the rock bed. Carmen waded in, halting to look back when I splashed into the current. I gave her the "it's OK" spiel, and immediately satisfied, she continued. Carmen was a different bear without cubs. She was now either more trusting or simply less concerned about my proximity. In the preceding weeks, I had begun following her more closely in an attempt to obtain "bite counts" of forbs and berries and the licks of ants she ingested. This proved difficult, as her head was often obscured by a stump or log when she was feeding on ants, and because I was usually behind her, she faced away from me while foraging on berries and the like. Without cubs, she tolerated me moving closer and into position as she foraged with her head down. The trick was to talk, stay in as clear a line of sight as possible, and move slowly. But it proved impossible to get consistent and accurate bite counts in all but the most open habitats.

Across the river, on the west shore, we emerged from a riparian stand of lowland brush into an upland stand of pole-sized aspens. Carmen began forage-meandering, investigating downed woody material in the stand for its ant content. As we walked through an area of crisscrossed logs, overgrown with grasses, I noticed that she walked right past a rather large fox snake. The snake lay coiled near the fusion of two decaying logs.

My olfactory capabilities have never enabled me to detect the scent of snakes at any distance. However, someone (presumably with a better nose for snakes) once told me that they smell like cucumbers. I could not imagine that Carmen, being so close to the reptile, would not have smelled it. I wondered if she had noticed the snake and ignored it because she was engrossed in foraging for ants, or if she was unaware of its presence. Curious as to how she might interact with the snake, I unslung my pack. Foraging fifteen feet ahead, she heard the sound of the rustling pack and halted to look back at me. I retrieved a fragment of doughnut from the pack and tossed it nearly on top of the coiled snake. (Up until now, I had never done anything to purposefully distract Carmen during our walks.) I didn't intend the tidbit to fall as close to the snake as it did but it was too late to retrieve or reposition it as Carmen came near. The snake held tight until Carmen put her head down to sniff the treat, when it uncoiled. Carmen immediately collapsed to her rump on an adjacent log. With outstretched forelimbs, she looked alternately down at the snake and then up at me. She obviously was unacquainted with moving doughnuts.

I do not pretend to understand to this day what happened next. In my most reassuring voice, I told her, "It's OK, Carmen." Well, obviously, it wasn't. Things were different. As the snake stretched to its full length of nearly five feet, Carmen vaulted to the side, trotted a few feet away, and stood looking back over her shoulder. I know I must have imagined it, but I thought I saw a slight raising of the fur between her shoulders. She turned away and resumed forage-meandering. Throughout the remainder of the walk, she never looked back again. And whatever passes for the "cold shoulder" in bear body-language is what I got for the rest of our walk. At dusk, nearly nine hours later, I trailed behind as we came to a patch of scrub dogwood along the shore of the Whitefish. It was a spot I recognized, and I broke off the walk there, heading cross-country for the Jeep. I knew I had screwed up.

The next morning, wanting to redeem myself in short order, I was positioned to make contact with Carmen at first light. Normally, on initial contacts for the day, the routine was for Carmen to halt her movement and wait, sometimes coming to the sound of my voice as I approached. This morning, as the steam rose off the mucky backwaters of the beaver flooding that separated us, Carmen never broke stride as she traversed the opposite shore. She appeared to jerk her head in the opposite direction as she walked away. Ignored again? The going was slow, but I slogged as hurriedly as possible through the mud and mire, talking to her as I went. She walked on—and it was a while before I was able to overtake her. After traveling about two hundred yards on winding game trails, she halted and looked back. Not knowing what my next step should be, I thought food the best avenue of approach. So I unslung my pack and pitched a few doughnuts into a pile on the game trail, then backed off a few steps.

Carmen approached the treats, but as she did, she began

circling the spot, testing the wind, and maintaining a steady gaze in their direction. She made three full circles, the third tightening to within only a few feet. Satisfied, she leaped in and grabbed a doughnut. Then she backed off several feet, dropped it, and began to daintily nibble it. She repeated the circling action a second time and was comfortable enough to eat two more in place, after which she walked off and began a forage-meander.

Bears do not hold grudges and minutes into the walk and on days thereafter, things returned to normal. I suspected then, and feel now, that I had violated Carmen's confidence the day of the snake. I told her it was OK when it was not, and she reacted to it. I vowed never again to artificially position Carmen, or any of her offspring, with food to test a hypothesis.

∽∘∾

6/23/94

Today I finally get a longer day with the bears. There are no trapped bears to handle, so I am able to join Nettie and June at midmorning after running the trap line. I find them in a northern hardwood stand near the eastern boundary of Nettie's range. Nettie is walk-meandering and clunking to June and pays surprisingly little attention as I fall in line. We meander to the refuge tree, where Nettie sits and grooms. June descends and we are off to an aspen seedling and sapling stand to search for ants. Nettie sniffs several stumps but does not bother digging them. Finally, when her nose locates the right one, she begins ripping it apart.[1]

Finished in the clear-cut, Nettie meanders to a hardwood stand and into a vernal pool. She finds nothing of interest to feed on here and moves on to a bog, where she forages on wild calla. June climbs and rests in a refuge tree at the bog's edge. While Nettie forages, I sit on a log. When June is rested, we cross the bog and meander into another clear-cut aspen stand, where Nettie feeds on more ants; I recognize them as *Camponotus*. (Until recently, I recognized all ants as simply LBJs— little brown jobs—unaware of their Latin epithets, which is the only way to distinguish some species, as they have no common names.)

From the clear-cut aspens, we head north and walk upon a hunting blind, which Nettie spends some time sniffing and head-rubbing. When we move north from the stand, we go only a short distance and walk out onto a well-used gravel road. Nettie appears apprehensive and walks gingerly westward along the edge for some way, then halts, sniffing the air and listening. June stands and watches, waiting. I lag behind. To my disbelief, Nettie walks to the middle of the road and heads west right down the middle of it. For nearly one hundred yards we walk the road to a point where we turn north up a grassy two-track lane. Nettie turns and looks back at me, and I tell her, "It's OK," but I know it is not, as I can clearly see a camp dead ahead at the end of the lane. The bears head straight for the camp, and both head-rub the protruding logs on its northeast corner. They walk around behind the camp, and Nettie head-rubs the opposite corner while June investigates a fifty-gallon drum, climbing on top. I follow as the bears move west from the camp into the abutting lowland conifers. June becomes preoccupied with a block of salt left by the camp's owner to bring deer into view. Nettie meanders to the north but returns to bat the block off its stand after seeing June dallying at the site. After licking the salt block briefly, June follows Nettie as she moves north.

I am glad to leave the camp behind, suspecting that some time in the past Nettie may have gotten a scrap of food from the site, perhaps discarded fish entrails or buried garbage (natives of bear country realize that leaving a clean camp goes a long way toward reducing visits by hungry bears—a fact lost on some newcomers). Momentarily, I lose sight of Nettie and

June as we enter a thick stand of spruce, but I am able to follow them by sound. When I catch up, Nettie is feeding on *Lasius umbratus* at the base of a balsam stump.[2] When she finishes, we meander north and come upon another hunting blind, this one dilapidated, and Nettie does not mark it. We are heading basically north and west when Nettie pauses to listen to a logging truck rumble by on the gravel road we traveled to the cabin's lane. After about a half hour of meandering with no feeding, Nettie nurses June near the edge of an alder swamp. Finished nursing and moving again, we encounter a plastic USFS boundary marker. The marker is springy, and the bears tussle with it for a few minutes, then go on. The next half hour is spent moving north with no feeding and only one brief stop for Nettie to groom. She nurses June again, after which we meander to another plastic USFS boundary marker, which she head-rubs. It proves a tough task for her to accomplish, however, as the marker will not hold still. The bears play and lounge for a few minutes as June takes over playing with and marking the sign.

Pressing on, we enter some hardwoods, where two deer flush from their beds. Nettie runs to the site and sniffs around for a while, then continues onto an abandoned logging road and into a lowland conifer stand. We cross a stream, and I again lose sight of them momentarily in the thick brush and sedges along the shore. I follow by sound into the uplands and emerge into a red pine planting to the sight and sound of Nettie ripping apart an old white pine stump. Here she feeds for nine minutes on a colony of *Formica* ants. When she is finished, we begin meandering through the pines, which are head high on me. I periodically lose sight of the bears walking cross-row in the pines. Looking for the bears in the pine rows reminds me of looking down the long aisles of a supermarket. Bears should be so lucky in a pine planting. Pine stands of this age contain little food of value to bears, and bears make little use of them. As we are exiting the corner of the stand, Nettie locates and approaches another hunting blind. There is no marking on this blind, and she acts tentatively and skirts it as we reenter the lowlands. North, and twenty minutes later, Nettie drops at the base of a cedar, and June climbs it to rest.

Shortly, Nettie begins meandering about the base of the cedar and feeds on swamp thistles. The thistle in this patch seems to have arrested development compared to those in other stands, and some are still small and tender enough for Nettie to select. When she finishes, she returns to the refuge tree, from which June descends and begins nursing. The session lasts just short of five minutes, after which no time is devoted to play, and we are off and moving north again. Farther north, Nettie investigates the root mass of an overturned spruce. Often, the spaces voided by such wind-throws contain edible herbs—anomalies in the ground vegetation of the otherwise thickly canopied conifers. Depending on the direction in which a tree falls, how big its root mass is, the underlying substrate, and moisture conditions at the site, it takes more or less time for herbs to grow in the voids. Thus, their phenology becomes spread out within the stand, making the stand of value to bears over a greater period of time. After investigating the root mass and getting nothing from it, Nettie continues north and into an area of dead balsam fir and black spruce. These are fairly large-diameter trees (six to twelve inches) lying amid clumps of sedge and shrubs, and we alternately walk on or under them to arrive at a hummock in the middle of the stand.

Here the ground is higher. My eyes are immediately drawn to a lone "wolf pine," perhaps one hundred feet tall, growing at the far end of the hummock. Wolf pines, alone and often limbless on their windward side from enduring decades of strong winds and ice storms, are icons of perseverance. Like the stalwart pioneers that came to eke out a living from forest and rock, they symbolize the essence of the Upper Peninsula. The Finnish people, who settled in much of the Upper Peninsula, have a single word to describe people of great mettle: *sisu*. If that term can be applied to other life, then wolf pines certainly have *sisu*.

As we start onto the hummock, I am surprised when Nettie drops and begins again to nurse June. This bout lasts for just less than five minutes and is only twenty-one minutes after the previous nursing, which is unusually frequent. The nursing bout finished, Nettie moves to rest at the base of the wolf pine, and June climbs up and out of sight in its windswept branches. At the base, Nettie grooms and then sleeps. Near dark I leave the bears in their secure refuge. Making my way through the fallen spruce and fir, across a stream, and around a beaver flooding, I arrive at the uplands. When I turn to look back at the bears across the picture-perfect setting, I can no longer see Nettie at the base of the wolf pine or June up its branches, but I know that they are there.

6/24/94

Today's bear activity is, in a word, ants. When I walk in on Carmen, she is in an expanse of lowland hardwoods that has been clear-cut and planted to pines. Many stumps and much downed woody material lies around as a result of the clear-cutting. Carmen is positioning herself to rip apart a big stump. She pauses to consider me as I come talking my way in, then returns to her business. Overhead, a male snipe performs his territorial loops and dives, his outspread tail feathers creating the unmistakable *woo-woo-woo* sound during the dives. It seems late in the year for the snipe's territorial flight, but Carmen pays no mind to the whir of wings; she is focused on ants.

Although black bears lack the longer claws that brown bears have evolved to unearth fossorial mammals, they have all the necessary equipment when it comes to raiding ant colonies. When ripping apart stump after stump and log after log like tissue paper, Carmen uses teeth, claws, and leverage. She positions herself to use her weight and powerfully built forearms to considerable advantage. She goes at each site with fervor, making it easy to conceive how a bear might break off a canine

138

in an attempt to expose ants. On more than one stump, I've noticed the blood of a torn claw or ripped footpad. Although the sites she is unable to exploit are few, some wood that ants colonize is too sound for her to tear apart. The moment she unsheathes ants, however, she begins licking and continues to do so as she peels her way into each honeycombed site. Her tongue moves in and out at lightning speed as she laps up the ant larvae and pupae. Many adult ants are ingested incidentally in the process, for it is, I believe, the subadult stages (larvae and pupae) that she is after. The bears rarely feed at sites where subadults are not present. When Carmen finishes with a site, I immediately move in to collect a sample of the ants. If I were to wait a day, the ant colonies would be long relocated.

Over the next several hours, Carmen moves about the cutting, leading the way to stumps and logs. Finished, she exits the cutting along its eastern boundary and onto a two-track road. After traveling a short way, she slinks through a gate and continues up the road. I know there is a camp about a quarter mile beyond, having previously obtained permission from the owner to cross his lands. Only a short distance beyond the gate, Carmen begins acting warily, looking about and sniffing. I attribute it to her feeling exposed on the two-track, and I log her actions into the data recorder as I stand awaiting her next move. After a few seconds she moves to the side of the road and wades a shallow ditch, crossing to the edge of a cedar stand. Here an area of the forest floor the size of a kitchen is trodden and beaten down. Carmen stands surveying an illegal bear bait.

It is legal to hunt bears with bait during Michigan's bear season. The placement of bait for the purpose of attracting bears is legal the month prior to the season. We are two months away from opening day. In addition, the use of any synthetic material such as glass, metal, or plastic is illegal at all bait sites, something that comes to mind as Carmen sticks her head into

139

a green, five-gallon bucket and licks at the tidbits of grease remaining in the bottom.

Finished with the bucket, she recrosses the ditch and continues north up the two-track. Her soggy footprints are a conspicuous sign for any nimrod, and I suspect that is why the bait was placed where Carmen found it. As we round a corner in the two-track, we come upon a new log cabin. We had been this way years before when there was nothing here but a game trail through the forest. Carmen sits and scratches behind her ear with her left rear foot. She makes the consummate lawn ornament. I fully expect her to continue to the cabin and arched-back rub or head-rub the porch posts. I begin to video the scene—a classic encounter, new humanmade stuff in the middle of bear range. Why some folks decide to build camps smack-dab in the middle of large chunks of forest puzzles me. Most people come to the forest because they love wildlife, but from a wildlife perspective, it is much less invasive if cabins are built on the periphery.

Surprisingly, Carmen ambles right past the front porch, alongside the cabin, through the backyard, and onto an exiting path at the rear. She stops to sniff a fifty-gallon drum and then continues down the path and into the surrounding cedar swamp. As the path fades into the cedars, I am glad to leave signs of the camp and human stuff behind. Carmen walks direct on a game trail for a piece and then stops abruptly to listen. I hear it, too. It is the *peeping* sound of nestling birds. She turns and immediately climbs an ironwood tree growing near the trail's edge. The tree is small, only about six inches in diameter. I can see a nest hole about twelve feet up. There are no branches for Carmen to grab hold of or rest upon, and she exerts considerable effort in her attempt to exploit the nest. As she disturbs the tree, the sound from the birds becomes louder— this seems to egg her on. But the situation proves impossible; the ironwood is much too sound for claws or teeth. In frustration, she begins to descend, and giving up totally, she drops the last five feet onto the game trail. Because of the angle of the tree, she lands on her rear in an awkward position. This leaves her in a bad mood, and she turns and blows in my direction. I tell her that it is not my fault as we head west through the cedars. Shortly after we cross a small stream meandering through the cedars, the ground becomes higher, and we emerge into a semi-open area dotted with Juneberry bushes.

Juneberries, at least at our latitude, are somewhat misnamed. The species flowers in May and does not produce ripe fruit until well into July during most years. Perhaps farther south, it fruits in June. Carmen stands on her hind legs to mouth a few of the berries. I can see that they are not ripe, but I'm curious as to how they might taste. So as Carmen stands mouthing the berries on the opposite side of the bush, I reach up and pull down a branch to begin a taste test of my own. This draws a harsh reaction from Carmen. Before I even get a berry to my lips, she drops to all fours and performs a blow and swat in my direction. I immediately discontinue my attempted berry feeding. Backing up a few steps, I wonder if she interpreted my actions as competition for her food. After registering her displeasure and apparently eliciting the desired response, she continues meandering through the small openings. We have gone only a short distance when, in keeping with the ornery tempo she has set, Carmen turns again to blow at me. This is fairly atypical behavior for her, especially as she is without cubs or yearlings. A lot goes through my mind as we stand facing each other. Is she still perturbed at my attempt to forage on her unripe Juneberries? Is she upset by her failure at the bird's nest? Or is it something unrelated? Whatever the case, I decide it best to leave her to herself and make my way back to the Jeep. We have put in a good day—besides, how would I feel if a bear followed me around everywhere I went. "See ya, Carmen, bye, thanks."

6/25/94

Some days work out better than others for walking with bears. In order for a bear walk to be successful, many things need to come together simultaneously. Not only must the researcher and all the equipment function properly, but the weather and the bears must cooperate, too. Antecedent conditions also play a role. I never know, for example, when I walk in on the bears, what has taken place in their life in the minutes and hours prior to my arrival. Many times the bears' behavior indicates that they are responding to some stimuli that I have not provided and am not aware of. Sometimes, especially on longer bear walks, I have been able to piece together how an earlier event played a part in present behavior—a bear's life is a continuum of events, and where we enter and exit will profoundly influence the interpretation of our observations. Part of ensuring the success of any bear walk is knowing when to push the walk just a little to overcome a rough spot. As a rule, the longer and more often I walked with the bears, the better it became. By now I have ridden out plenty of rough spots and have come to realize that future success also rests in part on knowing when to discontinue a walk—to quit on a good note.

As I move through the forest toward the sound of Carmen's radio signal, I see her chasing another bear and think that today I might have to opt for the latter strategy.

I see right off that the bear Carmen chases is ear-tagged with the small red tags reserved for yearling males. A quick check of frequencies reveals the yearling to be one of Carmen's— Aster. I hustle to keep up as she pursues him noncommittally through the forest. After a short chase, the yearling trees and Carmen stands huffing at the base. I witnessed a similar scene involving a yearling male form Carmen's first litter on numerous occasions. As mother and son face off, I begin judging my prospects for continuing this walk, based on my earlier experiences with "the Runt."

142

∾०∾

For good reason I named the smaller of Nettie's siblings the Runt. It was not a term of endearment. The Runt was timid. He had a hesitant and furtive nature. He was the first to climb to refuge at any slightly unusual sound. The coast clear, he was invariably the last to descend. Many a day's activities were held up so that the Runt could get with the program. He became lost several times, and Carmen spent much time looking for him. In fact, once when the commotion at a fawn kill sent his siblings up a nearby tree, The Runt spooked and tore out of sight. Three hours later, as Carmen rested at the kill site and his littermates alternately fed and nursed, I watched the Runt wander by, a hundred yards off in the forest, apparently unable to relocate Carmen and his siblings. He missed out altogether on the feeding and nursing and had still not returned more than four hours later when I left. In a word, the Runt was flaky.

Like this yearling male up the tree, the Runt was also tied to Carmen's apron strings after family breakup. While his littermates made a clean split, the Runt attempted to reassociate with Carmen on more than two dozen occasions while I was present. Once while Carmen was feeding in a raspberry patch during July, she suddenly stood alert on hind legs, front feet resting on a sugar maple—it was the Runt. His approach was tentative, and when he maneuvered to within a few yards, Carmen dropped and gave chase, cornering him. She delivered a swat to his head with such force, I actually saw his eyes roll back in his head and thought it was surely his demise. But he just shook it off and continued sidling up to her. Later in the day, Carmen gave in and allowed him to scrounge nearby, mooching leftovers. When I left them that evening at dark, they rested near one another in a cedar swamp. The following October, when Carmen denned in an aspen seedling-sapling stand, the Runt chose a nearby den site within the same stand. They were together in the aspens for four days, but when I checked on them the fifth day, only Carmen was present. The Runt was one and a half miles away, in a freshly dug den. Later that winter, when handling the Runt during den checks (of thirty-three juvenile males, he was one of only two that lingered until age two before dispersing) I found a four-inch gash across his muzzle. I am nearly certain he received it during a failed attempt to re-associate with Carmen in her den, something she would not allow and gave the Runt his final send-off. Nevertheless, not being the boldest, and lingering in familiar territory, undoubt-edly has certain survival advantages for subadult male bears, and the Runt was the only one of Carmen's five male cubs, big or small, to survive until age two. Three of the others died from gunshot; one died presumably of natural causes.

∽o∾

Presently, Carmen turns her back on the treed yearling, the runt of her second litter, and walks away. I start to fall in be-hind her, when the yearling scales down the tree and begins following us. Carmen turns on him abruptly and running past me (within inches), she chases him in a half circle, the yearling moaning and issuing pained bawls all the way as Carmen, huffing, tramples small saplings close behind. It is an impres-sive and tumultuous display and leaves me wondering how many times it will be repeated before something clicks to make this yearling realize that Carmen will no longer tolerate his presence. It took many lessons for the Runt.

It would be easy, while watching the dramatic events of family breakup unfold, to say that bears have emotions. And no doubt there are those who would flinch at the statement. However, just because bears, like children, tend to emote in a rapid and quickly dissipating manner does not mean that they do not have emotions. More likely, their emotions are too com-plex for our unraveling. The flinchers could never have witnessed the breakup of a bear family firsthand and thus could not fully comprehend what a stirring and significant event it is in the lives of bears.

After the yearling attempts several more times to reassociate with Carmen, I opt to conclude the walk and pay a visit to Nettie and June, where I know the maternal bond is still solid.

᙭ᴏᴧ

I manage to squeeze in five hours with Nettie and June. Today the pair traverses fourteen different habitat types. They spend most of their time in lowland conifers, where both feed on wild calla, cattails, and *Lasius.* Both drink after feeding on the ants. There is considerably more duff mixed into the ground-based *Lasius* nests, and this may explain the bears' greater water consumption. We discover another hunting blind (this one new to me), and Nettie urinates and Carmen-dances up to it, then head-rubs it. Afterward, both she and June play with the blue plastic tarp that serves as siding for the blind. Eventually, the bears shred and tear it off completely. Today marks the first testing of berries. Nettie mouths Tartarian honeysuckle and alder-leaved buckthorn berries, although neither are yet ripe. June nurses and then climbs a big maple growing at such an angle that upon her descent, she is required to use every bit of her climbing skill and nearly falls twice. I notice that the brown spots behind her ears have almost disappeared.

6/30/94

Laurie Johnson, the "ant girl," accompanies us today. Obligingly, Carmen spends most of the morning feeding on ants. As we near the edge of a red pine planting, a sandhill crane takes flight from a lowland meadow, and Carmen spends some time sniffing about the spot. I think maybe she will locate a nest or nestling, but she finds neither. Sandhills' tracheas are looped in the keel of their breastbone, and in mature birds it can reach a length of five feet. When air passes through the convolutions, it causes a deep resonant *garow a a a k* call that can be heard for miles. This bird seems to be vying for the Guinness Book record for issuing guard calls as it flies *garow a a a k-ing* out of sight. Moving through the waist-high pines, Carmen rises on hind legs to test the fruit on a black cherry tree. It is one of a few trees left unharmed when the stand was converted to a pine planting. But the fruit is not yet ripe, and we do not tarry here. We meander out of the pines and through some hardwoods, where Laurie finds an arrow near the edge of a well-worn game trail. Carmen walks direct on the game trail and remains on it throughout the stand. After crossing an old two-track, she comes upon a bird's nest in a dead tree. We identify it as a sapsucker's when we see the bird fly. Carmen stands on her hind feet and, with front paws wrapped around the tree, begins shaking the snag. When it appears that it is going to fall, she ducks out of the way and hunkers behind a nearby tree—it is obvious to both Laurie and me that she is practiced in this technique and knows when the tree is about to fall. After another shaking, the snag falls but catches on the limbs of another tree, still preventing Carmen from getting at the nest within. The failure brings about a bad mood. She meanders on, and at the edge of an aspen seedling-sapling stand she locates another bird's nest in a large snag. This one she climbs, but she can't get this nest, either— she blows at Laurie and me from fifteen feet above as if it's our fault. Descending, she moves huffily into the aspens for more ant feeding—Laurie thinks these look like *Camponotus spp.*

Moving on, Carmen arched-back rubs a balsam fir that has its top busted off about six feet above the ground (this is the same one Nettie marked last week) and appears to have received frequent use. Dropping down, Carmen rubs her flank on a nearby aspen. Finished marking and rubbing, she heads south-southwest paralleling the flow of the Whitefish River in the old riverbed now overgrown with knee-high wildflowers and stunted seedling aspens. Carmen flips rocks looking for ants—the clanking sound a dead giveaway for all within earshot. She locates some *Lasius* under a rock slab and feeds on them while holding it upright with her paw. While her head is down, a fawn bedded nearby flushes. Keying in on the leaf rustle, Carmen blindly gives chase. She starts too far behind to overtake the fawn but chases it out of our sight. We shortcut through a stand of lowland aspens and overtake her in an aspen seedling-sapling stand, where she is sniffing stumps. We move from the aspens up a hardwood ridge. In the hardwoods, Carmen stays mostly on game trails, until we come to a two-track, where she digs and feeds on ants in the stumps along its edge. Farther along the two-track, she digs at the overturned roots of a yellow birch stump for quite a while, and it appears as though she might be digging a den. From the yellow birch stump, we move into a semi-open area, where she feeds on the tops of yellow goatsbeard. She dances near the same spot in the opening where Nettie had earlier. Then she meanders to test the unripe berries of a Juneberry bush at the opposite side of the opening. The wind picks up, and Laurie and I decide to leave as she walks off into the hardwoods.

∽∘∾

If, as I did, you believed that black bears only investigate and construct den sites in the fall just prior to denning, you would be wrong. Carmen and Nettie investigated and constructed dens throughout the year. The first time I witnessed the bears experimenting with den sites, I was with Carmen in the summer of 1992. Walking along an abandoned two-track in the gated area, I initially thought she was digging for ants in the stumps there. But that notion was dispelled after standing and watching for more than twenty minutes as the dirt and dust flew out of the excavation. She bit into overhead roots and scraped the insides of the root mass and then backed her way out of the hole, digging as she retreated, her excavation for the most part obscured by the lush June vegetation. After she finished, she moved on along the two-track exploring for ants. She never used that site as a den that I am aware of. Initially, I attributed her diggings to a flush of hormones associated with the breeding season. However, that too was dispelled after I watched her dig several others over the course of the field season, including the construction of a nest in the cavity of a hollow tree.

In southern states bears frequently occupy dens constructed in the cavities of hollow trees. In Georgia's Okefenokee Swamp, many dens are located high off the ground in giant cypress. Tree dens have the advantages not only of being secure, but also of having greater thermal efficiency than dens constructed in brush piles or partially earthen dens. But few trees in northern forests are allowed to achieve the age and stature necessary to function as den trees. Most are cut well before they become suitable.

Construction of dens throughout the year may have several distinct survival advantages for bears. First, it provides alternate den sites to which they can flee should they be rousted from their original site (during the course of my study several female bears were spooked from their dens in the fall by recreational activity). Second, an early excavation will be obscured by newly emerging vegetation and later by falling leaves, as well. (Prior to the enactment of laws protecting denning bears, whole families of Michigan bears were annihilated in their dens during the firearm deer season by hunters possibly drawn to the sites by the excavation.)

∽∘∾

7/2/94

Nettie is resting at the base of a white cedar when I walk in on her and June today. They are near the edge of a stream flowing through a stand of lowland conifers. Nettie climbs the refuge tree and then descends with June following. Both meander along the banks of the stream feeding on jack-in-the-pulpit—they feed on the tops and dig and eat the corms. The vegetation along the banks of the stream is very thick, and, as we pick our way through it, I must follow them closely or lose sight of them. They are tolerant of my proximity. My observance of the rules of bear etiquette has strengthened their confidence in my predictability and is now paying off. We meander back to the cedar, where Nettie nurses June. June kneads Nettie's mammae with her tongue and "chuckles" as she nurses. Nettie is slouching in a position whereby her upper two sets of mammae almost touch one another, and June quickly moves her mouth from one to the other. After the nursing bout, Nettie drifts off to sleep resting recumbently at the base of the cedar.

7/3/94

We capture one of Carmen's yearling males, Corduroy, in a barrel trap again today. The smoked bacon and doughnuts we use for bait are big draws, especially because the berry crop is late this year due to a lack of moisture and an excess of cool days. Overall, there have been fewer growing-degree days than in so-called normal years. Trap baits are easy pickings for a bear so inclined. This is true especially for the young males, as they are overall less cautious than females and also travel about more and are therefore more likely to intersect our traps. As I release the young male from the trap, I recall an adult male bear that held the study area record for the greatest number of recaptures. When we first captured him, he weighed 225 pounds. Six weeks and many baits later, he weighed nearly 300 pounds.

∽o∽

When setting up traps, we placed them in the shade to prevent heat-stressing captured bears. In the back of the trap, we positioned a half-pound of smoked bacon in a mesh bag that was tied to the trap's trigger. When a bear pulled on the bag, the trigger tripped, the door fell, and the bear was caught. In addition to the bacon, we enticed the bear into the trap with a trail of doughnuts extending the length of the barrel. Outside of the trap, we covered a few strategically placed doughnuts with large-diameter logs. Disturbance of the logs would give an indication of the type and size of the animal that had come to the trap, should we fail to capture it in the barrel. All in all, it was a good "meal deal" for a bear that did not mind being captured. This particular adult male was adept at scavenging the doughnuts under the log pile, then eating every single doughnut leading into the trap before finally tripping the trigger and polishing off the bait. After his first recapture he was reluctant to leave the trap—and why not, it was located in a cool spot, and he had a full belly—and he seemed more than content to sleep it off in the shade. This created a problem because I needed to reset the trap and be on my way in order to finish running the trapline in a timely manner to walk with Carmen or Nettie. After failing to roust him from the trap, I left him in it with the door removed, figuring that when I returned after running the remainder of the trapline, he would be gone. But, when I returned, about two hours later, he was still there asleep. I could not wait around until he decided to leave the trap on his own, so we decided to attempt to shake him out of the trap.

Now, most people, when thinking about bear research, may think of biologists roaming sweet-scented forests, tracking and handling bears in glistening black coats—in general, envisioning it as a romantic adventure, perhaps even somewhat envious of the pursuit. For the most part, they would be correct. Some facets of the trade are hard work, however, and less than envious. One such task is the cleaning of barrel traps, particularly after a three-hundred-pound male has spent the night in one. Without fail, urine and feces are excreted in the trap, a condition sometimes worsened by the addition of rainwater. The trapper must squirm and crawl ten feet to the end of the two-foot-diameter conduit to clean it. Becoming soiled oneself is unavoidable. Herein lies the reason that we never minded catching the big male. When we elevated the end of the trap and shook him from it, he slid the length of the trap and very effectively scoured it as he went—we named him Bottle Brush, and his nine captures were a record and welcomed number.

∽◦∽

I locate Carmen in a lowland aspen seedling-sapling stand. More ants. I am with her for about six hours, and for more than four hours she nearly continuously works stumps and logs looking for larvae and pupae. Besides ant feeding, she eats one yellow goatsbeard, drinks water four times, and grooms five times before resting in a clump of balsam fir within the cutting, where she stayed for an hour and a half before I packed up and left.

7/10/94

June is up a big white pine in an upland conifer stand when I come upon her and Nettie today. As she descends, she looks big, especially her paws. She may weigh thirty pounds or more. There are plenty of claw marks on the pine, and I wonder how long the bears have been here. I have not been with them in over a week because of the time required to trap and handle bears. We meander to an old beaver meadow, where the bears forage on the tips of cattail fronds. Leaving the meadow, we meander to a lowland conifer stand, where Nettie nurses June; then both climb a white cedar and play. June weaves in and out of the branches while Nettie, straddling a branch, bats at her with a paw. We are all scolded by the longest-running series of *chinks* from a sparrow that I have ever heard, and I am glad when the bears come down and we leave the area. We spend most of the day in the lowland conifers, the bears feeding on cattails and jewelweed and occasionally *Lasius*. At one point Nettie stands motionless, sniffing and listening, I am certain there is another bear near but see and hear none. I begin to wonder how many encounters with other bears, if any, are prevented by my presence. Nettie sits and listens for a full five minutes before she continues feeding. While we are in a fairly open area in the conifers and Nettie is ahead feeding on impatiens, June approaches me, wanting, I believe, to play. She taps a paw lightly on my boot. I wish I could oblige her, but I cannot. Sorry, June. Later, she plays with a stick at the base of the refuge tree when the bears rest.

7/13/94

Nettie and June are in an aspen seedling-sapling stand feeding on ant colonies as I approach. Nettie meanders about sniffing stumps and logs. Here and there she finds a yellow goatsbeard and eats it. But the business at hand is mostly ants, and I follow for two and a half hours of sniffing and digging of stumps and logs and feeding on ants as the quest leads us on a stroll through the stand. Then Nettie moves to an adjacent stand of hardwoods, where she nurses June at the base of a white pine, after which she rests for an hour.

7/15/94

Today marks the beginning of the bear-hound training season in the Upper Peninsula. Houndsmen with strike dogs, dogs capable of detecting the lingering scent of bear for many hours, cruise the roads in the study area with their dogs perched atop vehicles, searching for the track or scent of bears. When any is found, the hounds are loosed on the bear's trail, and the chase begins. It is practice for the hounds, and for the bears. The consequence for bears during the hunting season is drastically dif-

152

ferent from that which they are conditioned to during the training season.

Often bait is placed before the legally allowable date to attract bears to a certain spot to make it easier for houndsmen to strike, or scent, a bear. This year, I have found nine illegal baits set by houndsmen in the study area for this purpose. I don't go looking for these sites. I discover them when a bear's telemetry signal indicates that it's frequenting an atypical habitat for an inordinate length of time. For instance, if I locate a bear for two or three days in a cedar swamp instead of the uplands, where I would expect a bear to be at the height of berry ripening, I walk in to determine its situation. More often than not, the bear has locked on to a bait. Often, I am led to baits on bear walks. This year I have been shown three illegal baits by Carmen. But neither Carmen nor Nettie has visited any of these baits in the last few days, nor has either one crossed a road where she chances being struck by hounds. For now they are safe to go about the business of bears.

∽◌∾

Nettie and June are back along the banks of the stream near the spot we were at on July 2. Nettie walks a log across the stream and stands midway to scratch herself with her rear foot. She clunks to June, who lags behind. Big white spruces hug the banks of the stream, their dense overhanging branches making it too difficult to follow along under them, so I wade the stream to watch the bears as they forage for jack-in-the-pulpit along the densely vegetated bank. Leaving the stream, Nettie leads the way inland and eventually steps out into a pruned lane emanating from a deer hunting blind. A bait barrel is chained to a tree at the opposite end some forty yards away. June goes to explore the barrel. Nettie sniffs the blind, then checks on June at the bait barrel. She stands on her legs to sniff the barrel. Her body appears thin. Dropping down, she walks past me on the narrow lane at a fairly close distance—less than five feet. June hesitates to pass by me, and I back to the side of the lane, allowing additional clearance. As she passes, she blows and swats at me. I talk to her, saying, "It's OK, June," but she runs to Nettie. I guess today this is too close for her comfort for some reason. We meander from the lowlands surrounding the blind into the uplands and to a semi-open area consisting of clumps of white spruce interspersed with small openings. The bears find the femur of a deer, and both crunch on it for a while.

The opening is fresh with the beginnings of summer. Violets, daises, clover, and grasses grow here. A few strawberries grow here also, and the bears eat the first ripe berries of the season. But mostly they just lounge and groom in the shade of the spruce on the edge of the opening. Nettie walks through the area from one small opening to the next, flipping rocks to look for ants and biting off clover leaves here and there. June discovers a green cardboard canister—I recognize it as a gypsy moth trap placed by foresters to evaluate the advance of the destructive insect. She climbs up and pulls it down from where it is tacked to a tree, then begins biting it and pushing it along the ground with the top of her head. This proves to be big fun, and she becomes engrossed in it—perhaps it is the pheromone in the trap that holds her attention. She treats it like it is bearnip. This is a good day in the woods. Nettie straddle-marks a choke cherry sapling and meanders about clunking to June. June tires of the canister and plays with a columbine flower and then feeds again on strawberries. (I have noticed that while bears do eat ripe strawberries on occasion, seldom is the fruit abundant or aggregated enough to command significant interest on their part; it is often bypassed.) Nettie sits and looks about for a long while before entering a connecting stand of pole-sized aspens. Here there is more ant feeding accompanied by the now diagnostic clanking of rock slabs as Nettie flips them over to uncover the ant colonies nesting beneath. A few of the slabs prove too big for her, and I feel an impulse to help but resist. Farther into the stand, June finds another gypsy moth trap tacked to an aspen. There is more play, and this time Nettie joins in. When they are finished, I leave them resting under a white spruce near the border of the stand.

7/16/94

Quite a bit south of where I left them yesterday, Nettie meanders about a cutting that is full of stumps and overgrown with balsam and spruce saplings, ferns, and raspberry bushes—the berries are not yet ripe. She is unaware I am watching her. I stand concealed on a wooded slope above her, and for about ten minutes I watch as she walks about the cutting. June is not with her, and I scan the tree line at the edge of the cutting for a likely refuge. There is a clump of white pines that looks probable. Walking down the west slope of the cutting, I begin talking as I move toward Nettie. She acts somewhat startled at my nearness when she detects me—I hope she appreciates the fact that I am getting better at the business of being quiet. Assured it is me, she resumes digging stumps and feeds on ants where she locates them. At one point, in a clump of the balsams, she makes a big dig at the base of a stump and I cannot tell if she is digging for ants or digging a den. During a pause in the digging, she tests a few nearby blueberries—they too are unripe. But she obtains no ants and does not finish the excavation. By my assessment, she has wasted a lot of energy to no benefit that I can tell.

Leaving the cutting, she meanders to the clump of white pines clunking to June and then drops to rest beneath the largest of the pines. I can see claw marks on several of the trees in the clump. I choose a tree only a few feet from Nettie and sit with my back to it, watching as she grooms. I can hear June's tiny claws as she starts down the refuge tree, and I look above Nettie to catch her movement. I can hear her but cannot see her and presume she is on the opposite side of the pine. The sound of claws on bark continues but still no June. Then a piece of bark bounces off my head and drops down the collar of my shirt. I look up to see June looking down at me. I am sitting under the wrong tree. With Carmen I would likely never have gotten away with this, but Nettie is more tolerant of my mistakes and sits watching me as I get up and move out of the way. June continues down and scampers across to Nettie, who nurses her as I watch from only a few feet away.

When the nursing is done, the bears groom and play briefly, after which we head east into an expanse of scrub-shrub lowlands. Having been here with Nettie as a subadult, I know this to be one of the most twisted, tangled, and torturous of places to walk with bears. And it just seems to go on and on. Pole-sized cedar and here and there a few scraggly black spruce make up the overstory. The midstory is a thick layer of shrubs—speckled alder mostly, but also dogwood and willow. The area is seasonally inundated, but at the time of year the bears visit it, it is dry to mucky. The ground layer is tufts of sedge spaced too far apart to walk across but too close to easily set a boot between. And because of the clumpy way the sedges grow, I have to raise my foot eight to ten inches to get it up and over the next clump, and invariably get tangled in the roots of unseen cedar and spruce with each step. Knees tire and hips want to give out after only a few hours of high-stepping through the stand. This is the part they don't tell you about. But the bears seem to like it, and they have the advantage moving through the area. They somehow find a groove in the sedges and just stay in the track. This places the surface of the sedge clumps about nose height on the bears, and they simply swing their heads side to side and sniff out the colonies of *Lasius* and *Vespula* nested here (the elevated portion of the sedges being the only suitable nesting habitat for the insects). The bears are also able to obtain calla and the occasional buckthorn berry held within the area's widely scattered microhabitats. The bears are difficult to see among

June climbs atop Nettie's back during a break from foraging in a wet meadow, spring 1994. (Terry D. DeBruyn)

Nettie and June playing on a fallen log in northern hardwood coppice, spring 1994. (Terry D. DeBruyn)

June walks a moss-covered log in a vernal pool. (Terry D. DeBruyn)

An insistent June is played with as Nettie takes a break from digging a fallen log in a northern hardwoods, spring 1994. Throughout the spring, females with cubs continue to lose weight. By the end of spring, taxed by lack of digestible herbs and protracted nursing bouts, they become stressed and while at feeding sites may swat or blow at their cubs rather than tolerate them underfoot. (Terry D. DeBruyn)

A sated and listless June props herself against a log, fall 1994. (Terry D. DeBruyn)

June feeds on apples at my bait site, fall 1994. (Terry D. DeBruyn)

On a warm spring day, Nettie and cubs lounge in a quaking bog, spring 1996. (Terry D. DeBruyn)

Nettie's evenly matched male cubs find time to play while foraging the banks of the Whitefish River, summer 1996. (Terry D. DeBruyn)

Nettie's cubs draped over a limb of a sugar maple, summer 1996. (Terry D. DeBruyn)

Nettie's cubs in a slow descent of a sugar maple refuge tree, spring 1996. (Terry D. DeBruyn)

Nettie's male cub at base of tree, 1996. (Terry D. DeBruyn)

the sedges and royal fern, and I must stay tight to them or quickly lose them. There seems to be no rhyme or reason to the route we take through this mess. After four hours of cruising the stand, Nettie rests and then nurses June. I can only hear their activity, even though they lie just a few feet away. I record the event with the appropriate codes on the data logger by sound. The bears rest and then sleep.

June has moved so that I can see her outline and am able to watch her rib cage expand and contract with each breath. She takes eighty-eight breaths a minute. Nettie sits up on her haunches and sniffs a lot, then lies back down. The wind is picking up, and a yellow-rumped warbler flits by with some-thing in its beak. I can hear a white-throated sparrow singing. An hour later, the bears still at rest, I decide to leave them. I strike out on a compass heading, as there is no skyline or ter-rain feature visible to reckon by. I miss my mark by a long shot and know it for certain when I approach the shore of a lake that is about one and a half miles south of my intended landfall. It takes an additional forty-five minutes of solid walking to reach the Jeep.

7/18/94

Today I drive the pie-plate road at first light and find the red pickup truck of some bear houndsman idling, door ajar, while he checks the illegal bait beyond the gate at the cabin road. Car-men has not visited the bait in the last few days that I am aware of, and I presume hounds will be of no concern today. I locate her in a clear-cut well north of the bait site feeding on ants. A sibilant cloud of blackflies descends. They are thick and biting as Carmen moves from stump to stump. I am not disappointed when she leads the way toward the Whitefish River; it is cooler along the shore under the cedars, and there are fewer flies. She walks a fallen log out into the river, then plunges off the end. Landing on her feet, she walks a rocky ledge across to the op-posite shore. I follow, and the cool water feels good, but the bottom is slippery. Carmen beats me across, and I must hurry to catch her as she moves upslope and inland. When I overtake her, she is sniffing around a bait site. A barrel is tied to a tree fifteen yards away, and a raised platform protrudes from an aspen twenty feet above—a perfect spot for killing. But this setup is for deer. Carmen meanders down the old shoreline of the river, now thick with sapling cedars, balsams, and dogwoods. She halts to dig in the root mass of an overturned tree and feed on ants. Then she disappears into a dense clump of balsams. I lower my head and barge through after her. As my eyes adjust to the dim light, I see that she has flopped to rest dead ahead, and I nearly step on her. She blows lightly, and I backpedal to maintain a respectful distance. I sit for a spell, but I can tell by her actions that she will be here a long while, so I decide to leave and visit Nettie and June.

∽◦∾

The twosome is in the hardwoods in the vehicle-excluded area. As I approach them, I can see Nettie sitting and scratching and June foraging on a jack-in-the-pulpit. When she is finished with the scratch, Nettie jumps upon a log and walks its length, pulling back the bark as she goes. I cannot tell what she is after, but she seems intent on it—yet she does not feed on a thing that I can see. June follows her by climbing a nearby tree then scaling onto the log, which rests too high above the ground for her to jump up on. They begin to play, and June scampers up a sapling growing against the log. Nettie stands, hind legs on the log, to play with June. Nettie's weight against the sapling causes it to sway, and June falls to the ground, then climbs back up the sapling and onto the log for more play. Nettie tires of the game and jumps off the log and rests with her back to it and begins grooming. June, left alone, scales down and meanders about feeding on vegetation as I watch from my seat at the opposite end of the log. As she works her way toward me, I can see that her upper lip is becoming extended, which usually signals displeasure or concern in bears and is often a precursor to more agonistic behavior. Somewhat tentatively, June swats the ground and blows at me. I am unable to discern what, if anything, I am doing wrong, so I keep my seat and begin talking to her calmly in an effort to diffuse the situation. At this stage I am not too concerned, although I do not want her to lunge at me (the next step in the progression) at such close quarters. There may not be room or time enough to sort things out before Nettie is obliged to intervene. Nettie, aware of our situation, continues grooming. To further demonstrate her point, June stands upright on her hind legs, her front paws resting against a maple, leans around it in my direction, and blows at me. This brings Nettie to investigate, and I talk to her in a steady voice as she approaches and sniffs June. Nettie looks directly at me across the few feet separating us. I remain seated and look directly back, not believing as some do that bears interpret direct eye contact as an act of provocation. Her ears are straight up, not in the forward position of an aggressor nor laid back as if threatened. The long hairs of her pelage appear normal, allowing for the shedding taking place. Absent is the pilar erection, or raised hackles, exhibited by some carnivores—a state I have never observed in bears and believe they seldom, if ever, exhibit. No, Nettie appears only inquisitive. I detect little from my probe of her small brown eyes; they are impossible to read. I wonder what signals she is able to obtain from mine, as I sit trying to look normal. Satisfied June is in no danger, Nettie breaks our eye contact and begins meandering through the hardwoods toward a clear-cut stand of aspen. June falls in line after delivering one final huff in my direction. I follow behind her, wondering if I have just been awarded my rank in this litter.

In the aspens, Nettie and June dig at stumps and logs and feed on *Lasius*. The sedges are headed out and stand above the bears' backs as they walk through low spots in the stand. Nettie mouths the first raspberries of the season and continues walking through the aspens, across a two-track, and into a lowland conifer stand. June runs ahead and climbs a white cedar, and we all rest here for a while. The woods are quiet and still. The bears do not nurse or play. Our rest is over in ten minutes, and we are on our way east toward a stream that separates the conifers from the uplands. The bears cross the stream on a small beaver dam, and Nettie stoops to feed aggressively on a clump of emergent vegetation. It is a soggy-looking salad, and I will never know the species, as she eats them all in short order before I am able to identify them—that happens occasionally. As we meander along the upland side of the stream, Nettie stands with her front legs on a round-leaved dogwood tree and uses her considerable weight and strength to attempt pushing the tree's top down through the tightly woven midstory canopy. When that maneuver fails, she climbs up a short way and bounces on the tree at intervals along its length. It slowly descends. Continuing the take-a-step-bounce routine, she eventually forces the tree down through the surrounding branches. Next, she walks as far out on the tree as she is able, bites the stem of the tree near the top, and swings to the ground while holding on with clenched jaws. On the ground, she straddles the tree and tests its berries. None are ripe, and the tree springs upright when released. I admire her technique but question the investment of energy, given the insufficient return.

Traveling a short distance downstream, the bears settle in under a cedar tree; June climbs and Nettie rests at its base. The stream cascades past. A brown froth, formed by the turbulent mixing of the tannic acids in the water, swirls in the eddies. A hen and drake mallard drift by. It's been one of those near perfect days with the bears. They have abided my transgressions and allowed a few more glimpses into their world. I find that more often this is where I feel at home and am happiest. When

I leave the bears an hour later, I hope for them that berries will soon ripen en masse.

7/24/94

At some point, usually by early summer, cubs seem to work out an order of hierarchy within the litter. In the case of multiple cubs, there is always a dominant cub and subordinates. It always impresses me how well littermates are able to get along with one another. Occasionally, subordinate cubs are even able to get away with taking food from a dominant sibling if their approach is slow and the other cub has enough food to occupy its immediate attention. But sometimes there are fights (short lived) over food sources that do not lend themselves to sharing, such as the small entrance hole to a colony of ants. I believe this is where dominance is decided, more so than when cubs are at play. Regardless of how and when it is decided, one cub is always destined to be the runt of the litter. In Carmen's and Nettie's litters it always worked out that I was it. Being the runt was inevitable and was the way I wanted it. I never did anything to assert myself when cubs attempted interacting with me. I certainly never competed for food (eating only a handful of berries now and then when the bears were not looking) and I always gave up any treats I carried. I often wondered what the littermates thought of me, their odd, "runt" sibling. I suspected that they viewed me as an eccentric cousin of sorts: too unlike them to be a member yet always hanging out on the fringes— a wanna-be. Occasionally, cubs tried to coax me into interaction. June, being a singleton, tried hardest of all.

The pair is in a lowland conifer stand today when I make contact with them. The stand is composed of an overstory of white cedars about four to six inches in diameter. Alder shrubs predominate the midstory. The soils are organic and patchily covered by much standing water. Sphagnum covers exposed areas. The bears are feeding on wild calla and ants. June is sprawled over a log, her belly flattened against it, feeding in a nearly inverted position on calla. There is probably little need for her to be serious about foraging with Nettie's storehouse of nutrient-rich milk so available (bear's milk is nearly 25 percent fat, compared to about 4 percent for dairy cows and humans). After about an hour of ant and calla feeding, the bears exit the stand into an adjoining stand of red maples and upland conifers. This is a bigger woods—sawtimber size. Nettie sits scratching herself at the base of a white pine. I sit so as to position the top of a fallen maple between myself and the bears to give them some privacy and hopefully lessen the influence of my proximity. June approaches me as I sit only a few feet away, my back against another big white pine. Working her way through the top of the fallen tree toward me, June squirms between the branches and the needle-covered ground. I sit motionless, awaiting the outcome. Nervously, she mouths the tip of the maple branch nearest me. When she releases it, it springs forward and slaps me on the pant leg. The noise is loud and strange in the quiet woods, and June runs back to Nettie, who stands alert to pinpoint the source of the sound. Nettie approaches to the opposite side of the fallen treetop and looks directly at me as I reassure her that there is no problem—at least on my side. Satisfied there is no intrusion, she returns to rest at her white pine. Nice play, June.

After a while, Nettie and June begin to play. Following a six-minute session, Nettie begins grooming herself and then nurses June. At one point during the nursing bout, June sits upright on Nettie's belly, scratches under her chin with her rear foot, and then returns to nursing, directing her attention now to Nettie's lower mammae. Nettie, lying on her back, is nearly asleep. The bout lasts just over ten minutes, after which June licks Nettie's mouth. Nettie yawns and begins grooming herself. June approaches me through the branches again. This time as she grabs a branch, it breaks off in her mouth. She walks back to Nettie, and they begin to play. Their play is interrupted when Nettie stands to listen to the overhead calls of a loon. The way she reacts makes me think this is the first time she has heard the call; perhaps it is. I wonder what the loon's call signals to her. As she stands listening, I notice how worn her coat looks and how thin she appears. She begins to rub her side on a red maple sapling. She braces all four feet and rigorously rubs the entire length of her flank along it, then faces away from the sapling to rub her butt up and down on it. The sapling's top sways in the midstory canopy. Finished rubbing, she walks off into a surrounding stand of northern hardwoods, and I follow. June parallels our course a few yards to the side and slightly behind me. June seems to have come into her own lately. Her hindquarters now appear fully developed, and her traveling skills are on a par with other cubs for this stage of the game. As Nettie leads the way through the open forest, I can see that June, having just nursed, is feeling her oats.

∽∘∾

In litters with multiple cubs, the cubs normally play with each other after nursing bouts, burning off some of their newly acquired energy. The year before, I watched as Corduroy and Aster, who were fairly evenly matched as cubs, played for some twenty-seven minutes, in the longest uninterrupted play session between cubs I have ever witnessed. They stood on their hind feet to spar, pushing and biting and swatting one another, one cub feinting high, then going low in an effort to outmaneuver his sibling. They used small saplings to steady themselves prior to lunging, always maneuvering, always looking for some advantage. They tussled over logs and wrestled on the forest floor, neck biting and pulling on each other's ears, searching for any good hold. Periodically, one pinned the other, then released him, and the battle royal continued. It was high-energy fun. And it all happened while Carmen, only a few yards away, slept soundly.

163

తింత

But June has no siblings to play with, and while Nettie often plays with her for extended periods, Nettie seems less inclined toward play after nursing, and it just isn't the same for June.

Today, June is rambunctious. She trots past me and begins running figure eights around Nettie and me as we walk through the open hardwood forest. When completing my end of her figure eight, she cuts in close and brushes me with her rump, trying, I feel, to rouse a response. When she does likewise at Nettie's end of the figure eight, Nettie obliges her, nipping or playfully swatting at her, and off they go, bounding in play through the open forest, with me, the consummate dud, bringing up the rear. (I always refrain from entering into any activity with the bears that I feel might be construed as a social or bonding activity. Of all the bear cubs, only June has persisted in encouraging it.) The bears continue the escapade for over seventeen minutes, running through the upland forest and splashing through the fingerlike wetlands that partition the uplands. I am happy for the reprieve when they finally pause to drink from the pock left by an overturned tree in a finger wetland.

I remain with the bears for several hours, during which time they feed mostly on wetland vegetation, wild calla, and the tips of cattail, located in the finger wetlands. I leave them resting in an upland maple-conifer stand crunching unidentified bones at the base of a refuge tree. As I walk a circuitous route back to the nearest road, I wonder about Nettie and June's play. Running through the forest, they had not seemed at all concerned about what they might have run into. We ran crosswind and with the wind, and it is quite possible that the bears might have failed to detect any immediate danger and have run headlong into it. Perhaps they just felt secure where they were, or perhaps what I took for play was serious training.

7/28/94

Today I contact Carmen at first light. She is in a stand of clear-cut lowland hardwoods, now overgrown with seedling aspens and sundry shrubs. The stand is thick with balsam poplars, timothy, mustards, ferns, and berry bushes. I park the Jeep at the south end of the cutting and begin talking to her almost immediately while shuffling my gear. Her collar's signal strength indicates she is close by. Approaching her signal, I walk a track of a two-track lane that spans the cutting. I spot her standing in the two-track, a hundred yards ahead, and begin to disassemble the telemetry equipment and stuff it into my pack. When I am at a distance of about thirty yards from Carmen, there is a crash in the brush on the west side of the two-track midway between us. Both Carmen and I stand still. My immediate assessment is that the noise was made by a bedded deer, frightened by my approach. Carmen, barely acknowledging me, moves to check out the origin of the noise. Her actions indicate that I am hasty in my interpretation, and that the noise was probably made by another bear. She sniffs around the area, then stands with front legs on an aspen stump looking in the direction of the fading noise. Dropping down, she trails the animal a short distance toward the edge of the Whitefish, where she abandons her languid pursuit. We cross the river at a shallow spot, and she meanders up a hardwood slope and out into a semi-open upland. Upon entering the patchy upland area, it is easy to read the sign scattered about the small openings—one- to two-inch-diameter stems of the bushes are bent at irregular angles. The pale green undersides of their leaves are immediately eye-catching and proclaim beyond a shadow of doubt: bears and Juneberries.

In most years, Juneberries are among the first berries to ripen in abundance; this year they have made a late appearance. Carmen is quick to stand on her hind legs and reach upward toward a heavily laden branch. Pulling it down to chest level, she throws her hind leg over it in a straddling fashion and then walks the stem out toward the tip, where she licks in the aggregated fruits while steadying them with a paw. This is the typical fashion in which Carmen and Nettie feed not only on Juneberries but also on berries that grow on taller shrubs. Berries are more efficiently consumed in this manner, rather than eating them one by one while standing on hind legs. When the bears finish with a bush, it often appears beaten down.

The bushes on which Carmen feeds are on the edge of the forest opening. Several more are scattered around its periphery, and all are laden with clusters of ripe berries. As the sun rises above the tree line, the dew on Carmen's forelegs and face sparkle as she goes methodically about her task. The morning is cool and the sky clear. The rising sun warms my back as I look on. It has all the makings of a good summer day.

Systematically, for well over an hour Carmen goes about her task; she does nothing but feed on the ripe Juneberries. Then, appearing sated, she meanders back down the forested slope, recrosses the Whitefish, and rests in a lowland conifer stand about a quarter mile north of where I located her at first light. We have not been situated long when in the distance well to the south, I hear a chorus of hounds. I watch for Carmen's reaction to the noise, but she appears to have none, still resting on her stomach, her head on her forefeet. I know it is bear hounds—I can hear the long bawl of the strike dog mixed with the shorter yaps of a chop-mouthed hound—but I cannot yet determine if they are in hot pursuit or are cold trailing. In either event, they are headed our way, so I saddle up my gear in anticipation of Carmen's move. If she has visited the illegal bait to the south during the early morning hours and the hounds are cold-trailing her, there is every likelihood that she will be struck and run. The morning dew is heavy, and her scent is sure to linger for several more hours. It will just be a matter of whether the hounds can sort out the cold trail and the river crossing. All there is to do is wait, with Carmen still appearing uninterested in the situation. Should she be struck and run by this pack of hounds, it will not be the first time it happens when I am along; nor will it be the first time that we sit it out and wait as hounds pursue another bear through her home range. Six times I've run with the bears as they are chased by hounds, and as many times we sat it out together.

∽ი∾

The first two times we were chased took place in August of 1991, when Carmen was with her first litter of three cubs. In both cases, after crossing a two-track in midmorning, we were set upon later by hounds having winded the bears crossing. My participation in those chases did not last long. I was quickly outdistanced by the bears. On both occasions, the bears were feeding on berries in cutover stands adjacent to logging roads. Carmen and the cubs fled immediately in an all-out run at the first caterwauls of the hounds. Curiously, Carmen evaded the hounds in a similar manner both times. After about a quarter mile of running through lowland conifers, I could no longer stay in contact with the bears but followed Carmen's radio signal to the edge of the Whitefish. I arrived there ahead of the hounds and watched as they lost the bears' trail in the thick patches of dogwoods and fallen cedars along the shoreline, and the chases broke up. Both times Carmen and cubs fled more or less along the same route and crossed the Whitefish River at nearly the same location. And both times the bear walks ended there, for I did not want to rejoin the bears in fear that they might somehow associate the chase with me. After those early chases, the seriousness of bear hounding was driven home to me. Carmen had not treed the cubs and fled the area alone, even though there was ample opportunity to do so. No, the cubs had fled with Carmen. Should a cub be separated from her during the pursuit it could prove fatal for that cub. A cub on the ground is no match for even one good bear dog, let alone a pack. Even though this is only training for the hounds, it is serious business for the bears, and I wonder just how much of the running and playing that takes place earlier in the year serves as practice for the cubs' response.

∾o∾

But today, there will be no chase for Carmen and me. She now sits upright, and we both listen to the steady brays of the approaching hounds. As they near the spot along the shore of the Whitefish River where she trailed the bear earlier in the morning, the hounds break into the unmistakable strike chorus and head west at the point our trails diverged. It suddenly dawns on me that the bear we encountered earlier in the morning might be one of Carmen's yearling males. I quickly assemble the telemetry equipment and check both of her yearlings' frequencies. Neither is within radio distance. If it is Corduroy or Aster, he has a good head start. After the hounds' cries fade out in the west, Carmen moves north through the lowland conifers for about a half mile and then crosses the Whitefish River at a favorite spot. We rest along the river's west shore in a stand of white cedars. There is no more Juneberry feeding this day, and there are no more cries of hounds, either.

∾o∾

The last time I was with the bears when they were run by hounds was the last time by choice, as events that occurred during that chase dissuaded me from accompanying the bears on later chases. On that occasion I had joined Carmen and her third litter early in the morning just after first light. She was in the northeast part of her range in a stand of aspen sawtimber. Her two cubs were up a huge aspen, each draped over its own limb, resting, with Carmen sitting at the base as I approached. It was only a few days after the start of hound training and the first weekend of the season. I was aware that there was an illegal bait close by. I had discovered it the weekend before. Carmen was listless this morning, and the handwriting was on the wall when the first dog bellowed near the bait site. She just sat and listened. I quickly connected her distended belly and indolent demeanor with the bait. At first, the chase sounded disorganized to me, as though the dogs were having a tough time of it, and I suspected that several dogs in the pack lacked experience. Slowly, the pack headed our way, and it became apparent to me that Carmen would be struck and run, if in fact she would run. I thought she might just climb the tree with the cubs and await the outcome. (I couldn't decide whether it would be best for me to leave them now or remain. I did not want to be on the ground with the hounds and have the bears associate me as one of the pursuing party. Likewise, I was uncertain what would happen if I climbed a nearby tree and remained with the bears.) Carmen made up my mind for me when she clunked and tongue-clicked to the cubs, which immediately brought them down the tree. They milled around the base of the tree as Carmen sat looking in the direction of the oncoming hounds. I had been thinking all along that it was none too soon for the bears to take off. Anytime now, Carmen. My guess at this point was that the pack of hounds was less than 200 yards from us. Apparently, Carmen wanted to be dead certain that they were on her trail. Now, with the hounds less than 150 yards away and closing fast, certain or not, she led the cubs off at a slow trot. As we moved south, we hit an area of overturned stumps and sedges at the south edge of the big aspens, where they blended into a clear-cut. A cub was waylaid by an overturned root mass, and Carmen stood on her hind legs on a stump in the cutting and clunked to the cub. When it emerged from the sedges, we all ran off across the open cutting. On the far side was a stream that ran south along the base of a hardwood ridge, and I thought we would cross it and head for the uplands, but Carmen turned us south along the east side of the creek, where we ran through the tangles and across several small mucky feeder streams. All I could think of was what a perfect scent trail we were leaving in the sedges and wet soils. I could hear the hounds behind as Carmen ran ahead with the cubs, slowly outdistancing me. The bears ran from tree to tree, stopping every so often to look back and listen to the hounds. I doubted they would be put off the chase now. The cubs went partway up a tree as if to determine whether it was the one Carmen wanted them in. When Carmen ran on, they scaled down helter-skelter and rejoined the route. We entered some lowland hardwoods, and the cubs were now keeping up fairly well with Carmen, but I could tell she was slowing for them. I was slowly falling further behind, and the hounds were closing in. I tried to cinch down my pack and while doing so took my eyes off the ground—this caused me to stagger-step in the muck along a feeder stream. Carmen halted, and the cubs instinctively went partway up a small red maple (any port in a storm). Then Carmen took a few steps back in my direction and clunked her jaws—to me. It was the "Come-on, I'm here" sound I had heard her deliver so many times to errant cubs, and I now knew it was me she thought was holding up the works. Not having a clue as to how to communicate "Go on without me" in bear language, I just stood there, hoping she would get the message. We all got a break when the pack reached the first refuge tree. Apparently, there was so much fresh bear scent up and down trees in the vicinity, and all mixed with mine, that it took a considerable amount of time for the hounds to untangle the trail. In the meantime, Carmen and her cubs—less a researcher—put considerable distance between themselves and the pack.

I stood along the stream for the better part of an hour waiting for dogs to appear on the trail, but they never came. While they were in turmoil at the refuge tree, someone blew recheat (on a car horn), and the dogs were gathered up. After that day, I never took flight with the bears again, not wanting to burden them with my lack of skill at running the woods. What was of scientific interest to me was a life-and-death matter for them. It was a strange feeling for me walking out of the forest that day. I felt more than ever a part of it but also realized what a great detriment I could be to the bears.

༄༅

I should say here that I am not against the *sport* of hounding. During the years I studied these bears, bear hunters cooperated with the study and showed consideration for study animals. It is likely that many of the research bears lived longer because they were deliberately passed up by hunters. However, I am equally obligated to say (and it would be cowardly to do otherwise) that hound training is allowed to begin much too early in the year. It occurs at a time when female bears are strapped with cubs that are not fully developed, in my opinion, to withstand the rigors of an all-out pursuit by a pack of hounds. It takes place when it is simply too hot for bears to be chased, and bears, particularly females with cubs, are on occasion deprived of their first decent opportunity to forage on ripening berries. The early and protracted training season is a tremendous impediment to bears' foraging efforts. It would do no harm to postpone the chasing of bears until the first week of August, thus giving the bears a couple more weeks to fatten unimpeded and affording their cubs further opportunity for development before being harassed by hounds. I have never chased bears with dogs, but I have been with bears when they were chased by dogs, and I considered it a hot, sweaty, and ornery business. If one considers it from the bears' perspective, they are pursued for nearly their entire "food year"—from before the time of first berry ripening, right up to and past the time of denning. I can think of no other game animal in Michigan for which this is true, and I am disappointed with the managers who cave in to the demands of those few who insist on seasons of such excessive length.

8/5/94

Carmen is again along the banks of the Whitefish River when I come upon her today. It is nearly two o'clock when I locate her signal and an hour later when I finally catch up to her. I considered not going to her this late in the day, but I am rewarded when I see her. The scene is as pretty as it gets. Several big white birches grow along the river shore, a beaver dam crosses the entire width of the river in the upstream background, and I can hear water tumbling through its openings. Beneath the white birch grows a continuous stretch of alder-leaved buckthorn bushes laden with ripe berries. The ink-blue berries sparkle in the western sunlight as it bounces off the riffling waters of the Whitefish. Carmen rises on her hind legs at my approach. I am forced to stop and etch the scene into memory. She holds the pose a few seconds, just long enough, then twists her body toward me and drops to walk in my direction. I quickly display outstretched palms and criss-cross my arms in the familiar "I don't have any treats today" pattern. With a slight huff and a temperamental about-face, she resumes feeding on the buck-thorn berries. I wonder aloud as to my worth to her, and why she continues to tolerate my company. There is no real reason or answer for it. I am simply fortunate that she does. This afternoon, it is all berry feeding as Carmen inhales the ripe fruits. I am always impressed at how much the bears use their loose, nimble lips and longish tongue when foraging on berries. Seldom do they bite or pull at them. When it comes to eating, the word "dainty" best describes bears, an observation first made by my wife, Annette, on an early bear walk in 1992 as Carmen foraged leisurely on herbs in a hardwood forest. Initially, I had some preconceived notions about the voracity with which bears

172

might feed. I envisioned headlong charges into food patches, the bears swinging their heads side to side, gulping in food, smacking their lips, toppling most everything in their path until all that was edible was devoured. Nothing could be further from the truth.

Here and there Carmen gets a dogwood or gooseberry, but for the most part, she consumes buckthorn. An hour later she meanders out of the berries and into a stand of lowland conifer, where she rests for over four hours. During the rest, I recall that it was just a year ago, about this same date, that I had been with Carmen and her cubs Corduroy and Aster near this very spot on the Whitefish River as they fed on buckthorn and dogwood berries. That day, I was accompanied by Dr. Rolf Peterson, renowned wolf researcher and my doctoral advisor. We followed as Carmen led the way across the Whitefish and up into the northwest corner of her home range. Along the way, she rousted a beaver out of its lodge along the banks of a small stream. As Rolf and I stood perched on a fallen log above the stream, the beaver swam beneath us, and we could clearly see scars along its back. We wondered if the beaver was a veteran of other close encounters with bears. Carmen chased the beaver downstream for about a hundred yards before giving up and returning to the cubs. Other than white-tailed deer fawns, that beaver was the only mammal that I witnessed her actively pursuing as prey. As I sit recalling the events of that day, I consider several times leaving Carmen here, but for some reason, I am determined to stick it out until dark.

When accompanied by cubs, the bears usually locate a suitable refuge tree just before nightfall and rest there until just before or after dawn. When alone, Carmen seems nonselective about her evening resting spots. She will rest for the night just about anywhere, including clumps of conifers in clear-cuts, thick stands of balsam firs, open hardwoods, and lowland conifers. After the first year of walking with the bears, I rarely tried following them, whether single or accompanied by offspring, as evening fell. It was just too difficult. The forest becomes dark earlier than the fields, and it is easy to bang a shin on an unseen log or get a stick in the eye. The bears seem edgy, too, mostly because of the difficulty I have keeping up with them and the consequent noise. Besides, for the most part, bears are not active much after dark, except later in the fall, when the increased human activity in the forest forces them to become progressively nocturnal. Often, I locate them at morning's first light exactly, or very near the spot, where I left them the evening before.

When Carmen arises, she meanders into a stand of balsam poplar seedlings. Where she finds them, she again feeds on alder-leaved buckthorn berries in addition to a single yellow goatsbeard. Entering a stand of lowland conifers, she feeds on more buckthorn berries, pausing once to drink. Initially, I am hesitant to follow her into the conifers, as I can no longer clearly distinguish her outline unless I am within a few feet of her. But as we meander into the conifers, the canopy opens and I can see her more clearly. Here, she concentrates her feeding activity on ants that she digs from woody material beneath the sphagnum-covered forest floor. When she meanders onto an old railroad grade running through the lowland conifer stand, I know it would be pushing my luck to follow. She nips at some buckthorn berries and then sits scratching behind her ear. Moving down the grade, she pauses to eat the tips of some cattail fronds, sits and scratches again, then resumes her northward heading. I stand talking to her, saying good-bye as she blends into the darkness. The old familiar chill runs up my spine as I turn and walk away.

8/6/94

Nettie is feeding on swamp thistles as I approach her and June in a lowland conifer stand. The bears have located a ripe patch of alder-leaved buckthorn berries and begin licking in the berries. After a half hour of berry feeding, Nettie moves to

174

rest under a white cedar. We stay here nearly an hour and a half before Nettie stands and walks a short way to drink. June leaves the refuge tree, and Nettie nurses her, then stands briskly and returns to berry feeding. Here and there the bears forage on wild calla or jewelweed, but for the next three hours they concentrate mainly on buckthorn berries.

8/9/94

Today it is bankers' hours for me. I locate Carmen at 9:00 A.M. in a clear-cut aspen stand feeding on berries and follow her until 5:30 P.M., leaving her near our beginning point. We traverse only five habitats including a clear-cut stand of softwoods that she just meanders through; a pole-sized red maple stand where she sniffs stumps and objects but does not feed; a poplar seedling-sapling stand where she feeds on cattails, drinks water, and feeds on buckthorn berries and raspberries; a lowland conifer sawtimber stand where she sniffs stumps and the ground looking for ants, feeds on swamp thistles, flushes a vesper sparrow from its nest and eats its eggs, drinks, feeds on raspberries, wild calla, and hazelnuts. Finally, she returns to the clear-cut softwoods where I originally came upon her, and I now leave her as she walks a two-track to the south.

8/10/94

When I approach Nettie and June this day, June is resting up a hemlock while Nettie rests at its base. A chickadee scolds my coming. June is getting big. Sprawled out on the trunk of the hemlock as she descends, she looks impossibly large for a six-month-old cub. She begins sniffing ferns at the bottom of the tree while Nettie sniffs her. Nettie clunks her jaws, and off we go. At 9:00 A.M. they enter an emergent wetland within the boundaries of a lowland conifer stand and begin feeding on cattail, calla, and jewelweed. June, all on her own, discovers and digs out a colony of *Lasius*. Nettie walks up a leaning spruce, where an insistent June is allowed to nurse. After nursing, June begins to scamper in and out of the branches of the leaning tree. Nettie descends and returns to feeding on cattails and vegetation. June climbs a split-trunk white cedar, against which the leaner rests. A white-crowned sparrow scolds a hard *chink* from a nearby balsam spire. That gets a jay going, and it sounds as if the whole avian community is aware of our presence. Nettie joins June up the cedar, and they play, after which Nettie rests on her back cradled by the limbs of the cedar and yawns as the sparrow continues its scolding. She rests in a nearly upside-down position for about ten minutes, then descends while June sleeps. On the ground, she begins foraging on impatiens, the tips of cattail, and wild calla at an ever increasing distance from the refuge tree.

Leaving the scolding birds behind, Nettie and I move quietly through the stand except for the splash of paw or boot in an occasional pool of open water. Less frequently, but more of a giveaway, the broken branch of a dead spruce or alder sounds. Bears are expert walkers of fallen logs and timber, and Nettie displays her skill. The space created by recently fallen timber is less restricting and allows the bears to navigate virtually noiselessly over the logs. While I believe that in many cases bears use logs as the path of least resistance, there are times when log walking offers a certain vantage point. I also believe that bears may walk fallen timber to avoid heat loss through the pads of their feet when traversing lowland habitats, especially in early spring when they do it more often. As she ranges wider in her foraging effort, Nettie habitually clunks to stay in contact with June. Eventually, we move out of sight of the refuge tree. After some thirty minutes of foraging on vegetation and the occasional ant colony, Nettie works her way back toward the refuge tree.

Looking around indifferently, Nettie sits at the base of the refuge tree and scratches her ear with her hind foot. Then she umphs and tongue-clicks to June and climbs the cedar to join her. But June is missing. Nettie descends the tree and begins a thorough scenting of nearby trees in an effort to locate her. It is not unusual for Carmen or Nettie to range a few hundred yards from the cub's refuge tree while foraging. It is unusual, however, for a sleeping cub to disappear from a refuge tree. I scan the canopy, thinking that Nettie may have overlooked a slumbering June. My inspection reveals no cub.

As a cub, Nettie was never separated from Carmen during our walks. Although her brother the Runt went missing on numerous occasions. Once, upon making initial contact with Carmen, I noticed immediately that a cub was missing. Carmen, with only two cubs, was searching from tree to tree. After sniffing the base of each tree, she stood on her hind feet while encircling the tree with her front legs and moved around it sniffing and clunking, often looking skyward. After nearly two hours of nonstop searching in this manner, we simultaneously heard the Runt bawling above a fifteen-mile-per-hour wind. Carmen quickly trotted toward his vocalizations, and the family regrouped at the base of his refuge tree.

It's a hard thing for a female bear to keep the family together while ranging through the woods. Imagine trying to corral and steer three or four cubs, each with a mind of its own, through the maze of a forest floor. It is a tough task to pull off. Cubs want to stick their noses into every nook and cranny and frequently go their own way to do so. They often dally behind as the family moves off, becoming strung out behind the females, sometimes fifty yards or more. Cubs lost or separated from their mothers provide a golden opportunity for predators such as bobcats, coyotes, wolves, and other bears to prey on, a fate that likely claimed the life of the largest cub, a male, in Carmen's third litter.

∽o∾

John Hendrickson, Upper Peninsula regional biologist for the Michigan Department of Natural Resources, and I had accompanied Carmen and her three cubs (Bows, Bigley, and Buttons) for approximately six hours. During the walk she flushed a fawn, but it got out ahead of her. She trailed it about twenty-five yards after intersecting the path where it had fled its bed. Soon the male cub flushed another fawn that went unobserved by Carmen; the cub followed about ten yards before abandoning the pursuit. Later, while we meandered through a stand of lowland brush between the upper branches of the Whitefish River, John and I witnessed Carmen kill a fawn after she encountered the birth site of a doe.

Upon finding the birth site, Carmen and her cubs sniffed and licked it for five or ten minutes. Carmen then meandered through the stand apparently "searching" for the fawn—returning to the birth site on several occasions, then meandering away from it again. This was the only time in the six years of walking with bears that I observed Carmen or Nettie behaving in a manner that could be considered actively searching for a fawn, and I attribute it to the freshness of the birth site. After approximately twenty minutes, we heard the bleats of a fawn, and Carmen carried it in her jaws to a clump of white cedar trees, where she and the cubs fed on it until we left the area two hours later.

When I returned to the site the next morning at daylight, I found Carmen desperately searching from tree to tree accompanied by only the two female cubs. The third, the big male, was missing. For the remainder of the morning, Carmen searched for the lost cub but never found him, nor did he ever rejoin her. Eventually, while moving along the shores of the Whitefish River in a patch of buckthorn, she lost interest in the search and began foraging on berries. Carmen and the two cubs then lounged in the river, and the cubs began a game of *bite-the-fur-on-your-sister's-back-and-let-her-tow-you-while-she-swims*. Then all three swam the river and thereafter never appeared to consider further the loss of the cub. I spent that afternoon looking around the fawn-kill site, trying to piece together the puzzle of the cub's disappearance. I found sizable bear tracks in the mud but was unable to tell if they were Carmen's or another bear's. There was no evidence of the cause of the cub's disappearance. It is my guess that the cub got up to feed on the fawn carcass on his own while Carmen rested at the refuge tree. This would not have been unusual. Carmen often slept intermittently several yards away as the cubs lounged or played near a kill site. It is quite possible that another predator, attracted to the site by the scent of blood or the bleats of the fawn, encountered the unprotected cub, killed it, and carried it away. That male cub was the only one out of eight cubs in three litters that Carmen did not raise to dispersal age.

~o~

Nettie's approach to the situation is measured; she has not begun the frantic loping and *umphing* I watched Carmen use when searching for her lost cubs. Methodically, Nettie moves from tree to tree, tracking the missing cub by its scent. We both receive a start when the wind plays a trick with a catbird call, making it sound just enough like the lost call of a distant cub to momentarily fool us.

Nettie searches in the same general direction that she foraged earlier. As we zigzag our way back and forth, I notice spots where she previously dug for ants. Then, above the wind, I hear the unmistakable bawling of a cub. I stand still until Nettie determines the direction of the alarm call and begins trotting toward it, tongue-clicking and clunking as she goes. I am unable to keep up and lose sight of her after a short distance, but I can hear her breaking brush and follow the noise trail.

When I arrive, I witness an especially affectionate greeting (licking and nuzzling) at the base of a small spruce. I surmise that June awoke to find Nettie gone, descended the refuge tree, and attempted to follow Nettie's forage-meander route. She had likely been gone only a short while when Nettie and I returned from the opposite direction.

June immediately attempts to nurse, and Nettie walks off a short distance to a thicket of sapling balsam firs and abruptly flops on her back in a small depression, where June nurses fervently. Nettie's movement is so unannounced that I am left standing barely ten feet away. I carefully unzip my fanny pack, withdraw the camcorder, and begin to video the nursing bout. I am hopeful that at this close distance, I will be able to capture the elusive "feeding chuckle" of the cub, a sound that previously has not recorded well. The vocalizations last about five minutes and then stop abruptly. June appears quite still in the viewfinder. I keep the camera in position in front of my face and peek around for a better look. Remarkably, June has fallen asleep with Nettie's mammae still in her mouth. It is as tender and touching a reunion as I have ever witnessed. Here is a place where lost cubs are safe and sound. Feeling almost a voyeur, I withdraw slowly. As I do so, June stirs slightly, her head slipping to the side. Nettie moves to cradle her with a forearm. "See ya, Nettie. Bye, June. Thanks."

8/11/94

Every bear walk is unique and memorable in all aspects. Yet every year, there is one walk that distinguishes itself from the rest. Today's walk is the year's standout for Nettie and June—not because it is the longest walk of the year, but because a lot of things come together during the walk, things that depend on having previously surmounted obstacles, on a display of tolerance and trust on the part of the bears, and on overcoming personal proclivities (sticking with it).

Shortly after 8:00 A.M. I hook up with the bears along the ecotone of a northern hardwood stand and an aspen seedling-sapling stand. I think the bears moved into the hardwoods at the sounds of my approach in order to be near a refuge tree. June is partway up, and Nettie stands below a hemlock; they are both watching me. June climbs down, and Nettie mills around and, finding a slow-to-develop sweet cicely, eats it. She urinates and then Carmen-dances. She clunks to June, and they move into the aspens and begin feeding on raspberries. They meander the ecotone for over an hour feeding on raspberries. I am wet to the waist from morning dew when we exit the stand onto an abandoned two-track. The bears forage their way south along the road, feeding on raspberries. I have traveled this way before with bears. There is an opening at the end of the road, an old log-decking area overgrown with grasses. Nettie stands to pull down the branches of a Juneberry bush, and with June's help she polishes off the berries in just under two minutes. She marks territory as we exit the opening. I have difficulty punching in the code, as instead of an arched-back rub standing on hind legs, she sits at the base of the mark tree and wiggles up and down, pressing her back against it. This is the first and last time I see this maneuver. We meander into an aspen seedling-sapling stand for more raspberry feeding, which lasts a little longer than fifteen minutes. Exiting the stand down a south-facing hardwood slope, we cross a two-track and move into a lowland conifer stand. Nettie feeds on swamp thistles, then drinks before Carmen-dancing and urinating.

As we meander south, the stand composition changes enough for me to code in white cedar and black spruce as the dominant overstory component. In the stand, there is more feeding on swamp thistle, and Nettie meanders to find a *Lasius* colony in downed woody material. She feeds on the pupae for a couple of minutes, then spends the remainder of her time in the stand sniffing stumps and the ground, but there is no more ant feeding here. Twenty-eight minutes after entering the stand, we exit into a stand of aspen sawtimber mixed with lowland conifers. There are hazelnuts here, and Nettie tests several before consuming them but never really settles in to feed. I wonder if they are unripe and grab a few for testing as I pass by. Nettie meanders, then stops to clunk to June, who is lagging behind fiddling with the hazelnuts. Nettie sits scratching as June plays catch up, but she is further delayed when June stops en route to bite at the flowers of a purple knapweed. When June arrives, mother and daughter play for a minute, then move on. The bears eat a few mouthfuls of jewelweed and test some more hazels—little feeding activity really for the forty-six minutes we spend in the stand. We cross a stream into a lowland conifer stand with many big cedar and white pines. Both bears drink from the stream and feed on impatiens near its shore. This stand provides more yield for the bears, and they feed on gooseberry, buckthorn berries, and raspberries and settle in for more than ten minutes of hazelnut crunching.

The hazelnut bushes in this stand are bigger than others we have encountered, and Nettie demonstrates a good technique for drawing the stems within reach. She climbs a pole-sized ash tree until she reaches a point above where the hazelnut branch crosses it. She then lowers herself onto the branch and rides it to the ground. As it turns out, there is only one nut on the branch. Luckily, other branches prove more worthwhile. Consuming hazelnuts is a tricky operation, but bears are skillful at it. Hazelnuts are sheathed in a long bristly covering (involucre) that is not only prickly to the tongue but also tart and bitter. Inside this coating, the edible nut is encased in a hard shell that must be cracked and the meat inside separated from it before being swallowed. Bears get at the meats by first putting the entire fruit in their mouth and then squeezing the nuts out of the sheath, catching them on the backs of their paws. They spit out the bitter prickly sheath using tongue and lip action, then retrieve the nut, position it between the molars, and crush it. The shell is shucked out the side of the mouth, again using tongue and lip action. The whole operation may take a bear fifteen or twenty seconds per nut. It always seemed to me to be a lot of effort for a miserly return. But the bears seemed to extract the nuts with relative impunity, and it must be worth it for them. They fatten readily on hazelnuts when they are available, and some bears travel great distances to get them.

Nettie and June remain in the stand for forty-two minutes,

then meander into a lowland conifer stand with more of a white birch and red maple component. Here, two stumps are dug but no ants found. At noon, we exit into a stand of pole-sized aspens. We meander until the canopy turns to an aspen–red maple mix, and we walk upon an old railroad grade into a cedar stand, where Nettie digs and feeds on a colony of *Lasius.* I drop a small transmitter and collect a sample of the ants and pupae. We move into another aspen–red maple stand, where the bears stop to play for a few minutes. June climbs an ironwood, and Nettie stands and bats at her in a game of escape and evasion. They run off in play, halting once to feed on round-leaved dogwood berries before we enter a stand of lowland conifers mixed with white birch and aspen. Some trees are more than two feet in diameter. Nettie and June dig and feed on more ants, and I drop another transmitter. Meandering, Nettie brings us to a beaver flooding, which we cross on the dam. The bears stop to feed on jewelweed and also on buckthorn berries at the edge of the dam. I stand off to the side of the dam on a log submerged in a few inches of flowing water to allow enough room for June to get past me without feeling threatened. She looks good. She has developed the side-to-side swagger of a confident bear. Nettie is doing her job, and the day could not be finer. June turns my way as she walks confidently past, then returns and walks out onto the log on which I stand. I talk softly to her, and she comes out on the log just far enough to place her nose right on the toe of my boot, then turns and walks to Nettie. I fall in behind.

Off the dam, Nettie meanders, then sits alert for nearly two minutes. I have no clue as to what she senses, but apparently satisfied, she resumes the walk, maneuvering through the stand and sniffing the ground. The bears play briefly, and we make our way to a familiar semi-open aspen stand. In one of the openings Nettie climbs an apple tree and feeds on a few green apples. While in the tree, she inadvertently prunes a few limbs and shakes some apples loose. June feeds on the fallen apples below. When Nettie comes down, June goes up, and Nettie feeds on fallen apples. Nettie walks the periphery of the opening, straddle-marks a balsam fir sapling, and then walks to the middle of the opening to feed on clovers and flip rocks for ants. She clunks to June, who descends the apple tree, and we move off into a lowland conifer stand, where the bears wade into a stream to drink and feed on jewelweed. We maneuver back to the aspen uplands, where Nettie uncovers an ant colony; both bears lick feverishly as the colony rushes about trying to carry pupae to safety. As the bears move off, I drop another transmitter. I can hear rocks flipping up ahead, but the bears get no more ants, and they meander toward the surrounding aspen–lowland conifer stand. Nettie stops to arched-back rub a balsam fir with a busted-off top—the same tree I have witnessed Carmen mark several times in the past. While Nettie takes care of marking, June moves catlike along the length of a fallen aspen. I see the object of her quest: the patterned shroud of a snake. I fumble for my camera but find I have shot the last of the color slides and must settle for black-and-white photos. June pauses a half-body length from the skin and, almost as if on point, sniffs, then reaches out and gives the shroud a tentative pawing. When it does not respond, she closes the gap and begins eating the skin. It makes a crunchy sound as she gulps down the dried remains. I think of it as her potato chips or pork rind. Finished marking, Nettie meanders into the surrounding aspen stand, where she sits to groom. June finishes with the snake skin and goes up a close-by refuge tree. She wants to rest, but Nettie climbs up after her and coaxes her down by tugging on her ear (this works better than I would have anticipated), and we resume the walk.

The next twenty minutes are spent feeding on buckthorn berries and a few hazelnuts. June attempts to nurse as Nettie lies cracking a hazelnut, but Nettie breaks it off after only a few seconds and is up flipping rocks again. She uncovers three colonies in the next five minutes (I am out of transmitters to drop). Both bears feed. From here we meander into an old river bottom, and in its rich soil the bears locate a few jack-in-the-pulpits, which they polish off in short order. Walking about the stand, Nettie pauses to sniff a game trail, which we walk into a mixed stand of red maples and aspens. The bears maneuver about the stand flipping rocks, rolling logs, and feeding on raspberries and buckthorn berries. Nettie stands on her hind legs to dig at a big knot on the side of a white birch. The tree is about three feet in diameter and the knot is about four feet off the ground. June joins Nettie and proves to be of help, as she crawls in and excavates the cavity. It is a squirrel midden, and the bears sort through the find of cones and nuts, then move to a stream and take long drinks. Refreshed, they begin to run and chase each other for a couple of minutes until we come to another beaver dam. Nettie and June move out onto the beaver's lodge and begin to explore it. June bites at the hewn end of a beaver-worked log; she looks as if she would make a good beaver. She stops her chewing long enough to Carmen-dance on a flat, muddy spot atop the lodge. I am impressed with her form. Nettie leads the way around the flooding as they sniff the beaver's runs and investigate recent activity.

We follow a run into the surrounding lowland conifers, where the bears feed on jewelweed and then play. Nettie walks to a clump of four white cedars and flops beneath them. June moves in to nurse. Nettie allows a seven-minute bout. The bears rest recumbently for forty-two minutes; then there is another nursing bout, which lasts slightly longer than the first. I cannot help but think how good June has it as she climbs one of the cedars to rest. It seems that we will be here awhile, so I start punching out of the data logger to save on batteries. I am on my second of the day, and only one remains. I have been with the bears just less than ten hours, and this is the first time we have stopped to rest. Whoever says that bears are lazy feeders would change their tune if they spent even a part of a day in the woods walking with a bear. Nettie is not of a mind to stay here long, after all, and an hour after she first nursed June, she stands and yawns and then walks off as June hustles down the cedar to join her. I thought surely June would be sound asleep and unwilling to resume, but not so. We meander to a red maple stand, where the bears feed once more on beaked hazels. For the next hour they course through the maple lowlands feeding on hazels and buckthorn berries, stopping once to dig out a colony of *Lasius*. We work our way back above the beaver dam and into a beaver meadow, where they feed on cattails and the shoots of a similar plant that I am unable to identify or collect. We are here until the sun sinks below the horizon and shadows close in on the scene. As Nettie and June make their way onto the dam and head west along it, I let them finish the day on their own, glad to have shared it with them and feeling privileged to be allowed. It is 7:47 P.M. A real day in the bear woods.

8/12/94

Carmen is feeding on ants in a lowland conifer stand today. She pauses, standing on her hind legs with one front leg stiff against the stump, the other poised in midair, as I approach, then resumes digging. The colony is mixed with much debris, and when she is finished feeding, she goes immediately to drink from a shallow pool of water. She stands in the pool, then sits and splashes around, and then lies down. It is only 9:30 A.M., but the temperature is already near 75°F and warm for the north country. After a rest in the pool, Carmen goes to the edge of a nearby stream, where she rests under a white cedar for nearly three hours. Then she stands to drink and lies back down to groom. She again stands and then walks to the stream to drink for a whopping thirty-six seconds. Carmen quenched, we meander into a northern hardwood–sawtimber stand, and she begins feeding on raspberries in the more open canopied areas of the tall timber. She alternates between feeding on ants and raspberries, and I drop a small transmitter at one of the ant feeding sites. At spots in the hardwoods, Carmen sniffs the ground under black cherry trees (I presume for fallen cherries), but none that are ripe have fallen yet. Four times she straddle-marks small deciduous saplings, and she pauses twice to rub—once on a maple sapling, then on a cherry tree. Along the edge of an overgrown, abandoned two-track, she investigates the earthen root masses piled there and sniffs the site of the first den I ever found her in—the one where Nettie was born. She straddle-marks a small beech sapling, then dances while urinating. This is her domain. She returns to raspberry feeding, and after more than forty-five minutes of it, I leave her to her business.

8/14/94

The sun is just up, big and red, and the sky is clear as I join the duo this morning in an ephemeral wetland amid a stand of hardwood sawtimber. Nettie has a bit of twisted stalk hanging from her mouth when I see her. I tell her she looks like a movie star—it does little to improve my standing. A few raspberries hang over the edge of the wetland, and Nettie eats them as she walks by, still in the wetland. Interesting. How do I code this? If I say she is in a wetland eating raspberries, someone is sure to remind me that raspberries are an upland food type and question my accuracy. I code it just like it is. The truth is always best. I turn to look for June and see that she has discovered a huge hollow log and is running in and out of it in what appears to be a solo game of hide-and-seek. Nettie finds a newly fallen maple, climbs atop it, and walks it out into the wetland. June joins her, and they play briefly. Meandering out of the wetland, they move into the hardwoods and begin feeding on raspberries and a few remnant sweet cicely plants that because of their location in the shade of a log are just now making growth. Nettie nips them off quickly and makes her way toward a clear-cut stand of aspens, where she continues to feed on ripe raspberries that seem now to be nearly everywhere.

In the middle of the cutting there grows a large sugar maple, greater than two feet in diameter at breast height. Limbless for nearly thirty feet up its trunk, it grows in a sweeping arch, then levels off nearly horizontal to the ground. At a point where a limb has broken off is a level spot that is easily big enough to accommodate a sleepy bear cub. June scales the maple and finds it. We have been here before, but never have I witnessed June or Nettie use the tree. It proves a good spot, and June sleeps while Nettie forages underneath on raspberries and vegetation. The berry feeding lasts nearly two hours. All the while, June sleeps above. By noon, I hear rumblings to the southwest; a front is rolling in, and it begins to sprinkle. I film the sleeping cub and also Nettie as she forages about but must stow all my gear when the rain becomes intense. The woods are gray and still from my vantage point as I sit huddled along the edge of the cutting under a maple canopy of my own and watch as Nettie climbs the arched maple and tries to roust June by the ear from her place of slumber. Her first attempt is unsuccessful; June is belligerent. Nettie descends and sits outwardly patient in the rain at the base of the maple. A quarter hour later, she climbs again, and this time encourages June to follow. The bears cross a two-track and move out of sight into the lowland conifers as I head for the Jeep in a pouring rain.

Fall

Bears are made of the same dust as we, and breathe the same winds
and drink of the same waters. A bear's days are warmed by the same sun,
his dwellings are overdomed by the same blue sky, and his life turns and
ebbs with heart-pulsings like ours, and was poured from the same First
Fountain. And whether he at last goes to our stingy heaven or no,
he has terrestrial immortality. His life not long, not short,
knows no beginning, no ending. To him life unstinted,
unplanned, is above the accidents of time,
and his years, markless and
boundless, equal Eternity.
—John Muir (1871)

I have not spent much time watching any bear unless he was
in a place where I could not get at him, or else was so close
at hand that I was not afraid of his getting away.
—Theodore Roosevelt
"American Bears"

189

8/15/94

Nettie and June are at a favorite stand of hardwood timber in the core of their home range. They are feeding on raspberries along an ecotone of hardwoods and sapling aspens. Nettie pauses now and then to sniff objects, but the business at hand is berry feeding. Both bears look to be in excellent condition. Their coats are shiny black and thick, and their bellies are becoming noticeably distended, especially June's. They have not yet developed the longer guard hairs of a fall coat, but that will happen in the next few weeks. Nettie strays into the hardwoods, and upon locating a solitary jack-in-the-pulpit, she first eats all its above-ground parts, then digs and eats the corm. We walk on, until the hardwoods blend into an ephemeral wetland. The wetland is desiccated, and sedges stand tall where water once lay in early spring. This is the same wetland Nettie frequented on numerous occasions in May, and where Carmen smelled, for the first time, the scent of her granddaughter June. Along the edge of the parched wetland, Nettie sniffs a fallen elm that lies concealed among the chest-high sedges. When she jumps atop the elm, I see her clearly again. She walks the log, pausing to sniff it intensively every few inches. When she determines the precise spot, she begins ripping the decaying wood apart with claws and teeth. Given the position of the log, its stage of decay, and Nettie's tactics, I suspect this to be hornet feeding activity and hang back to avoid being stung.[1] In short order, Nettie opens a hole in the log the size of a soccer ball and begins furiously licking and biting it, occasionally withdrawing her partially engulfed head to shake it vigorously. I am able to confirm hornet feeding when she pulls back, shakes her head, and trots to the end of the log. The swarm lingers in the air over the ravaged hive. I walk the log to the spot and record the scene while hornets swarm and fill the air. A remnant of the paper nest is left embedded in the wood, but its contents— larvae—are gone. Along the top of the log is a clear trail of wet footprints leading away from the cavity: unequivocal bear sign. I wonder how long they will linger in the rising morning sun.

I follow as Nettie walks another log and repeats the sequence, and I'm surprised that there are this many hornet nests available. When June moves in to investigate, I back to my end of the log, giving her plenty of room to maneuver. She attacks the site with all the fervor, if not the skills and might of Nettie. We all stand within a few feet of one another on the fallen log. I am respectful of the bears' space as they maneuver and am heartened that they have sufficient trust and confidence to tolerate me at this proximity. It is quite an impressive display to see, hear, and feel a bear ripping apart a log at this close range. As the log sways and vibrates, I like to think that I am making a contribution to the effort by steadying it with my weight, but in the fervor I am paid little mind—another example of the long hours of observing proper bear etiquette paying off. Finished, Nettie shakes her head and trots to the end of the log, and with a little hop she touches ground. June dallies, checking for any unfound morsel, then walks to the end, does an about-face, and backs off the log, her sharp claws holding her as she lowers herself to the ground. I follow closely behind just so I can step in their undefiled prints. It is one of the things I like to do when walking with bears—step right in their tracks as soon as I can after they take their foot away. Looking back, I see two sets of prints on the log, man and bear. Both will evaporate in a short while. Remarkably, over the next hour, Nettie locates two more hornet nests in downed logs around the periphery of the shriveled wetland. When the bears finish, we meander from the heat of the opening into the cool of a cedar swamp. The temperature drops as we move under the thick green canopy, a fact certainly not lost on the bears as they amble ahead plowing into the cool, moist sphagnum.

Today's is an unscheduled bear walk, and I must leave

Nettie and June to find out what other study-area bears are up to. I stand watching the dented sphagnum spring back from their soft tread, and when I lift my gaze, they have vanished.

8/16/94

Carmen, feeding on raspberries in a hardwoods, comes to the sound of my voice. As I near her on an abandoned two-track, raspberries appear to be everywhere, and she stops in front of me to feed in a particularly abundant patch that has invaded a sunny opening. The arching woody canes of the raspberries form the perfect grotto. When Carmen turns toward me, a berry rests perfectly centered on the top of her head.

Bears are perfect judges of when berries are at peak ripeness, as they must be. If the berries are not hanging-ripe and ready to come loose at the slightest touch of lip or tongue, bears must pull and tug at them, fewer are taken in for unit of effort invested, and their consumption is less efficient. For the next half hour Carmen feeds steadily on ripe berries along the two-track. We are near the very spot, where in 1992, she fed for more than seven hours straight on nothing but raspberries. It was so repetitive that I walked ahead of her a few dozen yards and sat down, then when she fed past me an equal distance, I got up and leap-frogged ahead of her again, all the while coding FBRB (feed berry—raspberry) into the field computer. Seven and a half hours—FBRB, FBRB, FBRD—with only an occasional break to mark territory or explore an overturned stump. But that's what fall is all about for bears. They are now in the business of fattening for winter and go from consuming a normal 4,000–6,000 kilocalories per day to gorging down a whopping 18,000–20,000 kilocalories per day.[2] Scientists call this period hyperphagia. It essentially means "pigging-out." And today, Carmen is in full swing.

She works her way westward along the two-track into an old log-decking area. Here she feeds on choke cherries that grow around the border of the opening. We walk purposefully to the north through a hardwood stand and onto an abandoned rail-road grade running through the hardwoods. The old grade is now overgrown with pole-sized maples and various shrubs. East on the grade and just prior to entering an abandoned log-decking area, Carmen stops to arched-back rub a balsam fir. It is the same mark tree that she used the day preceding the breakup of her litter in 1992. Then it's on to an adjoining two-track for an additional half hour of raspberry feeding. A hundred yards down the lane, Carmen abruptly changes direction, heading north into the hardwoods, and enters a small natural forest opening where she digs the ground and unearths a colony of *Lasius* from beneath the duff. I drop a transmitter to mark the spot. Meandering onto a game trail, she straddle-marks two sapling conifers only seconds apart and then exits into the surrounding lowland conifers, where she sniffs stumps and the root masses of windblown trees. She digs a stump and feeds on ant pupae. They look to be *Camponotus,* and here I drop another transmitter as I move past the site.

We meander on and off an old railroad grade, and Carmen continues sniffing the ground and stumps but locates no more ants. I suffer the brunt of a bluff charge when I follow too closely behind as she puts her head down to investigate a stump. I think she is perturbed at finding nothing there to eat, and I am simply handy for the scolding. I am hoping this will not turn into a bad day for Carmen and me. It is always easier following the bears when their attention is occupied with abundant natural foods. On days when Carmen does more looking than getting, she sometimes becomes perturbed. Today, her message comes through loud and clear, and I resume lagging back my usual fifteen to twenty feet as we move into an aspen clear-cut. Here Carmen feeds on raspberries, sniffs objects, and marks her territory. We meander the cutting for about a half hour, then she moves into a stand of pole-sized aspens. Here it is more raspberry feeding, and also gooseberry, choke cherries, and jack-in-the-pulpits. When we exit the stand about forty-five minutes later, she moves into a lowland area dominated by shoulder-tight aspen and willow saplings and stops to feed on a yellow jacket's nest, which she gouges from beneath a balsam fir stump. There is more stump and ground sniffing in the stand, but no additional feeding.

About twenty minutes later, we cross an active logging road and move into a lowland conifer stand. The stand is predominately white cedar in the overstory and feels about ten degrees cooler than the cutting. Here Carmen resumes feeding, and it's all hazelnuts. As she cracks them open one by one, it sounds like someone chewing ice cubes. I take a seat on a moss-covered log about ten yards from her and settle into the cool of the spot. About forty minutes later, she ceases her nut cracking and rests beneath a two-foot-diameter white cedar. I toggle through the data logger and note that I picked her up at 8:15 A.M., and it is now 1:05 P.M. She has gone nonstop for nearly five hours. We have traversed sixteen different habitats plus an additional six microhabitats within their borders. I have recorded more than three hundred activity codes. Although that is not an enormous amount of activity, I am struck by the diversity of food types she has consumed—nine different plant items, plus two species of ants and the yellow jackets. We have traveled more than two miles but are not much more than a half mile, straight-line distance, from our rendezvous site. This is what proximity to diversity affords a bear, a plethora of food items within a short distance of each other. It is an optimal situation—feeding on a diversity of food stuffs while being exposed to little danger.

Even though we crossed the active logging road, I am not too worried about a hound chase. It is the middle of the week, and most hounding activity, at least during the training season, takes place on weekends. It would be impossible for Carmen to fulfill all her food requirements without crossing a number of active roads, which makes me wonder if—at nine years old and experienced in road crossings—she has developed a feeling for the consequence of crossing different roads at different times of the day and year. Hard to tell, but I continue to wonder about it as I leave her in the cool of the conifers and head back to the Jeep.

8/17/94

Today I walk in on Nettie and June in a curious mix of habitat. They are in a stand of red maple–sawtimber mixed with large (more than two feet in diameter) white pines. Nettie is preoccupied with attempting to dig bees from a hole in the base of an ironwood tree. The hole looks like the characteristically shaped oblong hole of a pileated woodpecker that was chiseled into a softer part of the tree. Nettie is unable to fashion it further, however, and the bees continue their flights in and out of the hole as she lies digging at it. I imagine she can smell (or hear) the reward within, but I can see that she has slim chance of retrieving it. June is busying herself with peeling the bark off a fallen pine and licking the few ants that scatter as she exposes them. Both bears suddenly stand still to listen to the overhead calls of a loon. Nettie, now distracted from or tired of the bee quest, heads north into a lowland conifer stand, where both bears feed on wild calla. There is more sniffing and digging of logs, and Nettie uncovers the ground hive of a yellow jacket colony and consumes it. Then she returns to the woodpecker hole to give the bee nest one more try. But it is hopeless, and we head back into the conifers. Crossing the lowland, we enter an upland hardwoods containing many large beech trees. Nettie meanders beneath them sniffing the ground. Here and there she locates a beechnut and pauses to eats it, standing with her head down or lying on her belly. She interrupts her beechnut foraging to arched-back rub a beech sapling. June follows suit. Then it is more beechnut feeding, after which we meander back to the lowlands for additional calla and jewelweed feeding. Farther into the lowlands, Nettie drinks and then straddle-marks a sapling spruce and digs a colony of *Lasius* (and I drop a transmitter). After the ant feeding, she takes two more long drinks.

Over the next few hours we traverse hardwoods and swamp. Ants and vegetation make up the bulk of the bears' diet. Nettie stops to drink and groom, and June maneuvers under her elbow and nurses for five minutes. Nettie terminates the bout by blowing and standing when June get too rambunctious with her lower mammae. Moving on, we turn south, and the bears meander the lowlands for nearly a half hour feeding on nothing. As we approach a two-track, Nettie pauses to first listen to, and then wait out, a passing truck. She stands and waits nearly two minutes before crossing the road with June and heading into the hardwoods on the other side. I walk the road, erasing their tracks with mine, and stand watching as they disappear into the underbrush.

8/21/94

Carmen is in the northwest portion of her range when I find her today. She holds for me in a natural opening just behind the "Rusty Bucket," one of our bear trapping spots named for an old rusted pail hanging from the limb of a black cherry tree. It is very near, as bears walk, to the spot where we first captured Carmen four years earlier. It is 9:30 A.M. when she meanders through the aspen stand to a stream just south of the Rusty Bucket. Feeding on a few choke cherries en route, she appears lethargic and I notice her stomach is distended. Along the shore of the stream, she sniffs a hazel bush but does not feed, although I can see many nuts on its branches. She walks northeast on a game trail for about one hundred yards and directly into what is unmistakably a hunter's bait site. She sniffs around but finds no bait, and then walks a few hundred yards directly to a black ash swamp, where she alternates sitting and grooming for about a half hour. We meander out of the swamp and along the edge of a clear-cut stand of aspen. Cutting the corner of the stand, she heads for the stream, where she drinks. She eats a few choke cherries, and then it's back to the black ash swamp, where she rests and sleeps for nearly eight hours. She gets up only once to defecate. I can tell by the odor and composition of the scat that she has been feeding on meat, probably obtained from the bait site. At 6:15 P.M., she stands and yawns before meandering toward the bait site. This time as we draw near, she circles and approaches it from the rear. Seventy-five yards behind the bait, she stoops to feed, but the bracken ferns are too tall and thick for me to identify the food source. I maneuver around to see that what she is feeding on is the roasted head of a pig. She must have dragged it here from the bait pile earlier, and now she drops to her belly, lackadaisically rests a paw on it, and begins to halfheartedly bite and lick it. I leave her here and return to the bait site.

At the bait site, I wire a note to a limb of the tree in which the hunter has placed a tree stand. Baiting for bears has been legal since the tenth of August. This bait has been here only a few days. I know when the hunter placed it, having noticed and followed the trail of broken-down ferns. I wondered at the time how long it would take Carmen to ferret it out. This time of the year, I keep several laminated, waterproof notes handy in my pack. On each one, a polite message alerts the hunters that a research animal is frequenting the bait site and asks that they not kill a radio-collared bear if they should find one in their sights during the hunting season. My name and phone number are included at the bottom of the note. I hope to get a call on this one. In the past years several hunters have phoned, and for the most part, they are considerate, support the research, and agree to bypass collared bears. For Carmen's sake, I hope this hunter proves to be cooperative.

It can be argued that baits provide a worthwhile source of nourishment for female bears. Several bear researchers have concluded that females that fattened in fall had increased reproductive success. To know whether fall baiting actually enhances female bears' productivity would be worthwhile. But without a study in an area that lacks baiting, we will never know if bears would be just as fit foraging on natural foods. I have always wondered what Carmen would be doing if she wasn't lying around waiting to feed on hunters' baits in the fall. It's what she has done every fall I've walked with her, as have the other female bears in my study. The single exception was Nettie, who did not feed on any baits that I am aware of during either of the previous falls.

The practice of baiting bears for hunting serves to confound the impacts of the natural food supply on bear habitat use and demographics. Fall baiting of female bears in the study area was probably substantial enough to ameliorate the effects of any variation in natural foods on their reproductive success; thus it's likely that variations in reproductive success are attributable to a nutritional level established by food availability during another season, e.g., spring. If so, this further points to the pivotal role spring vernal pools play in maintaining adequate bear nutrition. But the fact is, we will probably never know with certainty what nutritional role baits play in bear reproduction.

In my view, although bears may fatten on baits, possibly enhancing reproductive success in some cases, overall, hunters' bait sites probably act as "population sinks," considering the frequent use of them by bears and the consequent high probability of a bear being shot. Dead bears don't reproduce.

8/22/94

Nettie and June run from me. The morning is windy (fifteen mph), and although I thought my approach a good one, they do not hold. I trail them, talking loudly until they come to a suitable refuge tree. Nettie stands at the base and then walks toward me when she is certain of what I am. It is my guess that during my absence they were chased by hounds. It is an unavoidable situation and happens every year at this time. Perhaps my voice was tangled by the wind and sounded like the bray of a hound. Taking no chances, Nettie fled.

Now, sufficiently settled, she moves off and a huffy June descends and follows. We move to a grassy two-track, and the bears begin feeding on raspberries. In the lower areas of the road Nettie feeds on swamp thistles. For nearly an hour, raspberry feeding and swamp thistle feeding are about equal. Nettie moves into the surrounding hardwoods and digs the larvae of beetles from three different logs within a half hour. Meandering back onto the two-track, she finds a yellow jacket's nest in the ground near the edge of the road, and she hurriedly digs and eats it, then runs from the site and stands scratching and rubbing her head. On other occasions, I have watched as she plowed her face into moist sphagnum or wet vegetation after yellow jacket and hornet feeding, possibly to cool the stings or remove stingers; however, there is no sphagnum handy at this site. After a short rubbing of her snout, she meanders along the two-track into an aspen seedling-sapling stand, where she halts abruptly, then tentatively sniffs another bear's scat. Urinating and briefly Carmen-dancing, she walks on to discover a rabbit carcass but strangely does not eat it, nor does June. We walk on, and as the aspens change to sawtimber diameter, I lose sight of the bears for a while in the undergrowth. When I rejoin them, they are digging a hornet's nest. June helps on this one and is allowed to polish it off as Nettie walks away. Nettie meanders and finds another ant colony under a rock; it is *Lasius,* and I drop another transmitter. She flips more rocks, then stops to drink as we enter a lowland conifer stand.

Next, we're off to a white cedar swamp for beaked hazelnut feeding and two long drinks. Then, more swamp thistle feeding. Nettie sniffs the base of a white cedar, then flops to nurse June. June stays on the ground with her, and we rest here for almost two hours. At 4:00 P.M. we are up and moving toward another aspen seedling-sapling stand. Nettie grabs a few raspberries, then turns and defecates (I wonder if there is room in the freezer). She rubs her vulva on a fallen log for forty-four seconds, then meanders to some swamp thistle and eats them. She drinks water twice in the next nine minutes in addition to grooming and much ground sniffing. Then, from a low swale in the stand, she feeds on cattails, both eating frond tips and digging and eating roots. We move onto a two-track for a half hour of raspberry feeding before we meander to a lowland conifer stand. Here Nettie feeds on hazels and must stand on her hind legs to pull several of them down. Moving on, she finds a patch of jack-in-the-pulpit and feeds on the corms. June sniffs a dead red squirrel, and Nettie, noticing her behavior, wanders over. But again there is no carrion feeding, and again I wonder why. After sniffing around the squirrel, it's back to jewelweed feeding, after which Nettie sits and scratches, then grabs a couple of mouthfuls of a grass, which I am unable to identify before she consumes it. Moving through the hardwoods, the bears are going strong when I let them walk on alone. I watched for just under seven hours, and what strikes me most is that the bears never played.

8/25/94

Today I follow Nettie and June into unfamiliar ground. Calling it ground is perhaps misleading. In knee-deep water, I attempt stepping from one clump of sedge to another. It's like trying to walk on an ocean of basketballs. The bears wade or swim casually. For the last several days Nettie has been expanding her territory east.

The area is characterized by black spruce bogs punctuated by "islands" an acre or two in size that are covered with big white pines and hemlocks. Here a foot or two difference in elevation makes a world of difference in flora. The bogs and islands are tightly interwoven with inundated sedge meadows (we are in one now) and are overgrown in places with tag alder and willow shrubs. In the bogs, spongy layers of sphagnum mosses cover ancient floating mats of acidic peat, which in turn cover old kettle-hole lakes left by huge chunks of glacial ice ten to twelve thousand years ago. The soils are relatively infertile, but sedges, showy lady's slippers, and stalks of cottongrass grow in open areas of the bogs. They are joined by the carnivorous picture plant and sundew, both of which supplement their nutrient needs by trapping and digesting insects. Low-growing shrubs like leatherleaf, Labrador tea, and sage-leaved willow invade stable areas of the mat and grow alongside stunted black spruce and tamarack. Tamaracks are favorites of mine. Here they grow on acid soils, but they are equally well adapted to calcareous peats. Tamaracks are known as turn-coat pines. Unlike most other conifers, they lose their needles in the fall much like deciduous trees lose leaves. In spring, their newly emerging needles are an indescribable shade of green. In fall, they turn a golden yellow, setting them apart from neighboring evergreens.

Walking in bogs is a cool diversion on hot fall days. But, while I deeply appreciate the beauty of the treed portion of bogs, the open areas prove to be an invigorating challenge. Unattached to the bottom by any root growth, the bog mat nearest the center "floats" over the water. It undulates. Walking on it is like walking on a water bed and surfing on a huge bale of hay at the same time. The gradual encroachment of conifers into bogs is the one reason I am disenchanted with plant succession—for eventually quaking bogs will no longer quake. Walking on bogs, or bog slogging, is an acquired skill. With practice, one learns to undulate with the rolling mat and trust fate for secure footing. If you can find your way to the center of a quaking bog in fall and immerse yourself three hundred and sixty degrees in its colors and essences, I guarantee it will beat any carnival ride.

Deep, slow-moving streams course the area in dendritic patterns, adding to the scenery of the bogs and meadows. Judging by the drift of bubbles that trail the bears as they splash across one now, its flow is southerly. This means that for the last few hours, we have been working our way east, into yet more new territory.

The bears feed here and there on wild calla located on rich organic soils in the shallower areas of the meadows, and on blueberries and huckleberries located on the acid soils of the "pine islands." Earlier in the walk, when the brackish water of a sedge meadow reached mid-thigh depth, I set the activity code on the GPS data logger to FM (forage-meander), stowed it in a waterproof bag, and stuffed it inside my pack. The manufacturers, in their product literature, tout the unit as being developed for and tested in Desert Storm. Supposedly, it is able to withstand sand storms and driving rains. In my experience, the unit is temperamental at best. While having no practice with it in sand storms, I know it cannot take a heavy dew, much less submersion. I can hear it chirping along now in my pack, trilling up like a metallic wood thrush and down like a metallic vireo as satellite connections are lost and reacquired. I am curious to see how the bears' route through the area will plot out when superimposed on the satellite imagery. With each additional waterlogged step, the route seems more of a zigzagged tangle. Yet back at the computer, if I zoom out, viewing the route from the perspective of an eagle, segments of it will appear more or less as straight lines, perception a matter of scale.

The longer I follow Nettie through this country, the more I wonder what she is up to. There appears to be scant food available. Even I know of richer food patches presently available elsewhere in her home range. In fact, we abandoned a patch of raspberries earlier this morning while abundant fruit remained. Certainly, it would have been better strategy to continue foraging in that more dense food patch. After all, isn't that what bears are in the business of: optimizing food intake and spreading their genes? Or is Nettie's exploration of this seemingly poorer food area an effort to supplement a particular dietary requirement that is unavailable elsewhere?

How bears move through the landscape and which habitats are most important to increase their fitness are of great interest to bear biologists, and using conventional radiotelemetry methods to determine bears' preference for and avoidance of habitat types can be misleading. Due to telemetry margin of error, it is nearly impossible to accurately locate bears in smaller micro-habitats. In fact, some forest stands (e.g., vernal pools) that are sought out by bears are not even mapped by forest managers. It is conceivable that one may miss entirely the bears' use of some critical habitats.

Observing wildlife at too coarse a spatial or temporal scale limits our ability to detect those areas of the forest that may be of greatest importance to them.

Walking with the bears in late summer and fall, I have watched them feed voraciously in an abundant patch of food, then abandon the patch while a profusion of food remains, shift-ing to an alternate food, as if bored with the former. What bet-ter time to go exploring for rich food patches than on a full stomach and when foods are abundant and widespread? If a new and particularly ripe patch is located, it can be exploited and its location stored for future reference, thus enabling a bear to "stay in the game" in a poor food year. On the other hand, striking out to explore new territory on an empty stomach when food is less abundant would not only constrain the search but might have potentially dire consequence as well.

Whatever the reason for bears' peregrinations during times of abundance, June appears to be a less than enthusiastic par-ticipant in Nettie's present endeavor. She is trailing. Periodi-cally, she bawls halfheartedly, pestering an unwilling Nettie to nurse her during our brief rest periods on the pine islands. The day is hot, and Nettie, having just finished swimming in a hole in a quaking bog, is now rigorously straddle-marking a tama-rack. From where I stand, only twenty feet away, I can see wa-ter being showered into the air as she shakes after toppling the larch with her chest. She quickly about-faces and marks it again. The surrounding sphagnum mat vibrates. I have watched Car-men perform the same ritual at a bog in the heart of her terri-tory on many occasions. Now Nettie is marking new territory on the fringe of her range, and it is a welcome sight to watch as the little-more-than-three-year-old bear comes into her own. I wonder if the swimming is in response to the heat of the day, or if it is part of the ritual, conceivably something that increases the quantity and detectable span of scent follicles she leaves behind. The change in tempo seems to divert June from her preoccupation with nursing, and she wanders about sniffing forbs and shrubs. Nettie bounds a short distance after marking the larch, pausing to sniff the leafless, weathered tip of a fallen black spruce that protrudes from the sphagnum mat. The spruce is inclined at such an angle and height that it makes a perfect back-scratch post, and Nettie stands arching and pressing her back up to it. When she is finished, the hair on her back is left standing. Had I not witnessed the scratching, I would surely think her hackles are up. But she acts as if there is little in the area that bothers her and begins feeding on wild calla. She works her way along the shore of a pine island and into an area of sedge meadow covered with tag alder. Underneath the alders she feeds on the leaves and flowers of jewelweed. Working her way to the upland, she leads June to a patch of huckleberries, where they forage briefly before Nettie splays herself at the base of a large white pine. June climbs the refuge tree and in short order drapes her belly across a branch and sleeps. Nettie rolls to her side and looks at me (ten yards away, my back to another white pine) until her eyes close and she begins REM sleep. I punch RR (rest recumbent) into the data logger (which I extracted from my pack earlier when we hit higher ground) and let it collect enough location points for a solid fix. I then change batteries and allow it to collect enough points for another solid location before shutting it off. I keep three batteries in my pack, and they add as many pounds to the load. But it is necessary, as I go through that many on a good bear walk. Today is stacking up to be a pretty good walk, too—no other bears, bungled stream crossings, failed river fording, bears' attitudes, or dead batteries.

I position myself to take advantage of a breeze and reach

into my pack for a canteen of Gatorade. We are more than six hours into the walk, and this is my first opportunity to drink. I find that I am able to get away with drinking something if I keep it to a minimum and drink only when the bears are sleeping or looking away. Otherwise, they become interested in my actions and approach to see if I have food—something I never bring on bear walks. On especially hot days I usually pack a frozen canteen of Gatorade. Placed in the pack against my back, it cools me during the morning, and by midday it is thawed and icy cold. One quart, which is all that room allows, does not last long. Today, I wish for another as I tilt the canteen for the last time.

Forty-five minutes into the rest stop, June scales down the white pine and bites at Nettie's elbow, which covers her mammae. Nettie gives in this time and maneuvers to prop her back against the white pine as June climbs aboard. After punching in the appropriate codes, I film the bout. Seven minutes later the nursing is over. Following fifteen minutes of grooming coupled with intermittent play, the bears are moving again. We head back toward the patch of jewelweed, and Nettie and June resume feeding. The jewelweed has grown tall in places, well over Nettie's back. The bears eat both the leaves and the orange flowers of the plant. When they have eaten their fill, we edge our way around the pine island and strike out across another quaking bog. Nettie pauses, looking back at me about midway across. I am causing too big a quake in the bog's mat. I try to reassure her, voicing my usual "It's OK, it's just me" stuff. She seems satisfied and goes on. We follow a well-worn game trail from the edge of the bog to another pine island, where the bears again forage on huckleberries. Meandering into an opening in the understory, Nettie becomes edgy and begins to sniff objects intensely. I realize that we are in a manicured shooting lane. Pruned spikes of brush protrude conspicuously from the ground. A quick glance reveals a hunting blind positioned at the end of the lane. It is the right spot for a deer blind, judging by the abundance of tracks and droppings. Nettie follows the lane to the blind and begins head-rubbing it as June climbs atop. June discovers a hole in the top of the blind and climbs inside, and the bears begin a game of tag through a window. After a few minutes, Nettie loses interest and walks off. June scratches her way through the window, and, clinging to the sill with front paws, she drops several feet to the ground and hustles to rejoin her mother. Nettie turns abruptly in the path leading from the blind and swings her rear end around toward a small balsam fir. I recognize the motion and, anticipating the outcome, punch DS (defecate solids) into the data logger. A good guess, too. When she is finished, she turns and, as is typical, sniffs her droppings. Walking away, she straddle-marks another balsam, her distended vulva hair now dripping wet with urine. I stoop to collect the scat as I pass, happy to expunge a sure sign of the bears' visit. It looks like an equally opportune site to kill bear as well as deer, and there is no sense leaving anyone clues.

Nettie makes her way south to the opposite end of the island. As far as I can tell, this is the farthest we have moved in any direction other than east all day. It is around six-thirty, and we have traveled for ten hours (including rest stops). I calculate that this places us about two miles in a straight line from where I left the Jeep near the raspberry patch this morning. Something has been troubling me all afternoon, and I feel anxious about the return trip for reasons I don't understand. I feel the urge to make it back across the big sedge meadow while daylight remains. So when Nettie continues south off the end of the island and into over-the-head alder shrubs, I say goodbye to her and June, thanking them for a fine day. I head west across the south end of the island, and when I reach the opposite side, where the lowlands begin, I stow all my gear in the pack and make ready for the walk out. The bogs will pose little problem; I am mostly concerned with having to cross the streams in the sedge meadows in the dark. Several of the deeper streams had given me trouble while fording them earlier, and

I do not want to have to negotiate them in the dark if at all possible. In this new territory, I am unsure of the direction of the nearest trail or two-track and think the best route to return by is the one Nettie took to get here. So I strike out across the lowlands, reckoning by upland features en route. It turns out that things actually go rather well. I negotiate the deepest streams in the sedge meadow with plenty of light remaining, and I do not get unusually wet in the process. After hustling through a stand of the lowland conifers and skirting a clear-cut, I handily intersect the old railroad grade on which I parked the Jeep earlier in the morning. I miss the mark by only a few hundred yards and feel pretty good about my reckoning skills. Barely an hour of sunlight remains as I walk the grade toward the Jeep. In the long shadows of the failing light, I notice that the Jeep seems to be listing starboard.

The right rear tire is flat. Nothing new here. It is easy to pick up a spike or shard of glass nearly anywhere on back-road two-tracks. I am notorious for flat tires and on a first-name basis with the entire crew of the Marquette tire shop. When I open the rear window to the truck's topper to toss my pack in, I notice a bear's footprint smudged in the dust on the glass and then spy another. Walking around the truck, I see bear footprints on all sides of the vehicle. A set of tracks crosses the hood, smears its way up the windshield, and onto the topper. They look to have been made by a small-footed bear, possibly a yearling.

Then it dawns on me that I made a huge mistake. I inadvertently stored in the bed of the Jeep the smoked bacon and doughnuts that I use for trapping. During the course of the day, the aroma must have wafted into the surrounding conifer swamp, where the roaming bear caught wind of it and followed the scent trail to the Jeep. Unable to gain entry, the bear has bitten all the tires in an apparent effort to obtain the prize within. (I have observed bear baits that were covered with old tires, and although such practices are now illegal, I wondered if they are connected with my bear-bitten tires.) On closer inspection,

I discover that the bear has also made a day bed under a tree near the Jeep. Sign indicates that the bear returned to it several times to rest, following repeated failed attempts to get at the cache within the Jeep. As I lie on my stomach under the Jeep to place the jack, I fully expect to see a bear's feet coming around. I am not particularly worried, though, knowing that the bear will likely scare easily if I make noise. I talk to myself and hum and sing a few bars of the Watusi just in case the noise of clanking hub caps and tire iron are not enough to dissuade it.

I finish changing the tire without any interference from the bear and have to chuckle to myself thinking how upset the bear must have been at being so near yet so far from the horde of goodies. I would have liked to observe its behavior. After hefting the flat into the back of the Jeep, I jump in and head for the truck trail, which is about a mile away via old railroad grades and two-tracks. Almost immediately, the right front tire blows out. Standing there in failing light, I see where canine teeth have penetrated its side wall. The strain of the first bump caused it to blow. The tire appears a total loss, so I decide to ride it slowly out to the truck trail, where a small hand-held radio kept under the front seat will be able to reach the receiver at Forest Service headquarters. By the time I reach the truck trail, the Jeep has overheated, and I wonder what else might go wrong. I prop the hood open, loosen the radiator cap, and steam bellows out. It is now dark, and I must look a sight when the mini-van filled with an Ohio family happens on the scene. Leaning out his window, the driver asks, "Need any help?" "No thanks," I respond. "Ya sure?" he says. "Yes," I reply. "Well, do you know where you're at?" he asks. "Pretty much," I assure him. "Well, I sure hope so, cause you're a long ways from nowhere," he says. I thank him again for his concern and inform him that help is on the way. He shakes his head as the window goes up and heads the family south on the truck trail. It has been my experience that Ohioans are some of the most recreationally deprived people in the country, and I do not wish to taint their camping trip "up north" with my bear tale.

An hour or so later, a good friend from the Forest Service, John Gregg (heeding an after-hours call), arrives to give me a lift. I put the box of smoked bacon and doughnuts down in the swamp to avoid a repeat performance by the bear during the night (after all, I still have a couple of good tires). There is a chance the bear will visit the Jeep again, and I don't want its signature left in the road. I figure I can retrieve the bait or clean up the area in the morning if the bear makes a mess of it.

I have a wrecker tow the disabled Jeep the twenty-some miles to town early the next morning. The bear did not return during the night. All told, with bear-bitten tires, broken water pump, lost antifreeze, and towing charges, the bill comes to $375. I can still hear the operators laughing to each other on the insurance company's toll-free line when I reported the claim. The operator, with one hand ineffectually held over the phone's mouthpiece, announces to her coworkers: "He says a bear ate his tires—like, yeah, right."

8/29/94

Today I'm back in the saddle, and Nettie and June are back in the hardwoods west of the truck trail. They have had the last three days to make their way back from the newly established eastern border of Nettie's home range. I would like to have made the trip with them to learn the route they took, but I spent the days with Jeep repairs. The bears are feeding on fallen black cherries. The ground is littered with them. This year's crop has all the makings of an excellent one for the bears. Nettie seems uneasy at my coming. I check to make sure I do not have another bear's scat in my pack. (In a day's walk with the bears it is possible to collect as many as half a dozen of their scats in addition to any others encountered from unidentified bears. In the haste to keep up with the bears, scats get stuffed in any and every pocket or corner of my pack—wherever room is available. It is easy to overlook one or two, only to discover them later.) There are none. Nettie and June return to cherry feeding, but not for long, as Nettie scents something on the wind. Nostrils flaring, she tilts her head at an angle to find out more. Both bears stand sniffing for a full two minutes, then resume meandering for cherries, June first. When Nettie nears a pole-sized maple, she stands on hind legs, sniffs it, then arched-back rubs it. When she finishes, June walks over and sniffs her mother's work, then rubs her flank against the opposite side of the sapling that Nettie has marked. Rubbing her way around the mark tree, June stands in the very same spot Nettie did and performs a near perfect arched-back rub herself (I give her a 9.9, only because her bite is a little sloppy).

As we move south through the hardwoods, I recognize parts of our route and have a hunch where we're headed. We come to a sedge meadow separated from a bog by a narrow strand of hardwoods. The sedges are nearly waist high, and I can barely see the bears' backs as I follow them through and on into the stand of hardwoods. Immediately upon entering the hardwoods, there is much ground sniffing as Nettie locates the scat of another bear. When I move closer to get a look, June executes a full-blown lunge in my direction. I suspect she is agitated by the unfamiliar bear sign, and that, coupled with Nettie's nervousness, has provoked her action. I talk calmingly to her and back off a few feet. She stands briefly to arched-back rub a sugar maple, and I again admire her form—she is becoming more bearlike in every way. Nettie, now sitting and scratching, yawns nervously and tips her head toward June and me as her claws rake under her jaw. She stands, then meanders north, pausing at a mark tree. Standing with her front legs on it, she begins sniffing it in earnest—I feel sure another bear has marked it, and recently. But Nettie does not mark here. She drops to all fours and begins sleuthing for beechnuts. She locates a few and eats them.

Fall

After standing briefly and sniffing the air, she leads us into the quaking bog. This is very familiar territory and where I anticipated we might go. I have been here with the bears multiple times every year. June head-rubs a maple on the edge of the bog, while Nettie straddle-marks a balsam fir sapling as she walks toward an opening in the bog mat. She stoops to drink from the water's edge, and June plunges into a hole in the bog about ten yards from her and splashes around. Nettie finishes her drink and begins sniffing and investigating objects. June climbs out of the pool and shakes off, then bounds over to Nettie. Nettie, her back turned, catches the movement out of the corner of her eye and wheels around huffing, unaware that it is June—the bears are really on edge here. Some of the tension is reduced when both bears walk to the hole Nettie drank from, and June plunges in. Nettie stands on the edge and leans out to paw in a strand of sphagnum, then eats it. June is busy splashing around, raising a great ruckus. Nettie bats at her as she comes close to the edge, and they play like that for a moment. But June soon tires of dog-paddling and hauls herself out of the hole and shakes. June and I fall in behind as Nettie leads the way back into the hardwoods. Near the edge of the hardwoods, June climbs a maple that grows in a curious manner, curving out over the bog. She walks the tree trunk back toward me as I follow in the bears' path. My route places me directly under her by only a few feet. It proves too close for comfort, and she blows at me. This brings Nettie trotting back to see what the problem is. Apparently, Nettie is taking no chances and feels she should investigate the situation quickly. She looks past me and, unable to detect the source of June's consternation, she climbs the tree to check on her. We both come to the same determination: June has overreacted.

Nettie and June stand looking down at me. We are all on edge now, and I consider bailing out of the walk. I do not want to interfere, should the situation become critical. We may get a visit from an adult male, though it has never happened before outside of the breeding season. On an earlier walk with Carmen and her first set of cubs, however, in August of 1991, we were very near this spot when she chased an unidentified bear.

On that day, Carmen and her three cubs stood alert while discerning the noises (vocalizations and leaf rustling) made by the incoming bear. Carmen popped her jaws at the approaching intruder the instant it came into sight. (Jaw-popping is a distinct agonistic behavior and is usually accompanied by lip-smacking. It is different from jaw-clunking, which has a throaty quality to it, is hollow sounding and more resonant, and is used to communicate whereabouts.) The bear was about twenty yards below us, down a slight slope. When Carmen popped at it, the bear stopped and looked in our direction. Before it could react, Carmen began chasing the trespasser, and it ran out of sight while the cubs remained on the ground in my presence (it was a good feeling to be trusted alone with the cubs that first time in a threatening situation). Carmen returned after about twelve minutes and, tongue-clicking to the cubs, located us, and we resumed our walk. She showed no signs of having had a clash with the other bear.

Now, the bears climb down the maple, and Nettie sits to scratch as if making a decision again. Apparently, she decides we will continue north. We travel only a short way up a slope in the hardwoods when, rising upright on hind legs, she looks toward the crest of the rise. She looks big standing there, and I am surprised at how long she holds her position. I know now there must be another bear close by and scan the ridge to detect any movement. I'll have a decision to make quickly should another bear appear. When I'm with Carmen, I figure she is pretty much the queen bee and does the chasing. Nettie, however, I'm not so sure about. She might get chased. Then what should I do? Before I have time to decide, Carmen appears over the rise. I recognize her right off as she stands stock still, taking a long look in our direction. June is spooked by Carmen's sudden appearance and runs partway up a maple close by. The three of us are looking at Carmen looking right back at us. Nettie alternately rises and lowers on her hind limbs, acting like she wants to run but is unsure if that is what to do. June hugs the maple with all four paws and leans her head and neck out from behind the trunk, huffing in her grandmother's direction. I wonder if they recognize each other, if they have it figured out through some keen scenting ability and have been maneuvering delicately for the last hour or so. Or maybe it is just happenstance. I am struggling to capture three generations of bears in the frame of the video's viewfinder when Carmen drops and runs huffing back over the hill. She apparently was not expecting the company. Nettie and June waste little time regrouping and trot away in the opposite direction. Within seconds I am standing alone, the sound of bears fading in the distance.

Walking out of the forest (I decided to let the bears work out the remainder of the encounter on their own), I am grateful to have seen the three generations of bears together. I wonder if I will ever be lucky enough to see four—not likely, but then one never knows. I also wonder if the notion that some female bears are not territorial might simply result from the observer being unfamiliar with the relationship of the bears—besides which, bears are most certainly individuals.

∽๐∾

That animals are individuals is something frequently diminished, if not overlooked, by population studies. Collective rates for attributes such as natality, fecundity, and mortality are ascribed, making it a manageable task to calculate various demographics. The truth is, however, that all populations are made up of individuals, and individual contributions to the population differ greatly. The fate of whole "populations" may in fact hinge on the behavior of a single member. This truth is poignantly illustrated by Rolf O. Peterson in his book *The Wolves of*

Isle Royale: A Broken Balance. Peterson describes how an old and barren female wolf (#450) usurped her sister as the alpha female, stealing her pups and banishing her from the pack. Later, over a four-year period, #450 bore ten pups of her own to the dwindling Isle Royale population, possibly saving it from extinction. Peterson noted, "The legacy of female #450 was much greater than that left behind by the 'average wolf.' Her late-blooming reproduction, modest though it was, allowed the dramatic experiment of wolf survival to continue on Isle Royale into the late 1990's. Though she would not care a whit, science owes something to this old wolf. . . ."

We can learn much about the whole from the observation of individuals. How much more informative and accurate it would be to make predictions about a population based on an intimate knowledge of all its individuals. Lamentably, in all but a few cases, we are relegated to managing the fates of entire populations of animals based on a scanty sampling of subpopulations and extrapolating the interpretations to the whole.

❧

As a follow-up, it is interesting to note that after the three generations of bears met in the hardwoods, neither Carmen nor Nettie and June went near the area surrounding the bog and hardwoods for the next six days. They all missed out on some quality raspberry and black cherry feeding in a secure setting. Scientists call that exclusion by mutual avoidance.

9/1/94

Nettie and June are across the truck trail and to the east today. Inside the rolling hardwoods, the forest floor flickers on and off with sunlight. Chipmunks sound from all around. The sound of so many chipping in makes as full a chorus as that of spring peepers in an evening pond. The chips turn off and on as my footfalls come and go. As I move toward the bears, I notice obtrusive dabs of blue and yellow paint squirted on surrounding trees, a sure sign that this stand will be cut in the near future. The sight of the fresh paint makes my work feel even more compelling.

The hardwoods we are in have a substantial black cherry component in the canopy layer, but once I contact the bears, they do nothing but meander and sniff the ground for twenty minutes without feeding. I am disappointed that they are not in the woods where we ran into Carmen a couple of days ago, as it appeared a much better woods for cherries and beechnuts than this one does. But I remind myself that the bears should know what is best, or at least possible. Nettie Carmen-dances for reasons known only to her. Then follows eight minutes of feeding on fallen beechnuts and black cherries. June completes a perfect Carmen-dance for her own reasons, and I wonder what cues I missed before arriving. We enter a lowland conifer stand, where the bears feed on jewelweed, swamp thistle, and golden saxifrage and then pause to drink. Most of the saxifrage is located in the shade of the roots of a wind-thrown tree. The roots extend nearly twelve feet above the forest floor, and Nettie and June climb them and play a game of bear-on-the-mountain. Nettie has weight and position to her advantage (she is on top), but June makes a good showing and claims the spot after Nettie loses interest in the contest and walks off. As June jumps off the root mass, she pauses to sniff the pale blue flowers of an aster, and the pose makes a pretty scene. The tranquility is interrupted, however, when a low-flying jet courses above and both bears stand bolt upright.

The Whitefish River drainage is a training ground of sorts for pilots stationed at K. I. Sawyer Air Base, south of Marquette. Jet fighters, bulky C-130s, and huge B-52 bombers maneuver through the area at what seems only treetop level. Their approach is sudden, the noise deafening. Once on a peaceful spring morning, as Carmen, her back resting against a hemlock, nursed her cubs, out of nowhere a jet fighter roared overhead, scattering the bear family in all directions including up. Anyone who supposes that animals, including bears, are unaffected by the roar and noise of aircraft overhead is mistaken. My only council for Nettie and June on this occasion is that the air base will be closing soon, so this will likely be one of the last disturbances from military aircraft that they will have to abide.

As we meander through the lowland conifers, I notice that some areas of the canopy are more open than others. This condition is due largely to spruce budworm defoliation of the balsam fir and black spruce trees. In many of these areas the trees are dead, leaving the ground below open to direct sunlight. It is in such an area that the bears now feed on vegetation, concentrating mainly on cattails, with intermittent wild gooseberry and bristly black currant feeding. Both bears interrupt their foraging to climb and play in the branches of a fallen white cedar that rests about four feet above the cool forest floor. There is much pawing at one another coupled with intermittent biting of the cedar's limbs. I do not notice the bears ingesting any of the bark, but they strip it from many of the smaller limbs. The reason is not obvious to me. When the play resumes, Nettie backs June far out on the trunk of the tree, and June retreats, falling from her position. She then runs to the butt end of the tree and climbs back up, reengaging Nettie, and the contest resumes. After a long play session, Nettie tires and leads the way to the base of a large white cedar, where she rests recumbently. June, however, has other ideas, and after prolonged coaxing, she is allowed to nurse. But partway through the tender scene, as I film it, it erupts in chaos.

What apparently happens (I am able to piece the sequence together only by watching the film later) is that June, while suckling Nettie's upper mammae, is bitten on the lip by a deerfly. Thinking the mammae has attacked, she bites back, shaking it vigorously. Nettie, startled by the attack, blows loudly and brushes June off with a forearm. As June runs for the refuge tree,

Nettie stands looking about bewildered. I quickly assure her that I had no part in the attack and remain seated as she moves to inspect June, who is poised partway up the trunk of the refuge tree huffing. In a few moments, June calms and descends the cedar, but neither bear attempts to resume the nursing bout. Together, they move off through the conifers. I sit watching them go.

9/3/94

Today I again find Nettie and June east of the truck trail in a stand of lowland conifers. My sister-in-law, Mary, the wife of my brother, Dan, is along for the walk. This will likely be the last weekend walk before the start of bear hunting season. It is nearly 9:00 A.M. when we locate the bears. I brought along a few doughnuts today so that the bears will spend some time in proximity to us and become used to Mary's voice and scent. The treats are gulped down in a hurry, and when crossed hands and empty palms are flashed, the bears are off. After a long drink from a depression in the conifers, they feed on wild calla and then both drink again. Nettie straddle-marks a balsam fir as we traverse a hummock in the lowlands on our way toward a stand of hardwoods. The only activity performed in the hardwoods is a sit-scratch by Nettie as she clunks her jaws to June, who has wandered ahead. From the hardwoods, Nettie leads us back into the lowland conifers for more calla feeding. As we meander through the stand, I can smell the rank "wet dog" odor of wild raisin well before we arrive. The smell permeates the air. I look about for the bush, but Nettie and June find it first and pause to eat the blue berries borne in clusters on the erect shrub.

The scent of wild raisin always triggers in me childhood memories of return trips from the October "rabbit woods." On those trips home, following cold wet days of chasing rabbits with my father, I shared the floorboards of a 1950 Ford with our sodden beagle hound, Dud. Curled up next to one another, both of us lay soaking up the hot air flowing from the car's heater. The heat catalyzed the scent of wet dog, and the olfactory memory lingers, triggered from time to time on fall bear walks.

After the berry feeding, Nettie leads the way onto another hummock, where Mary and I sit and watch as the bears engage in an earnest session of play. June uses a hardwood sapling to brace herself as she stands to paw and swat gently at Nettie. The bears entwine in nearly every conceivable position during the bout, which spans a half hour. Surprisingly, June is still rambunctious after the play session and plows ahead as Nettie makes her way from the hummock into the encircling lowlands. Here there is more calla feeding, but the real find is a mountain ash laden with clusters of bright red-orange berries. Mountain ash is an uncommon species in both Carmen's and Nettie's range, and its fruiting is sporadic, making this a rare find.

June climbs the tree only a few feet in front of Mary and me and begins feeding on berries near its top. Nettie bites the tree and then attempts to bend it over using her considerable weight and strength, but her efforts fail. So she climbs a maple tree growing alongside the ash and tries pushing the ash over with her back, using her feet to brace against the maple. When that proves somewhat successful, she climbs out onto the now leaning ash, which begins slowly bending to the ground under her weight. She inches her way outward along its trunk to bend it further. June is still up the tree ("up" is now relative, as the tree is nearly horizontal), feeding on berries as it continues a slow descent. When it looks almost as if Nettie will be successful in riding the mountain ash to the ground, it hangs up in a nearby red maple. Not willing to give up, Nettie walks further out on the trunk and begins bouncing to force it down. But the tree will bend no further, and she must settle for feeding while balanced precariously ten feet above the ground. When June maneuvers for a few more mouthfuls of berries near the top, the ash cracks in two, and both bears come tumbling down. Oblivious to the fall, they feed on the berries of the broken top where it lies on the ground.

When finished with that mountain ash, Nettie meanders to another and subdues it by pulling it down with her teeth, then straddling it the best she can, and walking its length out toward the tip, where June joins her for the feast. Nettie finishes before June, and the tree springs partially upright as she moves on. June, unsatisfied that the berries have been sufficiently exploited, climbs the tree and feeds while Mary and I watch. Nettie moves out of sight. When June is finished, we all play catch-up and find Nettie leading the way to a fourteen-inch-diameter white cedar, where the bears play and then rest. After an hour of rest, Nettie stands for a long drink and over the next hour works her way south through the lowland conifers, pausing to feed only twice, once on mountain ash berries and then on wild calla. The south end of the lowlands fingers into a stand of northern hardwoods composed of sugar maple, beech, and black cherry trees mixed with mature hemlocks. June races ahead and over a rise as we enter the uplands. Nettie follows, clunking her jaws. When Mary and I crest the slope, the bears are foraging on fallen black cherries. They concentrate their efforts in areas where the overhanging branches of cherries overlap. As Nettie and June move about the stand, we can hear the sound of falling cherries bouncing off leaves and striking the forest floor.

Yellow paint appears on the trunks of many of the trees under which the bears feed. This stand is destined to be cut in the near future. As I watch Nettie and June foraging voraciously beneath it, I hope that the message of managing for clumps of cherry trees as well as single trees will sink in before forest managers eliminate all such stands.

It is important to understand that not all trees are created equal. Some, by virtue of genetics or microposition in the forest (for example, soils, pH, drainage, climate, etc.), are better fruit producers than others. When it comes to the nitty-gritty of achieving optimal stand management for wildlife, it is imperative that this distinction be made. Those trees in the stand that are better producers and have the most potential for future production should be favored.

A similar distinction can be made for other mast-bearing species of value to bears, including beech trees. Several beeches in the stand show evidence of past use. Beechnuts tend to be a spotty crop. An abundant beechnut crop may be produced only once in seven years. Nevertheless, when beechnut production is good, it can dramatically affect the nutritional level and behavior of bears, actually prolonging the onset of denning for weeks as bears linger to fatten on this high-energy natural food. Some beeches are better nut producers than others. How does a forest manager go about telling them apart? Do they judge the worth of a beech by past generations of bear pugs etched into its bark? What might that tell us? Out of six fall seasons of walking with bears, in only one did I consider the beechnut crop to be abundant. Another year I felt it to be only marginal; all others failed. During the years of beechnuts, I never once witnessed bears climbing trees to obtain them. As with black cherries, bears seem to prefer to feed on them on the ground. It is probably easier and more energy efficient than climbing out onto slender limbs and gathering a few nuts at a time. I have always wondered if the beech trees bearing the claw marks of past bear use are simply those that retain their nuts longer (possibly due to a genetic difference?), thus forcing the bears to climb the tree to get at them. If we favor those trees with bear claw marks for retention in a stand, are we making more work for the bears? In truth, we do not know. One of my grandfather's favorite sayings was "The biggest room in this house, boy, is the room for improvement." Our forests stand as large homes to begin with—and there will always be room for improvement in our understanding of them.

While meandering the stand, June encounters the scat of another bear. She sniffs it intently and then performs a perfect Carmen-dance as she turns her back and walks away from it.

Nettie, seeing her behavior, walks over and smells the scat and then stands to arched-back rub a nearby ironwood tree. As she turns to bite the tree, I notice a blotch of yellow paint on its trunk. This mark tree it seems, will not serve future generations of bears. Nettie drops to all fours and meanders from the stand into a lowland hardwoods. Here the bears feed on wild calla and drink.

We meander south through the softwoods into a wetland where the canopy cover is less than 10 percent. The sun glistens off the bears' black coats as they walk logs over pools of water and meander through the mucky habitat eating copious amounts of wild calla. Mary, who has fallen behind while surmounting a particularly difficult fallen tree (I hear the splash—there is nothing worse than to be on a bear walk and realize that you're on cub legs), arrives just in time to see Nettie and June try to wedge their way past one another through the crevice formed by a pair of black ash poles. For an instant, the bears are stuck against each other, neither one able to give way. Eventually, Nettie wedges June out, and they continue in single file. I go around the obstacle, and Mary follows suit as we trail the bears, working our way to the opposite side of the wetland.

On the far side, we enter a mixed stand of large hemlocks and maples. The relative cool of the stand is welcome. June catches the scent of something on the wind and raises her head to sniff, then sits and sniffs while further assimilating the information. I remark on how developed she is becoming. She still has the headlong manner of earlier walks, but her approach to things has become increasingly measured. It is good to see. Satisfied, she stands and begins milling about in a manner that I believe indicates she is seeking a refuge tree. I assume we will rest here in the cool of the stand, but the bears proceed to the edge of the stand and then back into the sunlight of the wetland for more wild calla feeding. We are six and a half hours into the walk, and Mary and I decide to let the bears finish the day on their own. As I stand watching them feed across the wetland and move out of sight, I hope to get one more walk with them before the bear hunting season begins next week.

9/6/94

Nettie and June are back on the hummock in the lowlands today. I make my way into them through the surrounding swamp, the vegetation heavy with dew. Spider webs of orb- and tunnel-weavers are adorned by tiny droplets of moisture. Now I understand why they are always in my face while following the bears—they are everywhere.

June actually appears fat. I cannot wait to see what her weight will be in the den this winter. The largest yearling I have handled in a den weighed ninety-seven pounds. That was A.J., the largest male in Carmen's first litter. Nettie weighed eighty-six pounds as a yearling. I think June may be even heavier than she was. When we reach an appropriate spot during the walk, I extract a doughnut from my pack and toss it on the ground in front of Nettie. I made a decision over the weekend to forgo additional walks with the bears for the remainder of the year. It is hard to imagine that this year of walking with bears should end so soon. But hunting season is now only four days away.

This year, the study area is included in a zone that is part of an experimental "third" hunting season for bears. The third season is scheduled to start a bit later than the first two, but it will extend nearly to the end of October. Additional kill-permits are issued for the third season, and as a result, there are many novice hunters about. In fact, there are too many to take any chances, so I decide to establish a bait of my own for the bears in a secure portion of their home range. I hope this will curtail their movements and reduce the chance of their finding a bait or being struck by hounds and killed. I received some good news over the weekend; the hunter whose bait Carmen is hooked on called to say that he would not kill a radio-collared bear should the opportunity arise. For his consideration, I offered him the opportunity to visit a bear den during the upcoming winter, and he accepted.

As Nettie stoops to sniff the treat, I dump my whole pack, which contains several dozen doughnuts carefully wrapped to prevent the bears smelling them earlier in the walk. As I sit upon a huge, fallen white pine log, on an island surrounded by wetland, I watch Nettie and June indulge. We had our first hard frost of the season a few nights before, and hints of autumn are about. That certain incipient scent of fall is in the air. In the swamps, the delicate airy fronds of the maidenhair fern and the royal fern have turned a golden color. Already deciduous trees on marginal sites are ablaze. From where I sit, the tiny, leathery, glossy leaves of shining club moss form a dark green mat that contrasts beautifully with the fall colors in the surrounding canopy. As I finger a specimen of the moss, I note the yearly constrictions of growth on the branches forking from its main stem, which trails just under the soil's surface. It reminds me of the generations of bears and of an earlier fall walk with Carmen and her first litter.

∽◦∾

As Carmen and her cubs rested, I concentrated on the moment, knowing it was among the last I'd have with the bears that year. I had decided not to accompany them on walks after that day, for the next day was September 10, the beginning of bear hunting season, and I did not wish my presence to hinder their actions. Nettie and A.J. were resting part of the way up a large cedar while Carmen and the Runt, his head against her back, rested beneath. I sat with my back to a cedar about ten yards away. The bears had put in a long day and appeared tired. The trio of yearlings had just finished nursing and had proceeded immediately to rest, skipping the play that normally followed.

The cubs had grown big. I guessed their weights at between fifty and seventy pounds; A.J. was the biggest, Nettie was in the middle, and the Runt—well, he was the Runt.

I had joined them earlier in the day as they foraged for the fallen fruits of black cherry trees on the floor of a mixed northern hardwood forest. The day was unseasonably warm. High winds had pushed a warm front north the day before. In its wake, the wind left many fallen ripe black cherries. The bears had capitalized on the windfall.

Carmen had meandered through the forest licking up the ripe berries while standing on all fours. When she located a concentration of berries, she lay on her stomach and elbows, and moved her head side to side, licking up all nearby berries. When the berries in close proximity were depleted, she propelled herself with hind feet until she was again surrounded by fallen berries and began to lick up all berries within reach. In this manner she moved through the aggregated pools of berries until they were depleted. This was the first time I had witnessed bears feeding in this manner, and I enjoyed the performance. The cubs followed suit with a similar version of their own, licking and pushing, licking and pushing. It was thirsty work, and even though there was nearly 100 percent canopy in the bower, the temperature beneath was hot and the air was still. For the bears in their black coats it must have been very hot indeed.

The bears seemed to be concentrating their efforts in areas where the cherry trees grew in clumps. Probably the overlapping branches in the canopy translated to greater concentrations of berries on the ground. Where the microtopography of the ground was such that the berries were funneled into large aggregations, the bears fed *ad libitum* and virtually licked the place bereft of berries.

After nearly two hours of feeding on black cherries (I had to sit down at one point, my back to a huge beech tree, tired of standing and punching FBBC [feed berries—black cherry] over and over into the computer), the bears were actually panting as they moved from the hardwoods into an adjoining quaking bog. Here they plunged into a room-sized hole in the sphagnum mat. They swam and lounged for twelve minutes in the cool of the bog. As they exited the bog, Carmen, dripping wet, arched-back rubbed a spruce, the top of which was broken off at head height from previous markings. From the bog, the bears went directly back to feeding on black cherries in the hardwoods. After nearly two more hours of feeding, they returned to the bog for more swimming and lounging, after which they returned again to forage for cherries in the hardwoods.

After the third berry-feeding session in the hardwoods, which also lasted nearly two hours, Carmen struck out to the north, foraging now more haphazardly on the black cherries as she moved toward a lowland conifer stand. The bears appeared satiated. When we entered the conifers, the Runt and Nettie propelled themselves with their hind feet and skidded along on their sides, taking advantage of the cool sphagnum floor. I was enjoying the cool myself, the conifers probably fifteen degrees cooler than the hardwoods. Carmen, sniffing along the ground, began digging and quickly unearthed a paper wasp nest. I had watched as she uncovered basketball-sized nests in the past—this one was smaller, the size of a softball, but the occupants were no less perturbed. Because of their sting, wasps are my least favorite insect that bears encounter—luckily, I have been stung only once. That time, I followed too closely behind Carmen after she dug up a nest in a lowland conifer stand. In the failing light, I did not detect the swarm until I blundered into it—the buzzing in my ears tipped me off, but by then it was too late. Fortunately, I was stung on the leg, but that bear walk ended there.

While the Runt finished up on the wasp nest, I gave the spot a wide berth and filed in alongside the trio of bears. The Runt played catch-up as we headed northwest. We covered a little over a half mile in the next two hours as the bears worked two more wasp nests along with several patches of nannyberry and dogwoods, in addition to feeding on the tips of cattail fronds. Following that, we came to rest at the clump of cedars.

The bears trailed off to sleep, and I began to count Carmen's respirations, watching her side rise and fall as she slept. (In the early years, I counted or noted nearly everything, including which side of their bodies the bears slept on and for how long, their respiration, and whether or not they exhibited rapid eye movement during sleep. Occasionally, when Carmen or Nettie slept close enough to me, I was able to count heartbeats by watching the fur over her chest cavity palpitate. Similarly, I could count respirations by watching small herbs shiver in front of the bears' nostrils during exhalations. The range of breaths bears take during sleep is great, from eleven to eighty-five a minute, but averages around forty.) Watching Carmen in REM sleep I wondered if she dreamed. On only a few occasions had I observed her feet twitch during her sleep like those of my Brittany spaniel, something I take for a sure sign of dreaming in dogs. If Carmen dreamed today, it must certainly have had something to do with black cherries. That is all I was able to visualize when I closed my eyes.

I had recently taken to resting my eyes for short periods while the bears slept—although not for long, as my worst fear was that they would get up silently and leave me behind. So I checked on them every few minutes or when they stirred. Mostly though, I stayed lucid and catalogued vegetation surrounding the site and made notes on the walk. When I opened my eyes this time, I noticed movement to my left through the cedar trunks about thirty yards away. I saw right off that it was a small bear. I took a quick head count, thinking that one of the cubs might have gotten up to forage on its own, without my noticing. The count revealed two bears up the tree and two at the base. All accounted for and still asleep. The fifth bear approached from downwind of our position, and I felt it must be able to smell the bears and me. But onward he came. He halted at about ten yards from the sleeping bears. Placing both front feet on a fallen log, he surveyed the site. He was now perhaps fifteen yards from where I sat off to the side of the sleeping bear family. I thought surely that Carmen would detect his presence and we would have a chase or maybe even a fray at hand. But all four bears remained sound asleep. Without giving it much thought, I asked the intruder, "Who are you?"—not, of course, expecting an answer. Judging by its reaction to the question, the bear had been unaware of my presence. He fixed a look in my direction, and in the unmistakable manner of a bear that knows he has screwed up, he rolled his eyes while slowly turning his head to the side and then bailed off the log, retreating huffily and with all due speed back the way he came. Carmen and her cubs slept through the whole thing. When they awoke a half hour later, I left them, feeling more than ever a part of the clan.

∽o∾

I sit on the white pine log and watch Nettie mark a small white spruce tree. I know the bears will return to the spot, just as they would to a natural stand of mast. My hope is to use bait to lock them solidly into the area and prevent them from crossing roads and becoming susceptible to hounding or wandering into hunters' baits. The most important element dictating when and where bears are likely to be found at a particular location is food availability. This is especially true in the fall when they are compelled to fatten for overwintering. Bears may move considerable distances to forage on the crops necessary for fattening when nutritious fall foods are not found in proximity to adequate cover. This movement places them at greater risk of exposure to roads and encounters with humankind.

Likewise, I plan to set up a bait for Carmen tomorrow. Carmen is notorious for making excursions in late August and early September to the northwest portion of her home range. Her ultimate destination is a single stand of highly nutritious food, and to get there, she must negotiate a gauntlet of roads and homesteads. She is aided by her experience and, on more than one occasion, a measure of luck. I learned how much of each in an earlier year.

❧

Carmen made her move on the evening of September 14, 1991. With her three cubs in tow, she headed out. Leaving a stand of abundant black cherries in the heart of her home range, where she had fed for several days, she covered a distance of about four miles sometime between 7:30 P.M., when I left her, and 8:30 A.M., when I located her the next morning. How and why bears make these moves is a mystery to me. Are they able to smell ripening crops at such a distance? Is it a learned behavior? (Four years later, Nettie would visit this same food source, not once to my knowledge visiting it in the interim.) Why would Carmen leave abundantly available foods—is she bored with them? The answers prove elusive.

The morning of September 15, I checked her signal before first light. She was nowhere to be found. I had a bad feeling and was fighting it off. It was opening day of bear hunting season with hounds. I had felt that Carmen and her cubs were secure in the portion of their home range where I'd left them the evening before. Vehicles were excluded from that area, and therefore she was unlikely to be struck by hunting dogs if she did not leave the area and cross a road. I lost no time in checking for her signal from all the likely spots.

After looking for a solid hour and coming up empty-handed, I anticipated the worst: that she must have been shot over bait (although it would have been illegal, as I had arrived well before legal shooting time this morning). Pulling out all the stops,

I drove to a reference point known to researchers as the Mondo Tree Fort. It was an old archery hunting blind constructed some twenty-five feet above the ground in a snag-elm tree. At one time it overlooked a game trail in a lowland hardwood stand; now it stood ostentatiously above a knee-high red pine planting. Because of its height I had a better chance of finding a signal. I climbed the rickety steps and pulled myself onto the decaying platform. Hooking up the antenna and receiver, I began making slow deliberate circles with the antenna, straining to hear the familiar ping of Carmen's collar. In the past, I had heard the sounds of elk bugling on their fall ranges, mating bobcats crying in the night, wolf pups howling at rendezvous sites, and wild turkeys gobbling from their roosts in the spring dawn. These were all exhilarating sounds of the outdoors, but lately, my favorite had become the highly prized ping emanating from the radio collar of a found bear. Nothing to the south or west, then a faint ping to the northwest. Could it be? Her collar was in active mode. A good sign. But what in the world was she doing way up there, and why did she pick the opening day of the hound season to go and do it?

From my perspective, Carmen and her cubs had no business being where I found them. They were in a twenty-acre cornfield. Bordered on the south and west sides by knee-high alfalfa fields and on the east by a field of barley stubble, the cornfield abutted lowland hardwoods along its north edge. Against the backdrop of the red and yellow leaves of the hardwoods and coupled with the more than one hundred sandhill cranes profiting from waste grain in the barley stubble, the senescent corn made for a real slice of Upper Peninsula fall. Under any other circumstances I would have gaped.

I moved in close enough to determine the bears' exact location but held off making contact, fearing that I might cause them to move out of the field and across nearby roads in the process. I had encountered no fewer than four groups of houndsmen traveling the roads on my trip across—all with strike dogs perched on the hoods and in the beds of their trucks. Good strike dogs are capable of smelling where a bear has crossed a road up to twelve hours afterward. I had talked with all but one of the groups before the beginning of the hunting season and had obtained assurances that collared bears would not be killed by members of their groups. I was somewhat buoyed by their promises; however, not killing did not necessarily mean not chasing, and anything can, and does, happen during the calamity of chasing bears with hounds (more than one research bear has been killed during a ground fight with a pack of dogs in the owner's effort to 'save' a valuable hound).

The fall before, when Carmen was pregnant with her litter, I located her radio signal near this same cornfield. New to the game of bear activity, I walked slowly south through the lowland hardwood stand toward the sound of her radio signal and came to a halt at the edge of the cornfield. What I saw was a real eye-opener. An area the size of a football field had been decimated. Row upon row of the farmer's silage corn lay bowled over and stripped. Among the cornstalks and chewed cobs were numerous tracks and scats. The sign read unmistakably . . . bear. Carmen (and other bears) had made forays into the cornfield testing the ears for ripeness. Dainty little bites were evident on several ears. When the corn had reached the late milk–early dent stage of development, the bears hit it hard. I went directly to contact the landowner.

The farm was a working dairy farm (they are all work; I make the distinction only because many neighboring farms have recently gone under). It also functioned as a refuge for geese and other wildlife, as the owners allowed no hunting on the property. Many people fail to recognize the profound positive benefit that farmland can have on wildlife and the price that landowners pay to provide this public benefit. Management plans and habitat suitability indexes that fail to recognize these impacts and incorporate surrounding agricultural lands into the planning process are, in my opinion, less than desirable.

After introducing myself to the woman who answered the door and explaining the situation, I offered to reimburse the owners for the depredated crop. She looked me straight in the eye and said, "What for? The bears were here first," and then added, "You should get back to your work and learn as much about them as you can." It seemed that Carmen & Company were safe here for the time being. If the sentiment of that good woman were universal, a major problem for bears would be resolved. Perhaps the real root of our ecological crisis is embedded in the fact that people are simply too many generations off the farm. It is easy to forget our connection to the land and how we fit in. We have a responsibility to ensure that our "fit" does not force other pieces apart. Farmers see, on a daily basis, how the air, water, soil, and plants and animals are interconnected. They understand just how much land it takes to support something as large as a cow, let alone a bear. To lack this understanding is to be unable to conceptualize and support the conservation of blocks of land that are large enough to maintain viable bear populations and ensure their perpetuation. In the years following that conversation with the farmer, I was allowed access to the farmland and occasionally obtained permission to climb the sixty-foot silo there. From its top I was able to reach out and touch the radio signals of all the bears in the southwest corner of the study area.

For whatever reason, Carmen was not long for the cornfield that day. Perhaps other bears were too much for her to contend with while she was burdened with the cubs. At 9:30 A.M. she and the cubs exited the corn to the north and then headed east through the hardwoods. I joined them, and we walked for some way while they fed here and there on the fallen fruit of a few scraggly black cherry trees. The bears appeared wary as we approached a major gravel road about a half mile east of the farm. I decided to hang back when it became apparent that Carmen would cross the road (in broad daylight at 10:30 on opening day of the hound season no less). In a straight line, one after the other, the bears promenaded across the road. I stood concealed inside the tree line watching them go, disbelieving that any bear, especially a female with cubs, could be so foolish. Standing there, I heard a vehicle approaching from the south. It rounded the corner a quarter mile away, a pickup full of hunters and dogs with a strike dog ornamenting the hood. Now, what to do? If they saw me, they would surely surmise what was going on. Maybe I could talk them out of the chase, something I felt was worthwhile to attempt, even if it was a long shot this late in the morning. If they were still cruising the roads, it meant they had yet to find a track and would be anxious to run. There probably wouldn't be much point in discussing the matter. And there was absolutely no hope of the evidence disappearing either. The tracks were plain in the areas of the road shoulder where it had been "dragged" the night before with an old bedspring weighted with cement blocks—something houndsmen do nearly every evening to allow them to distinguish fresh tracks at first light—and Carmen's scent was fresh and would linger for hours.

Just as I was about to move to the road's edge, I heard another vehicle rounding the corner to the north . . . more hunters and dogs. This truck was fast approaching the spot where Carmen and the cubs had crossed the road and so was the northbound group. There was absolutely no hope now that the bears would not be struck and chased. But propitiously, the southbound truck, in an effort to raise more dust than the other truck, accelerated and the groups passed each other at the exact spot the bears had crossed. The dogs exploded in a crescendoing chorus. And as luck would have it, both groups of hunters mistook the pandemonium as a "dog to dog" thing rather than a "here's a bear" thing, and their pickups churned along their way. I felt a sense of victory. Score one for the bears.

Carmen & Company turned south after crossing the road and crossed only one other road (a narrow two-track) on their way to the Whitefish River corridor, which they then followed south back into the vehicle-excluded area. There, the bears resumed foraging for black cherries. I did not walk with the bears after the road-crossing episode but tracked their progress by vehicle instead. I made the decision during that trip to establish a bait of my own in a secure portion of Carmen's home range. I would forgo the science in an effort to curtail her movements and keep her alive. It would become a ritual I performed yearly.

∽o∾

9/12/94

Nettie and June have abandoned my strategically placed and well-tended bait to forage on black cherries. I find them just two hundred yards north of a well-traveled gravel road in the south part of their range. June forages far up a towering black cherry tree. As she maneuvers to obtain its ripened fruit, many are shaken to the ground, where Nettie scrounges the fallen bounty. Whether by design or default, it proves a good system and one that keeps both bears actively foraging for over an hour. Shifting my gaze toward June I notice a group of seven red-tailed hawks kettling on thermals high above a skein of geese winging their way south to wintering grounds. Returning my gaze to the ground, I watch Nettie as she forages ever nearer my position. When she is just a few feet away, she stops and eyes me briefly where I sit. I say nothing, and the look in her eyes gives nothing away—we just look, and then she resumes her task.

When the wind picks up and rustles the golden brown leaves in the overstoried hardwoods, it draws my gaze back to June, now precariously perched at the end of a limb, trying to haul in a branch laden with cherries. As she reaches out unsteadily, I am reminded of last winter's visit to Isle Royale, where many a moose enticed by the last tidbit poised just beyond its reach took a tumble off the sheer north face of the island onto Lake

Superior pack ice to become fodder for wolves. But the present scene remains peaceful as June maintains her balance and handily rakes in the berries. Soon she descends the tree (some sixty feet), pausing about fifteen feet above the ground to check out the situation below. When she reaches the ground in a hail of bark and limbs, she and Nettie head north into a cedar swamp, pausing to drink as they cross a stream near the edge of the stand. I do not follow.

⁓ↄoↄ⁓

A day later, I locate Nettie's signal indicating that she and June are within the gated area. I reestablish a bait for them and another for Carmen. By their radio signals, it's clear that the bears use the baits in the safety of the vehicle-excluded area, for nearly a month. But the September day I watched June feeding deftly on cherries while silhouetted against the pale blue sky with hawks circling overhead is the last I ever see her alive.

⁓ↄoↄ⁓

10/3/94

If you are early to rise, and mindful of the day, there are windless and frosty mornings in early October when you can be the first to commute the Rapid River Truck Trail following the bulk of the leaf fall from the overhead bower of hardwoods. What awaits is a carpet of red and gold embers. I try never to miss it. Today the crimson leaves swirl up in the rearview mirror as I pass. All the while I walk the woods roads toward Nettie and June's location, I think what a great day it is to see the sights, hear the sounds, smell the smells, and soak it all up. The two bears would have denned only a few days ago based on Nettie's inactivity signaled by her radio collar. But an alarm

234

sounds the minute I raise the receiver to my ear. There is no signal, Nettie is gone.

I hadn't approached Nettie's stationary signal closely to confirm it, not wanting to disturb them in the early stages of their slumber. The bait upon which they had consistently fed for the last three weeks had remained untouched the last two nights, and there were plenty of opportune brush piles in the aspen stand they occupied in which to den. It was the logical assumption. But why, I ask myself, would the bears leave a secure area after they've denned? Surely, it can only mean trouble.

I locate Nettie's signal about one and a half miles outside the vehicle-excluded area in the middle of an expanse of swamp conifers near the southeast border of her range. I do not go in to her but instead return to her earlier location and try to determine the cause for her abandonment of the presumed den site while the sign is still fresh. I had walked around a likely clump of brush within the stand the day before and have it in mind as a place to begin my search.

Returning to the aspen stand, I start in toward what I think might have been the den site. I have gone but a few yards when a raven flies up and into a hardwood on the border of the stand. I think perhaps a piece of bait has been dragged into the aspens and the raven has found it. As I shoulder my way farther into the sapling aspens, I notice a number of recently established but well-worn game trails and begin following one. The trails converge at a center point like the spokes of a wheel, and there, at the confluence, lies June—motionless. Gradually, I realize that the trails must have been made over the last few days by Nettie, as she returned over and over to the fallen cub, perhaps to encourage her to resume the walk of life. All efforts failing, it is apparent that Nettie remained and slept near June for several days before abandoning the carcass. I wonder how Nettie interprets June's death. I know that I feel an overwhelming sense of loss. I can not help but think that had I not ceased walking with the bears at the beginning of the hunting season, perhaps things would now be different. I wrap June's carcass in my poncho, lash a rope to it, and drag her from the woods. I place her in the back of the Jeep and drive to the U.S. Forest Service office, where her remains are put in a freezer. From there the carcass is sent to the Rose Lake Wildlife Research Station in the Lower Peninsula, where necropsy will determine the cause of June's death.

~o~

I'm told that June died from natural causes. Five porcupine quills penetrated the right atrium of her heart, and three lodged in her left lung. Porcupine quills have evolved with minute barbs designed to insidiously work their way inward once impaled in the victim. Michigan Department of Natural Resources wildlife veterinarian, Dr. Steven Schmitt, estimated that it took a month for the quills to work their way into June's chest cavity and to her vital organs. I imagine that it was a slow and painful natural death.

One of the most dramatic realizations that comes from walking with bears is that it is a life-and-death matter every second of every day for them. Tranquil and tender family scenes can change in an instant into struggles for life. Some die, others live. Nowhere is this truer than in the bear woods.

~o~

A day later, Nettie is back in the gated area. I walk to her in a hardwood stand. In a hillside above a desiccated vernal pool, she has dug a den. Outside the entrance is a day bed constructed of grass, sticks, and bark stripped from a close-by maple. Nettie dozes inside the den, and when I see the arrangement, I talk to her softly and exit the area. Over the next two weeks, I monitor her day and night. She makes evening forays into a grove of beech trees, and on two occasions I am able to sit with her and watch as she forages on the fallen nuts—the pulse of life goes on. I will miss watching June grow. She possessed the most character of any cub I have ever known, more in fact than some people. But it was her independence and headlong manner that in the end proved her undoing. Perhaps there is a lesson to be learned here about being bold and first in the animal kingdom. It might serve a cub well to hang back just a little. Headstrong and heedless are apt to be maladaptive as survival traits.

10/4/94

Today Carmen dens in a huge cutting in the central part of her range. It is the same clear-cut stand of lowland hardwood in which she denned with her litter in the fall of 1991. Surrounded by roads and probed by hunters of all sorts, her choice is, in my opinion, a poor one. She makes the trek to the den under blue jay-skies coursing the one and one-half miles between 10:00 A.M. and noon. She begins from an aspen seedling-sapling stand that has been her daytime resting spot for the last week—and where I sit reconnoitering her position from a ridge above. There are calm frosty mornings in October when a red squirrel scrambling across the crisp leaves sounds as loud as a moose busting through the woods. There is no mistaking the noise Carmen makes as she moves through the aspens some hundred yards below as that of anything smaller than a bear. Slash cracks like rifle shots as it is pressed down under great soft paws. It is easy to hear and follow her raucous movement, and I trail from afar.

At this stage of the game, bears compelled for weeks by physiological pressures toward denning appear nearly oblivious to their surroundings. Once perceptive eyes drift. Previously sharp hearing is inattentive. It is almost as if they are somnambulant. I liken it to getting up during the night for a glass of milk—you have a vague notion of where you are and a recollection of how to get to the refrigerator, but your response time is considerably less than optimal. Shortly before noon, after following a drainage north, skirting a hardwood, and crossing a two-track, Carmen enters the clear-cut. A few hours thereafter the signal from her radio-collar indicates that she is stationary. I wait nearby until nightfall. She does not move the remainder of the day.

∽o∾

The average den-entrance date for all reproductive classes of female bears in this study was October 17—nine days before the legal end of bear hunting season. Pregnant females denned nearly two full weeks before all others, and an average were in their dens twenty days before the end of the hunting season. Much evidence—beyond my observations—suggests that bears function at a reduced physiological capacity up to three weeks prior to denning, which means that under present Michigan regulations, it is legal to hunt and kill female bears that are likely functioning in this foggy, inattentive state. I believe that the bear hunting season should be shortened to preclude hunting and killing bears in the weeks before denning, to remain in keeping with the ethics of "fair chase." In addition, Michigan's *third* bear hunting season serves only to concentrate the hunting effort during the latter part of the hunting season when bears are in a state of reduced physical capacity. There is little good reason for this. If additional recreational days of hunting are deemed necessary, they should take place earlier in the hunting season rather than at its end, when bears are disadvantaged. The management that allows this, in my opinion, is certainly not management by science, it is hunter-centered and not bear-centered, as it should be.

Fall

∽o∾

The next winter, when we handle Nettie in her den, it takes the strength of several researchers to pull her from her subnivien world. As we approached the den, I hoped for a split second that somehow June would be there, that I had made a mistake last fall and the carcass I disposed of was not hers. But Nettie is alone. She has fattened considerably on beechnuts (and bait) and weighs a whopping 210 pounds following five months of hibernation.

Later that spring when I visit her den to sit and talk, I discover she has moved. She has redenned in a hollow tree in the hardwoods a few hundred yards distant. The first and only research bear to use a tree den during the study. Searching for her signal, I walk right by the den and over the next rise, only to discover the signal behind me. I turn around, thinking she has circled and is coming to my voice. When I discover my mistake and locate her in the hollow tree, she is fast asleep and does not stir when I peer in through a slit in the base of the tree. I retreat to sit upon a log near the site, thinking how much I will miss in the life of a bear, unable to follow June as she matures and has cubs of her own. After an hour or so of reflection, I feel an urge to get up and go but decide instead to stay and enjoy some more peace and quiet in the bear woods. When walking with bears, part of what I enjoy most is being a committee of one. When it comes time to make a decision—whether to go or to stay, leave the woods or follow the bears—I always have the last word, whether or not I agree with myself.

Sitting here, I begin to consider the worth of bears and just what place they have in the scheme of things. My thoughts drift to a "bear talk" I gave to a class of schoolchildren several months earlier. The reason I have a lot of hope for the future is because of bears and children.

I should say that I believe the true test for earning a Ph.D.

239

ought to be that of presenting and defending a thesis to a third-grade class. If the candidate can come close to exhausting the pool of questions, let alone answering them all (without prevarication), then he or she should pass automatically. For seven consecutive years, I talked about bears with Sandy Bonsall's third-grade class at Teal Lake School in Negaunee, Michigan. The questions I fielded were straightforward and unabashed, and I'm still looking up the answers to some of them. As I sit watching Nettie's den tree, a particularly tough one comes to mind.

A student, quite open-mindedly, asked: "What are bears good for?" The question took me aback. My instinctive response was to quote Aldo Leopold, who said: "The last word in ignorance is the man who says of an animal or plant: 'What good is it?' If the mechanism as a whole is good, then every part is good, whether we understand it or not. If the biota, in the course of aeons, has built something we like but do not understand, then who but a fool would discard seemingly useless parts? To keep every cog and wheel is the first precaution of intelligent tinkering." But that response didn't seem fair for such a young student. The truth is, I don't remember how I responded that day, but I have always felt it was less than adequate. Since then I have thought a lot about the worth of bears. The student touched the crux of matter. For too long, biologists have concentrated their efforts on gathering habitat-use data so as to be able to identify and protect critical habitats. But at some point, we must begin to turn our minds to figuring out just where bears fit into the scheme of things. What is their role in the ecosystem they occupy? A paucity of data exists to answer that question.

There are a few canned answers I could have given that student, such as: Bears are an "umbrella species." As such, the preservation of the vast amounts of habitat required for their existence will consequently ensure the life requirements of many other organisms are met in the process. There is something to be said for this notion, but I would prefer that people see bears as bears and understand them for all that they are and not as an icon for all else. [I am of the opinion that bears should, can, and do stand on their own in regard to any values we assign.] Besides, other mammals, such as the wolverine, have home range requirements that are as large as, or larger than, those of bears. Does it then follow that bears are somehow worth less? I think not. Yet in some ways, it does seem fitting that other species should ride the coattails of bears.

Another response might be that bears are a "keystone" species. Keystone species are species that play such an important role in the ecosystem they occupy that without their presence the system is doomed to fail. A classic example of the keystone concept is the relationship between a huge, flightless bird, the dodo, and the tambalacoque tree of the Mauritius Islands in the Indian Ocean. It was observed, in the 1970s, that the tambalacoque tree was becoming rare and no longer reproducing. The reason for the tree's decline was discovered to be the requirement that its seeds pass through the digestive system of a large bird in order to become viable. And the only bird large enough to perform the task, the dodo, was exterminated from the islands some three hundred years earlier. Fortunately for the tambalacoque, it turned out that its seeds could be germinated by passage through another large bird, the turkey, and its possible demise was thus averted.[3]

Bears might well aid in the germination of some seeds and the dispersal of others and therefore might be considered a keystone species in some systems, although the truth is that birds probably do as much for the dispersal of some small seeds as bears. But larger seeds, such as those of the mountain ash and the black cherry, perhaps owe much of their dispersal to bears.

Another possible response (although it always seems selfish when I hear it) might have been that an understanding of bears' physiology may have potentially beneficial health implications for humans. For example, answering the question of how bears overwinter for periods as long as seven months without getting osteoporosis would be of benefit not only to the bedridden but possibly to space travelers as well. (Bone-building processes in humans are suspended after only short stays in the hospital.) Understanding the mechanisms by which bears regulate their cholesterol levels—which may rise into the 800s during fall hyperphagia and denning, only to lower into the mid 200s during summer with no apparent adverse effects (such as plugged arteries)—could also benefit human health. (I question whether bears, if they had a say in the matter, would vote to contribute to this understanding, given that an extension in the life span of our species will inevitably result in the continued and accelerated shortening of theirs.)

There are other conceivable responses as to the worth of bears. I have a few of my own, but they are by-and-large soppy and, some would no doubt say, anthropomorphic. I subscribe to the notion that there is a great deal of intrinsic worth in just knowing that bears are out there. Just fathoming that something as big and powerful as a bear can still roam wild and free somehow greatly improves my attitude.

For me the real worth of bears is that they can put us in our place. Alone, and eye to eye, bears can treat us any way they want. I can only hope there will always be that choice for bears—and for us.

Bear Walkers

Bob Bati
Diane Bati
Joe Bauer
Tom BeVere
Dean Beyer
David Binder
Sheri Buller
Thresa Chase
Annette DeBruyn
Dan DeBruyn
Mary DeBruyn
Kevin Doran
James Ford
John Frey
Bob Gwizdz
Steve Harriman
Jodi Helland
John Hendrickson
Bruce Johnson
Jamie Johnson
Laurie Johnson
Dan Kote
Yu Man Lee
David "Buck" LeVasseur
Mike Lewis
Ann Maclean
Rolf Peterson
Ed Rumbergs

243

Dick Schellenbarger
Jan Schultz
Kevin Shinn
Richard P. Smith
Larry Visser
Frida Waara
Guy Wallace
Kerwin Werner

Notes

Introduction

1. B. McLellan and D.C. Reiner, "A Review of Bear Evolution," *International Conference on Bear Research and Management* 9, no. 1 (1994):85–96.

2. The Kermode bear is named after Francis Kermode, who as curator of the British Columbia Provincial Museum, at Victoria, British Columbia, confirmed its existence in 1905. Kermode set about his task after being apprised by Dr. William T. Hornaday, director of the New York Zoological Park, that he had traced the orgin of the hide of a "white" bear to British Columbia.

3. J. Van Wormer, "The World of the Black Bear," in *Living World Books*, John K. Terres, editor (New York: J.B. Lippincott Company, 1996).

Physiography

1. N.D. Strommen, "Climate," pages 133–134 in *Soil Survey of Delta County and the Hiawatha National Forest of Alger and Schoolcraft Counties, Michigan*, L.W. Brendt, editor (USDA Publication).

2. Climax communities are the final stage in a successional series of vegetation types. They are relatively stable communities in dynamic equilibrium with the climatic, physical, and biotic environment.

3. M.S. Coffman, E. Alyanak, J. Kotar, and J.E. Ferris, *Field Guide Habitat Classification System.* CROFS; (Houghton: Michigan Technological University, School of Forestry and Wood Products, 1984).

Winter

1. S.M. Herrero, "A Comparison of Some Features of the Evolution, Ecology, and Behavior of Black and Grizzly/Brown Bears," *Carnivore* 1, no. 1(1978):7–17.

2. R. Peters, "Communication, Cognitive Mapping and Strategy in Wolves and Hominids," pages 95–108 in *Wolf and Man: Evolution in Parallel*, R.L. Hall and H.S. Sharp, editors (New York: Academic Press, 1978).

3. It is curious to note, however, that during winter den work, while I was disturbing more than one hundred bears in their dens, never once did any bear act aggressively toward me. Mostly, they just turned away, shielding their young and appearing too lethargic to do otherwise. But on two occasions, yearlings were able to muster enough energy to run from their mother's dens during researcher disturbances.

Spring

1. L.L. Rogers, "Effects of Food Supply and Kinship on Social Behavior, Movements, and Population Growth of Black Bear in Northeastern Minnesota," *Wildlife Monograph* 97(1987).

2. The nitrogen content of sweet cicely at the time the bears forage on it averages about 4 percent, which equates to approximately 24 percent crude protein. The other herbs growing nearby, such as Dutchman's-breeches, trout lilies, and violets, which the bears do not eat, have lower nitrogen concentrations.

3. Theodore, J. Karamanski, *Deep Woods Frontier: A History of Logging in Northern Michigan* (Detroit, Michigan: Wayne State University Press, 1989).

4. A.W.F. Banfield, *The Mammals of Canada* (Toronto: University of Toronto Press, 1974).

Summer

1. I believe that Carmen and Nettie locate ant colonies by smell. Many ants give off hydrocarbon compounds as a form of recognition

and as alarm pheromones. (See M.S. Blum, "Alarm Pheromones," *Annual Review of Entomology* 14[1969]:57–80.) *Lasius umbratus,* a favorite of the bears, emits citrinellal ($C_{10}H_{18}O_6$), a terpenoid compound, from their mandibular gland as an alarm pheromone. The odor is distinct at sites where Carmen and Nettie have fed on this ant. More noticeable still is the odor of formic acid (CH_2O_2) that comes from the poison gland in *Formica* and *Camponotus* spp. and is typically emitted as an alarm pheromone. When foraging for ants, whether in aspen seedling-sapling or lowland conifer habitats, Carmen and Nettie always sniff stumps, logs, or the ground prior to digging for ants. On occasion, while in aspen seedling-sapling stands, the bears stopped a forage-meander, tilted their heads to sniff the air, walked directly to a stump up to ten yards away, and then, after a confirming sniff, began digging for ants within the stumps.

2. The ant species *L. umbratus* has no stinger, has soft body integuments, and is relatively slow compared to *Camponotus* and *Formica* spp. It is likely selected by Carmen and Nettie because of these characteristics as well as the fact that most of its colonies are ground based and pupae and larvae tend to be aggregated and thus more easily exploited. The preference of *L. umbratus* for lowland conifers probably accounts in part for the high use of these habitat types by all study bears during summer. In contrast to *L. umbratus, C. noveboracensis* and *F. subnuda* are found most often in wood. These ants have relatively large bodies, are faster than *L. umbratus,* and they bite. However, they also have relatively large pupae and larvae and soft body integuments, and may be preferred by the bears for those reasons. Clear-cuts provide ideal habitat for *C. herculeanus, F. subnuda,* and *C. noveboracensis.* The colonies are located in stumps and slash (primarily balsam fir) from previous logging operations.

Fall

1. The only hornet species in North America is *Vespa crabro,* the European, brown, or giant hornet. It normally builds its nest in hollow trees. The bald or white-faced "hornet" (*Dolichovespula maculata*) is not scientifically considered a hornet—it is a wasp and builds a paper

nest with a single opening above ground in trees or shrubs. Yellow jacket wasps (*Vespula vespidae*) build a paper nest in the ground or at ground level in fallen logs. All three species belong to the family Vespidae. I collectively termed them hornets.

2. Ralph A. Nelson, "Protein and Fat Metabolism in Hibernating Bears," *Federal Proceedings* 39, no. 12(1980):2955–58.

3. Malcolm L. Hunter, Jr., *Wildlife, Forests, and Forestry: Principles of Managing Forests for Biological Diversity* (New York: Prentice-Hall, 1990).

Afterword

After den work in the spring of 1997, I was offered a job with the Florida Game and Fresh Water Fish Commission as head of their Bear Management Section. The bears there suffer from the age-old problems of bears everywhere: human encroachment into their habitat, fractionation of the habitat by roads, *nuisance* losses, and hounding. What with maxed-out credit cards and student loans I knew it was time to go to work— they only let you have so much fun. Diploma in hand, Annette and I headed south. That fall I received a phone call from an outdoor writer. While he read me the ear-tag numbers of a female black bear that had been registered in the opening days of Michigan's hunt, I went through the motions of checking my list of numbers. But I knew those numbers like the back of my hand—Carmen was dead, killed by a hunter over bait. A year later, I walked in on Nettie to find that she had died a lingering death by a hunter's arrow. A hunter who lacked even the basic skills required to recover her carcass. And so it goes.

It seems a bitter irony that the bears which contributed so much to increase our knowledge and understanding of their kind would, in the end, be killed by those who obviously knew and cared so little. Carmen was with her cub when she was killed and the fate of the orphaned cub, Frida, remains unknown. Likewise, Nettie was with three cubs-of-the-year when she was shot. It is unlikely that they survived. In

Michigan's bear hunt, it is illegal to kill a female bear in the company of a cub. Yet like so many of Michigan's bear hunting regulations, it is largely unenforceable. At best these laws only keep the honest man honest. As someone who believes in the hunt and the ethics of fair chase I try to reason out the *good* in Carmen and Nettie's deaths. For now, I can see none. The only consolation I find rests in the realization that each moment in time is as real as the next whether it occurs in the past or future. There will be no future moments with Carmen or Nettie. Yet, I have a bounty of recollections—vivid moments of times we shared together at large in the northwoods.

I will always wonder if bears are capable of measuring their days. I'd like to believe they are. And that on at least one day the bears measured me as something of worth